Idea to iPhone

The essential guide to creating your first app for the iPhone and iPad

Carla White

WILEY

This edition first published 2013

Reprinted June 2013

© 2013 Carla White

Registered office

John Wiley & Sons Ltd, The Atrium, Southern Gate, Chichester, West Sussex, PO19 8SQ, United Kingdom

For details of our global editorial offices, for customer services and for information about how to apply for permission to reuse the copyright material in this book please see our website at www.wiley.com.

A catalogue record for this book is available from the British Library.

ISBN 978-1-118-52322-3 (pbk); ISBN 978-1-118-52323-0 (ebk); 978-1-118-52324-7 (ebk); 978-1-118-52325-4 (ebk)

Set in 10/12.5 Chaparral Pro Light by Indianapolis Composition Services

Printed in the UK by Bell & Bain

About the Author

CARLA WHITE is a designer, writer and business-Mac-Gyver whose apps have been featured by Apple, USA Today, NPR, Oprah, Successful Living Magazine and many other major publications across the globe. As both a speaker and a consultant, she helped software giants and small businesses bring breakthrough ideas to life. She's a Human Factors specialist with an MBA and MIS and has launched business practices and products all over the world for companies as big as Microsoft and as small as her own two-person startups.

Born to a farmer and a photographer, Carla inherited her dad's work ethics and resourcefulness and her mom's artistic eye. She was also born with an insatiable curiosity, which earned her an alphabet soup of degrees, but more importantly provoked her to travel solo coast-to-coast in a beat up Chevy (twice). She lived in California to learn how to surf (and failed) and Colorado to learn how to snowboard (and loved it). She got her first "big girl" job working for the Pentagon and was also a translator for the 1996 Olympics. She's since ventured to all corners of the globe, lived in Europe for over ten years, and speaks multiple languages. Her life recently has come full circle and she now resides back in her home state of South Dakota with her husband, son, and dog. When Carla isn't having adventures with her family, she enjoys yoga, running, and throwing a mean dinner party.

Today Carla runs her app agency Happy Tapper, creator of the apps Gratitude Journal, Vision Board, and Little Buddha, where she offers consulting as well as design services. Carla is on a mission to show everyone how to find happiness through gratitude and giving back as well as motivating women to succeed.

Publisher's Acknowledgements

Some of the people who helped bring this book to market include the following:

Editorial and Production

VP Consumer and Technology Publishing Director: Michelle Leete

Associate Director–Book Content Management: Martin Tribe

Associate Publisher: Chris Webb

Associate Commissioning Editor: Ellie Scott

Senior Project Editor: Sara Shlaer

Copy Editor: Chuck Hutchinson

Technical Editor: David Loewenthal

Editorial Manager: Jodi Jensen

Editorial Assistant: Annie Sullivan

Marketing

Associate Marketing Director: Louise Breinholt

Marketing Manager: Lorna Mein

Senior Marketing Executive: Kate Parrett

Marketing Assistant: Tash Lee

Composition Services

Compositor: Jennifer Mayberry

Proofreader: John Greenough, Joni Heredia Language Services

Indexer: Potomac Indexing, LLC

To Colin and Nico—I love you beyond words.

To my parents, John and Jeanette—I owe everything to you.

Gratitude

"I honor the place in you where the entire universe resides. I honor the place in you of love, of light, of truth and of peace. And when you are in that place in you and I am in that place in me, there is only one of us."

--posted on my Facebook wall

First, I want to thank my loving and above-and-beyond supportive husband, Colin. You put your life on hold while I worked early mornings and weekends. You believed in me and I'm forever grateful. I love you dearly.

I also want to thank my son, Nico, for constantly reminding me to live in the moment and for filling me with endless inspiration. I hope it ripples to every person who reads this book. As your mom, I want to make you proud and show you that every dream is within reach.

Mike Rohde, I want to thank you for answering my emails and agreeing to do this project. Your illustrations have transformed this book. I feel honored to have my creations on the same pages as yours.

Sara Shlaer, you've been a world-class editor, molding all my half-baked ideas and cutting the lame jokes. Your endless striving for absolute perfection has taught me a great deal, something that I will carry throughout the rest of my career. *Much* obliged.

I want to thank Wiley for believing in me. Your team has been nothing but the best to work with. They were always professional, helpful, and understanding. A special thanks to Ellie Scott for making all of this happen. I also want to thank Chris Webb for being open to my ideas and embracing them, as well as the rest of the thoughtful and creative team at Wiley.

Thank you David Loewenthal for reaching out to me all those years ago and helping me get this far in the app business. Hopefully one day we'll actually meet.

Featured Developers: Thanks to Loren Britchter, Mark Jardine, Bobby George, Christopher Taylor, Alain Hufkens, Paddy Donnelly, Andy Skirvin, John Casasanta, Patrick Wetherille, and Shelby Meinzer. Your insights have made this book all that much better.

Friends, family, and colleagues, thank you for your encouragement throughout the project. A special thanks to my book coach, Jan B. King, as well as my incredible friends in the Downtown Kite Flyers Club; the most supportive and inspirational women this side of the Mississippi. Also, Gin, Linda, Dan, and Daryl, thanks for embracing and supporting me as the black sheep.

I want to thank everyone in the app community who took time to answer my emails, tweets, and posts over the years, both fans and developers alike. I'm constantly taken aback by how helpful and supportive people can be, and am forever grateful to each and every one of you for getting in touch. I look forward to seeing it grow.

Last, but certainly not least, I'm forever grateful to my dear mom for always letting me leap, no matter how much it scares you. Our friendship is my cornerstone.

Contents

Introduction. 1

CHAPTER 1
Kicking Off Your App Adventure 9

Eliminating Doubts and Debunking Myths 10

"I'm not a developer or even the slightest bit techy." 12

"I don't have the money to create an app." 12

"The app market is saturated. I don't stand a chance." 14

"I don't have the time." 14

"I'm not artistic, and I don't know how to use design software." 14

"I don't live in a tech center." 14

"What if I fail?" 15

Financing Your App with Your Time and Talent 15

You need less money than you may think. 16

You have more to offer than you know 16

Keep doing what you do best 17

Filling in the missing skills 18

The Journey Ahead 18

The Mobile World We Live In 19

Apps must be understood in 15 seconds or less 20

We see only part of the screen and it's blurry 21

Think thumb, not fingers 22

What You Need to Know About Working with Apple. .23

Apple may take months to answer a question 23

Handling rejection. 24

How to grab Apple's attention. 24

How iTunes helps (or hurts) sales. 25

Getting paid by Apple 26

Getting Organized and Setting Up Shop. 27

Learning how to talk the talk. 27

Getting the right Mac and iDevice 29

iDevice 29

Mac computer. 30

Downloading the software. 30

Developer tools 30

Design tools. 31

Tools to manage your team and project 31

Registering as an Apple Developer 32
Purchasing the iOS Development Program membership 32
Snagging the best domain names 33
One Small Step to One Giant Leap. 33

CHAPTER 2

Shaping Ideas into Apps People Want 35

Your Target Audience: Finding Your Tribe 36
Go tribal 36
Find your proxy 38
Making the most of your research 40
Creating Apps That People Really Want 40
Strategy 1: Fix a problem 41
Strategy 2: Amuse, charm and captivate 41
Strategy 3: Connect us with people and places 42
Ingredients for Magnificent App Ideas 42
Don't be afraid of crazy ideas. 43
Let your passions inspire you 43
Add a dash of personality. 44
Spice it up with surprises 45
Mix in some viral goodness 46
A Brief Introduction to Integrating with Facebook 49
Which Device Is Right for My App? iPhone, iPad, or Both. 51
The benefits of targeting both iPhone and iPad. 52
Why the iPhone's smaller touchscreen might be best 54
Why the iPad's extended views are the way to go 54
Doing Your Research 56
Making a (Mission) Statement 57
Avoiding Scope Creep: The $120 Bottle of Shampoo. 58
Prioritize your features 59
Save some killer features for updates 60
Avoiding headaches: Features to leave out 61
Avoid features that require you to own a server 62
Avoid features that require moderating 62
Avoid anything that requires a Terms of Service agreement. 64
Keeping Your Idea Confidential and Protected. 64
Testing Your Idea's Pull Power in Three Easy Steps. 65
Step 1: Create a site for your app. 65
Step 2: Run an ad campaign. 65

Step 3: Watch it for a week 66
What to make of the test results 67
Kicking Off Your Marketing Campaign 67
You're not just creating an app; you're putting on a show 68
Your tribe already loves you; they just don't know it yet 68
Jumping on the social media bus 69
Concocting an enticing teaser video 70
Try for some humor 71
Keep it clean and simple 72
When friends refuse to be actors 72
Where to share your masterpiece 72
Growing your audience with a teaser site 73

CHAPTER 3
Designing Luxurious and Stunning Apps **77**
Getting the Ballpoint Rolling 78
Understanding the Navigation Models 80
Nested dolls 80
Tab bar 81
Breaking the tab bar ceiling 82
Swiping tabs 83
Slide-out navigation 84
Bento box 85
The sliding cards 87
Immersive designs 88
Navigation found on the iPad 90
Layered navigation 90
Sidebar navigation 91
Button and Tab Combo Navigation 91
Taking a Peek at the Standard Controls 92
The bars 92
The status bar 93
The navigation bar 93
The toolbar 94
The table view 95
Inputs and outputs 97
Stealing Good Stuff 100
Finding design inspiration 100
Building your collection 101

Creating Natural Flow in Your App 101
    Map out the flow with boxes and arrows. 102
    Turn the flow into a story. 104
Shifting Your Ideas into a Killer Design. 104
    How anyone can design like a pro. 104
    Why prototyping is the best thing since sliced bread. 105
    Start by sketching 106
        Creating paper prototypes in a flash 106
        Test, edit, repeat. 107
    Creating working prototypes: No coding required 108
Putting Your Designs to the Test 110
    Capture useful feedback 111
        The "Get it?" test. 111
        The key task test 112
        Five-second test 113
    Edit, edit, and edit again. 113
From Mockup to Masterpiece 114
    Preparing your designs for Retina Display. 114
    Building designs that scale using Photoshop. 116
    Creating your layout 117
        Shortcuts to layouts. 118
        Stealing some templates 118
        Making each image. 118
        Naming files 119
Creating Designs That Really Stand Out 119
    The importance of pixel perfect design. 119
    Make it subtly real 120
    Make it easy and effortless: The ABC's of design 121
        The power of contrast 122
        Repetition and grouping. 122
        Give it some space 123
        Same, same, same. 124
    Make it delightful 125
        Tuck it away 126
        Be careful with the interruptions. 126
Making That Critical First Impression Count. 127
    What you need to know about icon design 127
    Shortcuts to creating an icon 129

It's all in the name 130

Launch screens of love 132

Outsourcing to a Professional 137

Finding a ~~good~~ *great* designer 137

What the designer needs from you 138

What you need from your designer 139

Signing the contract 139

Doing without the designer 140

Marketing Ideas Checklist 141

CHAPTER 4
Developing and Testing Your App 143

Finding Dependable and Talented Developers 144

Reaching out to the iOS community 145

Where to scout out the talent 145

Making the most of Elance.com and other sites 147

Search for the developer you want 148

Post your project and let the developer find you 150

Find other places to circulate your job description 151

Selecting the Best Developer for Your App Project 152

The developer review checklist 152

Interviewing prospective developers 154

Questions to ask 154

How to review the developer's prior work 156

Where to find honest feedback on a developer's skills 157

Understanding that cheap can be expensive in the long run 158

Comparing apples to apples 158

When can work start? 159

When will I get my app? 160

Test-drive with a mini project 160

Learning to trust your gut 160

Signing the contract 161

Working with Developers 162

The secrets to keeping your developers happy 162

1. Listen to them 162

2. Don't keep changing your mind 162

3. Be specific 162

4. Have realistic deadlines 162

5. Check in but don't micro-manage...................................163

6. Make decisions quickly...163

7. Don't use any four-letter words.................................163

Be nice and be boring 163

Money as a motivator 163

It's more than a short courtship 164

Kicking Off Development 164

Creating a spec that says it all 164

Remember to include the kitchen sink 166

A six-year old can understand it..................................168

What your developer needs from you...............................168

What you can expect from your developer 168

Issues, Bugs, and Tweaks: Testing Your App 170

Have you downloaded the SDK and Xcode? 170

The absolute beginner's guide to Xcode 171

Setting up your device for testing................................175

Taking a look at Apple's iOS Provisioning Portal 179

Adding in Game Center, Push Notifications, or In-App Purchases..........180

Find bugs and create buzz by enlisting your tribe 181

Distributing your app using Test Flight 181

Keeping track of bugs 182

Breaking the news to your developers 184

Tweaking design after development: Don't do it 184

When It's All Gone Wrong...185

What to do if your developer disappears 185

Knowing when to fire your developer.............................185

Knowing When to Go Live...186

Marketing Ideas Checklist 186

CHAPTER 5

Raising the Curtains and Going Live **189**

The Ultimate App Submission Cheat Sheet.........................190

Selecting a Powerful Launch Date 191

At Least One Month Before Submitting Your App 191

Get set up on Apple's iTunes Connect 192

Prepare for customer care...194

Select a support site..194

Add a contact link in your app 195

Offer an FAQ page 195

Identify launch tricks you must start now. 195
    Make the most of promotion codes 197
    Prepare your website for the red carpet 198
    Recognize the beauty of a great newsletter 199
    Build your press kit 200
    Produce a viral video 201
At Least One Week Before Submitting Your App 201
  How people really scan the iTunes store 202
  The formula for an effective product description 203
    The perfect elevator pitch 204
    Reaffirmations, reviews, ratings, and rewards 204
    Craft an awe-inspiring benefits list 205
    Share upcoming enhancements 206
    Add in a personal note. 206
  How to design screen shots that sell. 206
    An entire story with five images. 206
    Screen shots that say it all. 207
  Improve discovery with the right keywords 210
Submitting Your App for Approval. 211
  Complete the app details on iTunes Connect 211
  Set up certificates, App IDs, and profiles 212
  Create the distribution build yourself 213
  Let your developer create the distribution build for you. 214
Countdown to App Approval. 214
  Prepare your message 215
  Close shop. 216
  Backstage sneak peek event 217
  Announce your launch date 217
3...2...1...Launch! 217
  Double-check the important stuff. 217
  Roll out your new site 218
  Blog your big news 218
  Get the word out on social media 218
  Ready, set, email! 218
  Get fans in on the fun. 219
Keeping Track of Sales 219
  Add a free analytic service 219
  What Apple tells you and doesn't tell you 219

Building Customer Love. 220

Answer emails early, often, and sincerely .220

Be real and they will reward you 220

CHAPTER 6
Promoting Your App and Making a Profit. 223

The Art of Attracting Attention and Creating Hype 224

Give people a story to tell. 225

Pull on the heart strings 225

Build identity 226

Make it cute as kittens. 227

Make us laugh. 228

Create nostalgia 229

Try taboo, unusual, or outrageous 230

Monitoring buzz to create more interest .230

The $5 Marketing Plan 231

Have a sale 232

Give out promo codes 232

Promote your app inside your app 233

Build in social and sharing features. 233

Request a review. 233

Tell a friend 234

Reward handsomely. 234

Teach to reach 235

Write, write, write 235

Reveal your secrets. 235

Praise other apps 236

Create videos and presentations 236

Share everything 236

Share customers 236

Share your brand 236

Put your name on everything. 240

Hit the streets 240

Speak Out 240

Pull a stunt 241

Promotion Tactics That Don't Work 241

Press releases are spam. 241

Think before leaping into banner ads 241

Never slam competitors' apps 242

Creating a Compelling Website. 242

    Registering a domain name 243

    Purchasing web hosting 243

    Tips for creating a memorable teaser site .243

        Should you use a landing page service?. 244

        Collecting names and addresses. 244

    Tips for an effective app website 245

Tips for a Successful Email Campaign 247

    Repeat after me: no spam! 247

    And you are?. 247

    Boring subject lines actually work better .248

    Use space wisely. 248

    Make it quick and reward them. 248

    Use images sparingly. 248

    Make it easy to share. 249

    Answer replies 249

Making Money from Your App. 250

    Pricing your app in the paid model. 250

    When to give it away for free 251

        How the free-to-paid model might be the ticket 251

        The difference between free and lite 251

        The latest fad: In-app purchases. 252

        Making money with iAd and other advertising options. 253

    Think outside the app 253

The Generosity Principle 254

    Donate to a charity 254

    Find a launch sponsor. 254

    Create a promotion 254

    Order some business cards and freebies 255

CHAPTER 7

Maintaining Your App and Going the Distance **259**

Working on Your Business as Well as Your App. .260

Tweaking Your Way to the Top. 260

    The boomerang theory 261

    The addicts model 261

    It's an easy sale booster. 262

What to Tackle First 264
    Feedback and reviews 264
    Fix the bugs first 265
    Improve usability. 266
    Examine the analytics 266
    Localize the description on iTunes 266
    Localize your app to expand your market 267
Adding New Features to an App. 268
    Rocking the boat 269
    Taking your time to release 271
    Should you create a whole new app instead?. 272
Managing Your App on iTunes Connect 272
    Keeping your app fresh and current 273
    Submitting new updates. 273
    Understanding software versioning 273
        Major updates. 274
        Minor updates 274
        Revisions and bug fixes 274
Keeping Up with Apple and iOS Releases 274
    What new iOS updates mean for your app 275
    Porting your app to a new iDevice 276
    Expanding to Android. 278
The Law of the Vital Few 278
Let Your Inspiration Guide You 279

Index. 281

Introduction

I have no special talent. I am only passionately curious.
—Albert Einstein

In early 2008, when I got my first iPod touch, I knew instantly that I had to create an app for that darling little device. I wasn't a programmer, had never used a Mac, and had a measly $500 budget. In fact, I didn't even have an iPhone, just my iPod touch. But none of that was going to stop me. A few months later my app stormed into the top position on the App Store and was hailed in major news publications around the globe.

If you had peered in my window during those few months, you would have seen me huddled at my computer, absorbed in design tools, messaging developers, and fumbling with Xcode—all before going to my day job. I was determined to figure out how to create a hit app on a shoestring budget, without learning how to code.

It wasn't easy, but I managed to teach myself how to do all the designs, outsource the development, and grab people's attention—all on a budget that paid for itself by noon on the first day of sales. My apps have since graced the front page of *USA Today*, been featured on *Good Morning America*, and been praised in the media from Fargo to France as proof that anyone can create a killer app.

Now I'd like to share everything I learned with you, so you can do it too.

Who Should Read This Book

I'm writing this book for people whom I like to call "ideapreneurs"—folks who come up with innovative and breakthrough ideas but don't know how to design or build them. You might be a business owner, project manager, marketing genius, or the one-person shop doing all the work yourself. Or maybe you're a developer or a designer who already created an app, but it's not getting the attention and downloads you hoped for.

Perhaps you attempted to study the technical manuals with computer languages you don't understand, and discovered that even the most basic books assume some knowledge of programming. Then you scoured the Internet for information but still don't know what to believe or where to begin. You just want a simple and affordable way to shift your idea into a top-selling app that appears on iPhones and iPads all over the world.

You might not have created anything artistic since grade school or know the first thing about software development, but you're willing to roll up your sleeves and make the most of your greatest talents. Step by step, I walk you through the technical jargon, breeze you past the time wasters, and help you jump through Apple's hoops, making the process as simple as possible. I show you ways to build on the skills you already have by engaging in activities that excite you.

My experience alone isn't enough of a solution to all the different challenges, so I interviewed some of the most successful app developers out there. These incredible folks have apps that blasted the App Store charts, including *tap tap tap*, *Tapbots*, *Montessorium*, *Weetaps*, and creators of *Lose It* and *Wood Camera*, and *Letterpress*. These people have mentored me over the years and are now sharing their insights, mishaps, and advice with you.

If I Can Do This, So Can You

When I started, I owned a flip phone, had no programming skills, and worked at a job so remote the building was in the middle of cornfields. For the longest time, blogs or books for app developers simply didn't exist. And because I was financing everything myself, I had to hold down my day job, too.

That was quite a few years ago, back when George W. Bush was president and Beijing hosted the Olympics. I create apps full time now, but I'm still not a programmer. I shy away from venture capital and haven't added a single person to my payroll. I outsource the development, and everything else I do myself.

Over the years I have witnessed firsthand how this industry and the tools to create apps are evolving at an insane pace. App designs continue to get better and the competition fiercer.

Still, my overall formula for creating apps remains the same. But the formula alone won't produce successful apps. It also takes drive and courage. While some are dreaming of success, the real winners wake up and work hard to achieve it.

A Glance into the App Development Process

To keep things simple, this book is organized to reflect the main phases of an app project. It aims to shorten development time and keep costs low, with the goal to start earning within a few months.

To do that, there is one important rule to remember: **Go for the quick wins.**

Break the development process into short phases so you can get things done and move on to the next thing. This approach keeps momentum going and keeps your project from fizzling to a slow death.

The process can be broken out into six overlapping and repeating phases. Some phases, such as development and promotion, never truly end. In fact, promotion actually kicks off before anything else, and is part of every phase of the project. The illustration on the following pages provides a brief overview of the process that will be discussed in more detail throughout the book.

- **Conceptualize—Idea, Discover & Brainstorm.** Decide exactly what your app does and who it's for. Narrow down your target market and mold your app idea into something they want.

- **Design—Flow & Story, Prototype, Test, Final Designs.** Establish a clear blueprint of the features, screen layouts, and navigation. Test your designs and build on the ideas of others, then polish it all off with a design tool.

- **Develop—Code & QA Test.** Create an app that is efficient, bug free, and well tested.

- **Distribute—Submit & Go Live.** Send the app to Apple with images and a description for approval. Execute a launch strategy that gets Apple's and the media's attention.

- **Promote.** Market the heck out of it while you're building your app as well as after it's on iTunes.

- **Maintain—Update & Expand.** Support your customers as well as your app by working on new releases. Expand to new markets and platforms.

Idea to iPhone Process

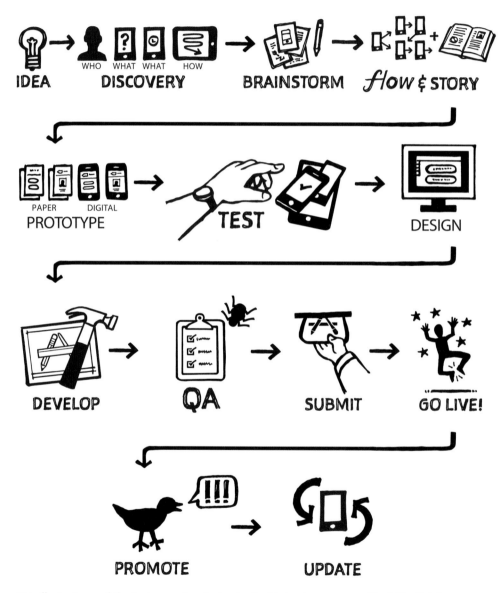

This illustration and the first page of each chapter in this book were created by Mike Rohde (http://rohdesign.com/). © 2013 Mike Rohde.

A Few Things You Won't Find in This Book

Not only is this book nontechnical, it also won't sell you a get-rich-quick scheme in which you quickly create an app and then live in the comforts of your private island, sipping cocktails out of a coconut shell. Creating *successful* apps takes hard work, and I'm not about to sugarcoat the process. But if you have the drive and passion, the rewards can be phenomenal.

Here are a few other things you won't find in this book:

- **A one-size-fits-all solution**—I've been creating apps since they first hit the market, and one thing I know is there isn't a process that fits all situations. It's just not that black and white. You will come across roadblocks that will force you to change course. Technology changes so quickly; what works today may not work tomorrow. I do think, however, that there are some guiding principles that don't change, and I will do my best to convey them in this book.

- **Facts and figures to wow you**—If you're holding this book, you don't need me to hear a jaw-dropping figure about what app developers are earning or how many apps are downloaded each day. Apps are selling like hotcakes, and there is no sign of that slowing down. If anything, the flood is just getting started. Some of the best apps are yet to come, and hopefully, from you.

- **Programming languages or jargon**—This book isn't another technical manual about iPhone and iPad development. I don't know any Objective-C or Cocoa Touch because I had to do things a little differently. I will share just enough technical details so you can hire and manage your developers, test and submit your app, and understand the limits of the software development kit (SDK).

- **Online app builders**—If you have a lot of content that you want to distribute in the form of an app, an online app builder might be all you need. I've never used an app builder because my app ideas don't fit the mold, so they aren't discussed as a solution in this book.

- **Half-truths and overselling**—I only give straightforward real-world advice. I practice what I preach and honestly tell you everything about my process in terms as basic as I possibly can. Creating apps can be frustrating, confusing, and exhausting. My goal is to make the process simple, straightforward, and most of all, fun.

What I Really Mean to Say Is...

Throughout this book when I refer to the iPhone, I mean both the iPhone and iPod touch. Likewise, when I refer to the iPad, I mean both the iPad and the iPad Mini. My use of these terms is mostly a repetition factor and in no way is a reflection that the iPod touch or iPad

Mini is less important than the iPhone or iPad. It's anything but that. Here are a few other word clarifications:

- **"Customer" refers to "user."** I purposefully try to avoid the term "user" because it seems degrading to those important people who will be the reason for your success. Those guys will be downloading your app, enjoying it, and telling others about it for you.

- **"I" refers to me, the author.** Sometimes I speak as the voice of an app developer (such as "I recruited some testers…"), and other times it might be as an app consumer (such as "If I have to log in first…").

- **"You" refers to you, the reader and app developer.** In my view, if you are reading this book, you are an app developer also. You are designing, building, and promoting apps.

- **"We" or "people" refers to everyone who uses apps.** Including you, me, and my dear, sweet mom.

As with all rules, I have to occasionally break these, but I hope this list will prevent some confusion.

A Small Book for Such a Big Subject

I did everything I could to keep this book simple and short. My hope is that you can read it in a single rainy afternoon, or flying across the continent. I did this for a few reasons.

- **You don't have the time.** Your days are already full with your day jobs or running a business. You're busy keeping your boss or customers happy, and your family warm and well. You just want some straight answers.

- **You don't need to know everything.** Too many details will bog you down and confuse you, creating inertia. I share just enough so that anyone can create an app.

- **It's a guide.** This book is designed to walk you through the process of creating your first app. I hope you dog-ear it, highlight it, underline text, and refer back to it often. If we ever meet one day and you have this book with you, nothing would flatter me more than seeing it has been feverishly used.

App Developers Who Contributed to This Book

Throughout this book you will discover bits of advice from other app developers. This is a brief introduction to their backgrounds and apps.

- **John Casasanta, Co-Founder of Tap tap tap**—The Tap tap tap (www.taptaptap. com) team is comprised of the guys from the popular MacHeist, the leading Mac software promotion site, so they're no strangers to Mac development or promotion. They were one of the first developer teams to break the mold of app design and continue to top the iTunes charts today. This team has sold millions of downloads and nearly every app they created has been featured on iTunes or an Apple ad. Today they have seven apps on iTunes, include the number one Camera +, Classic, Voices 2, and Faces.

- **Mark Jardine, Co-Founder and Designer at TapBots**—Chances are you have a TapBots (http://www.tapbots.com) app, and you probably downloaded it simply because it's so incredibly beautiful. Starting with their first app, Weightbot, the simplicity and functionality of their apps have set them apart. This team of two, Paul Haddad and Mark Jardine, has been awarded best design app and has apps featured in iTune's Hall of Fame. TapBots' apps are a great example of how a slick design can take a simple concept and turn it into a bestselling app. There are other weight apps available, but none enjoyed as much success as Weightbot. TapBots also has three other top selling apps: ConvertBot, PasteBot, and TweetBot.

- **Loren Brichter, Founder of atebits 2.0**—Design prodigy Loren Brichter is the founder of atebits 2.0 (www.atebits.com) and creator of the Letterpress, the 2012 runner up of game of the year. You might be familiar with some of Loren's earlier work, including the popular Tweetie iPhone app which won a 2009 Apple Design Award.

- **Bobby George, Founder of Montessorium**—Husband and wife team Bobby and June George began Montessorium (www.montessorium.com) one day when they were talking about how they could offer the unique methods of Montessori on a grand scale. They went on to create four top selling apps, all of which have been featured either on the App Store or in an Apple ad. In Chapter 1 you'll read how Steve Jobs wrote to them personally. Their apps include Intro to Letters, Intro to Math, Intro to Geography, and AlphaWriter.

- **Andy Skirvin, Founder of Blimp Pilots**—Koi Pond was the first app I ever purchased and was the most downloaded app in 2008. It has rested nicely in the App Store's top 50 for years after its release, and became the second most downloaded app of all time. The creators, Blimp Pilots (www.theblimppilots.com), have since released two other apps: Distant Shores and Name in Lights. They also released an iPad version of Koi Pond.

- **Patrick Wetherille, VP Product Marketing at Lose It!**—The weight tracking app, Lose It! (www.loseit.com), was another app that I first downloaded back in 2008. The app has graced the number one spot on the App Store Health & Fitness category for years and continues to be featured by Apple. Their app has helped people lose over 15 million pounds (and counting).

- **Alain Hufkens and Paddy Donnelly, Co-Founders of WeeTaps**—WeeTaps (www.weetaps.com) is a joint venture that is rather new to the app scene. I discovered their app WeeRocket after noticing the icon on design forum, and am thrilled with the simplicity and style of the app. Using the same formula they had for their first app, they created a second one called WeeSubs, and it's just as marvelous.

- **Christopher Taylor, Co-Founder of Playtend**—My son for introduced me to Playtend's ingenious apps (www.playtend.com). Before he was even two he was counting in four languages thanks to their clever Counting Ants app. Focusing solely on education apps for children, this partnership of Christopher Taylor and Victor Johnson has created nearly 40 apps, some of which have been featured by Apple as well as praised by major publications and blogs.

- **Shelby Meinzer, Founder of MindTapp**—I first met Shelby Meinzer shortly after the launch of his app, PhotoNest. Shelby and Dan Martin founded MindTapp, a design-based company that focuses on simple aesthetically pleasing tools for the iOS platform, in 2010. Neither Shelby nor Dan were developers but they had an idea and knew that they could make it work. They teamed up with the developers at Clever Coding and brought PhotoNest to life. While MindTapp has been idle for some time now, you can expect PhotoNest to make a return as a totally free app as well as a new offering from MindTapp at the beginning of 2014.

Reach Out

As you'll soon learn from this book, I encourage you to reach out to other app developers and share ideas. I hang out on my Facebook page (**www.facebook.com/carlawhite.happytapper**) a lot and would love to hear about your project. You can also contact me through my personal website at **happytapper.com**, my blog **carlakaywhite.com,** or on Twitter at **twitter.com/carlawhite**. I not only look forward to hearing from you, but also using your marvelous app one day.

CHAPTER 1

Kicking Off Your App Adventure

"You only live once, but if you do it right, once is enough."

—Mae West

There's something alluring about the wide-open frontier of the app business, where a piece of software has made legendary millionaires out of folks writing code from their kitchen tables. While some say that striking it rich comes down to pure luck and that the gold rush is over, I disagree. As mysterious as app success might be, the truth is that it's not reserved for some elitist club who manage to get lucky. There's actually a formula to creating successful apps and still plenty of unexplored territory out there to apply it, making this an opportunity open to everyone, including the person reading this book.

This chapter starts by debunking the myths of what it takes to create a first-class app. It outlines the talents needed and reveals the eye-opening fact that you already have most of the skills. You'll learn important insights about the mobile market, what people want from apps and what it's like to work with Apple. Finally, you'll roll up your sleeves and take your first exciting steps on your journey from idea to iPhone.

Eliminating Doubts and Debunking Myths

For those who think that app success is reserved for software giants with budgets the size of the Gobi Desert or technical geniuses that rival Mark Zuckerberg, pull up a chair and hear this. Although the app market might seem impenetrable to the average person who has wonderful app ideas but not necessarily the technical wits to produce them, the truth is that creating a great app is not rocket science. Just like you, some of the most successful app inventors began with an idea, and working in their basements and bedrooms created apps that millions now enjoy. These apps catapult birds at pigs, transform a dull photo into something cool and retro, or hail a taxi with just one tap. Figure 1-1 shows the Instagram and Taxi Magic apps.

Whether you're so passionate about an app idea that it robs you of sleep, your boss asked you to create one, or you just want to figure out how to do it, jump in with everything you've got and enjoy the ride. Once you discover that by using the simple methods explained in this book pretty much anyone can do it and experience how thrilling app success feels, you'll wonder why you waited so long.

FIGURE 1-1: Instagram app (left) and Taxi magic app (right)

Source: Facebook, Inc and RideCharge Inc

To watch Koi Pond climb up the charts and sit at number one for almost two months was completely unbelievable, and drastically changed how seriously we were taking iPhone development.

—Andy Skirvin, co-founder and engineer at The Blimp Pilots (Koi Pond app)

Throughout this book, you'll learn how to bring your app to life by using the skills you already have and engaging in activities that excite you. The question isn't whether you have what it takes to pull off a great app—because you do. You just need to understand the basic steps and know where to find the best resources. The real question is whether you're ready to play like a champion and overcome the doubts standing in your way.

"I'm not a developer or even the slightest bit techy."

So you don't know how to code. App development is one of the fastest growing technical skills on the market, so you have plenty of great talent to choose from. This book shows you where to find great app developers online using sites like Elance and oDesk, as well as in your own backyard (see Figure 1-2). It explains how to reach a fair contract that will keep your project on time and within budget, and how to get the best work from your developer. It also walks you through any technical hurdles and clearly explains each step in the app development process.

"I don't have the money to create an app."

You actually need a lot less money than you might think. By contributing your own talents and time and doing some of the production yourself, you can save thousands in up-front capital. Saving money means you won't need outside investment to fund your app project, freeing you from requesting a loan from your bank, pitching your idea to investors, or risking family ties.

Making this effort may cost you in early mornings, and you may have to live on dinners of rice and soy sauce. But in the end, you will pick up some new skills and lower your financial risk, which in turn makes your odds for success that much greater.

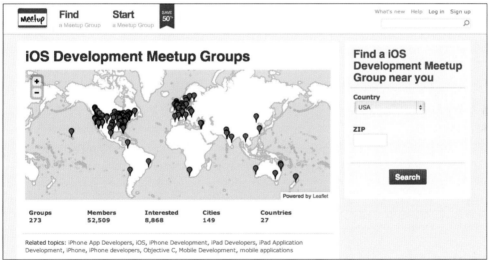

FIGURE 1-2: Websites like oDesk.com have thousands of iOS developers for hire. You can also discover developers in your community using sites like Meetup.com.

Source: oDesk.com and © 2013 Meetup

"The app market is saturated. I don't stand a chance."

The App Store has only been around for less than six years—it's just getting started! It's one of the fastest growing industries in history and has no signs of slowing down. With over 400 million App Store customers, it's also the largest collection of accounts with credit cards on the web. These people *want* new apps.

Sure, the low hanging fruit is gone, but there are still plenty of unexplored possibilities. Even if your app idea already exists, there are always ways to make it better. The incredible success of Clear app is a perfect example. There are thousands of to-do apps, but the developers of Clear discovered a way to take make the experience better by removing all the clutter and creating a simple yet striking design. Stories like this prove that the app revolution is just beginning. In fact, the mobile analytics firm Flurry predicts over *one billion app downloads a week* in 2013. There's *plenty* of opportunity for your idea.

"I don't have the time."

If you're waiting for all the stars to align and a massive block of free time to suddenly open up, you'll never get started. You have to make the time. We're not talking all-nighters or 80-hour workweeks to pull your app together, but you will have to squeeze in some extra hours each week—early mornings, evenings, and weekends. It's enough time to get your app rolling. Gradually, creating your app will progress from there.

"I'm not artistic, and I don't know how to use design software."

If you can draw a circle, a box, and some arrows, you can design an app. If your artistic talents tap out at stick figures, and design software is as confusing to you as the plot of *Lost*, you most likely will have to hire someone to produce a polished interface. But you can save money on a designer if you spend time blueprinting your idea first. You'll learn basic steps on how to do this as well as how to outsource the design work in Chapter 3.

"I don't live in a tech center."

Residing light years outside Silicon Valley didn't hurt my apps one bit. If anything, it probably helped. It forced me to connect with other developers online, and I discovered a welcoming and generous community that is also incredibly knowledgeable and helpful.

Like you, many of these developers are also rolling the dice at something new and somewhere along their journey, they were insanely grateful to get help from a total stranger in another hemisphere. Tweet about an issue, and you may be surprised at the new friends you make. Google it, and you'll find forums filled with others who had the same issues and shared their solutions. I share app developers' favorite hangouts in both the real and virtual worlds in Chapter 4.

"What if I fail?"

Most successful developers *did* fail before they struck gold. And not just once; they belly-flopped over and over. Rovio, the maker of Angry Birds, released 52 unsuccessful games before it finally hit the jackpot. The company persevered and not only became the most downloaded game of all time, but one of the fastest growing consumer brands with those colorful birds appearing in everything from movies to coffee mugs.

The good news is that you probably won't have to go through 52 fiascos or risk the family farm before someone other than your mom downloads your app. Following in the footsteps of successful developers takes a lot of the guesswork out of how to create apps that become chart busters.

This book shares the behind-the-scenes process, breakthroughs, and slipups from me and other developers who were just like you. We reveal what worked for us and what didn't, and what to expect every step of the way.

Financing Your App with Your Time and Talent

For many of you, there are two things standing between you and your app—money and knowhow—so let's address funding your app project and the skills you'll need first.

Almost half of the people who come to me with their app idea say they'll pull the trigger after they secure venture capital to pay for everything. Inevitably, I never hear from them again because their app project never leaves the ground. It went stale and grew mold in the months they dedicated to pitching their idea to investors rather than creating their app.

The beauty of app development is that it actually doesn't require that much investment up front if you're willing to commit your own time and talent. A better approach is to establish a budget you can afford to finance with your own precious money and do some the work yourself. Even if you have never managed software development, designed something, or started a business, you still have what it takes do this.

TIP If outside funding is essential to your project, look into crowdfunding sites like kickstarter.com and indiegogo.com. These funding platforms are great alternatives to a bank loan or private investors.

You need less money than you may think

Outside funding might seem to be a quick and safe way to bring your app idea to market, but I've seen gorgeous apps that launch with $30,000 marketing campaigns suddenly outsold by an 11-year-old punching out code in his tree house.

The App Store is a game of chance, and the best way to reduce risks and increase your odds is to bootstrap your project:

- Instead of buying expensive advertising and hiring a PR firm, start marketing early and use creative methods to get your app noticed.

- Instead of hiring a team of ten, outsource part of the work to one or two really talented people.

- Instead of going nuts with features in your app, start with the bare minimum and focus on a beautiful design instead.

If you happen to be sitting on a hefty budget for your app project, by all means hire an experienced team to do the whole thing for you. But if you want to lower your risks and save money (who wouldn't?), you can do plenty of the work yourself and cut costs in other ways as well.

You have more to offer than you know

Being an app creator is like being the CEO of your own company. At this point, you're more like the CEO of a lemonade stand than Amazon, but that's a good thing. It means you're small, lean, and fast. You can make decisions quicker and fix your mistakes faster. You can change your priorities, focus, or mind. Less is a good thing because it forces innovation and creativity.

As CEO, it's your job to find the right mix of talent to pull your idea together. Here's a cheat sheet to help you understand what skills you'll need to move your idea from your head to a hit on iTunes. Start by figuring out which of these talents you already have (or have access to), and which you will need to acquire (by partnering, hiring, or learning how to do it yourself).

Essential Skills		Additional Skills		Personal Skills	
	iOS Development Objective-C Xcode		**Software Testing** Test app Report bugs Track fixes		**Time Management** Goal setting Self-discipline Task tracking
	Design Graphics /illustrations Usability or UX Design software		**Website Creation** Web programming Web design SEO		**Critical Thinking** Open-minded Nonjudgmental Honest
	Marketing and PR Writing Video Blogging Social networks		**Outsourcing Experience** Remote workers Scheduling Cultural sensitivity		**Decision Making** Intuitive Analytical Commitment
	Project Management Communication Budgeting Teamwork		**Accounting** Budgeting Planning Bookkeeping		**Having Fun** Relax and let go Love your app idea Accept criticism

Keep doing what you do best

I bet you nodded your head at a few items in this list, but you probably have more talent to contribute than you know. You just might not recognize all the skills you use naturally. Have you ever organized a trip? Great! You're adventurous, can communicate, and are good at getting people fired up. Do you enjoy writing? Excellent! You can pen all the promotional messages. Are you good at fixing things? Superb! You understand the nuts and bolts of engineering. Do you arrange all your canned goods in alphabetical order? Then you're wonderfully organized. You might think that these things have little to do with creating an app, but they do.

These skills are just as critical in an app project as the coding because a good portion of what's involved is management and marketing. For example, I'm crazy about yoga. That interest helped me to connect with thousands of others who share my same passion and they were my first fans. Even though my app had nothing to do with yoga, simply talking about something I love helped build my audience and hype for my app.

Beyond your golf swing and record collection, you have other experiences that will impact your app. Have you ever managed a group? Pitched an idea? Sat in a meeting? I'm guessing you said "yes" at least once. Warren Buffet, one of the world's richest men, attributes a great deal of his success to his childhood paper route because it helped him think like an entrepreneur. Chances are you have similar experiences that will contribute to your app project.

Filling in the missing skills

You have several options for filling in the gaps where your skills fall short. You may have to dip into your pocket and pay freelancers to design or program your app for you, but this book shares ways you can save money on outsourcing costs. You can also partner with someone whose skills complement yours. Many app teams consist of two or three people, and among them they have all the talent needed.

Another option is to find the time to learn some new skills. The fact that you're reading this book is evidence that you're willing to make that investment, but don't feel you have to do everything. Very rarely is there a designer, developer, promoter, and project manager all sushi-rolled into one person. In fact, adding at least one other person to your project, if even briefly, helps to give you a refreshing new perspective and outside opinions.

Do it because you love it. Don't do it because you see stories of people making zillions off iPhone apps. But if you're passionate about it, jump in with everything you've got and enjoy the ride.

—John Casasanta, founder at tap tap tap (Convert, Camera+, and other apps)

The Journey Ahead

Now that you have some insight into the skills needed, it's time to think about the basics of app development. The steps are pretty straightforward, but let's get one thing clear right away. You're not just building an app. You're producing a product that people *want* to download, use a lot, and tell their friends about. Your success hinges on focusing your time and energy on two critical tasks:

- Creating a simple and elegant solution.
- Marketing your app as soon and as often as possible.

Did you notice that coding isn't on the list? This might leave some developers up in arms, but the truth is it's not the core to successful apps. A well thought out design and a strong marketing strategy are the crux of any successful app. Obviously, I'm not suggesting you can do without coding. But if you spend most of your time and budget on coding grand features and leave the design as an afterthought, people *won't* be drawn to your app because it's confusing to use or as dull as cardboard. Likewise, if you wait until your app is almost complete before you start promoting and connecting with your audience, most people won't even know your app exists. You need to focus on both the design and marketing throughout your project to make it work.

These are the basics of any app project: a well thought out design and a strong marketing strategy that connects you to your audience. Take a closer look – it's essential to formulate app ideas that people want with the key ingredients to become addictive and viral. You must also take the time to ensure you have a bug-free app, meaning both the code *and* the design work.

Throughout this book, I'll explain the entire process in detail, identifying exactly what goes into a quality app, affordable ways to promote it, and how you can maximize your talents in every step of the process.

Let's start by noting what people expect in an app—any app. In the next section, you'll look at how we really use our iPhones and iPads, because that plays a big part not only in the design, but the app idea itself.

The Mobile World We Live In

Whether we're completely obsessed, a little ambivalent, or even slightly bored with our iPhone or iPad, we're usually distracted when we're using them. Most of us have a pretty good idea of what's competing for our attention at any given moment, like our kids, other apps, or the slippery sidewalk. But it's actually a lot more complicated than that.

To give you an idea, Figure 1-3 illustrates the layers of distractions we face when using our mobile devices. See that tiny purple sliver in the middle labeled "interface"? That small part of the surroundings is *your app* and it's in a tug-of-war with all sorts of other demands on the user's attention. Besides the fact that we all might be safer with padded light posts, let's take a closer look at how this set of circumstances affects an app's success.

FIGURE 1-3: The overlapping spheres of distraction in our mobile environment.

Original image by Nadav Savio, Giant Ant Design (www.giantant.com). Reproduced under the Creative Commons Attribution 2.5 license.

Apps must be understood in 15 seconds or less

Apps get used in short bursts interrupted by text messages, phone calls, and the changing traffic light. For your app to be successful, people must be able to understand exactly what it does in 15 seconds or less. We should "get it" without having to invest any extra brain cells thinking about it.

Your app needs to be so obvious and intuitive that your neighbor who just purchased an iPad yesterday understands it (see Figure 1-4). If your app confuses people, they get frustrated, lose confidence in you, and move on to the next app. Even worse, they'll leave bad reviews on the App Store so your app never gets out of the starting gate.

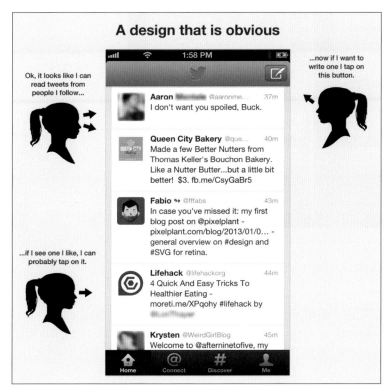

FIGURE 1-4: Obvious designs lead to comments, not questions in our minds.

We see only part of the screen and it's blurry

We use our devices one-handed and often while engaged in another activity—watching *Jon Stewart*, eating stir-fry, or catching the bus. This means the screens are constantly moving around and are partially covered by fingers that are trying to control the app while holding the device in place.

Try this little experiment. Open your favorite app, move it back and forth, and notice what you see. Small fonts become blurred, images and icons stand out, and whitespace makes a huge difference in recognizing grouping. This is how your app will look when people are using it while running on the treadmill, down the stairs, or after their kids. Figure 1-5 illustrates this point.

FIGURE 1-5: How the app is designed (left) and what we typically see (right).
Source: Clock app by Apple

Think thumb, not fingers

"Fat thumbs" rapidly paw their way over buttons while one eye stays glued to the TV. That chubby digit also scrolls down content as we're walking to the coffee shop, and snaps a shot of the winning goal while we're jumping with excitement. Thumbs have come a long way from simple hitchhiker helpers.

For the majority of people, the left thumb does most of the dancing around the iPhone screen. Sometimes it partners with the right thumb when playing a game, typing text, or using an iPad (see Figure 1-6). Other times it tangos with a finger on the right hand. This is important to remember when designing your app.

Also, our chubby thumbs need nice, big sure-hit targets. Buttons should be big, optimally located, and obvious to everyone. Labels need to be simple, easy to read, and understood at a glance. Colors and images are cleverly used to guide us quickly through the app.

FIGURE 1-6: How we hold our iPhones and iPads.

What You Need to Know About Working with Apple

Now that you understand more about these devices that have transformed our lives, let's talk about the company behind it all: Apple, the gatekeeper to all of our eager app shoppers. Without Apple's blessing, your app doesn't exist. Apple also holds onto all your sales earnings until they pay you your share. In a way, they're like a business partner, or maybe your boss.

The next sections give you an insider's take on what it's like to be in business with Apple. What can you expect in terms of support, and how can you make Apple sit up and take notice of your app.

Apple may take months to answer a question

Apple works hard at being a modern-day *Willy Wonka's Chocolate Factory*, where everything is done in a mystery of silence. This holds true with its interaction with the developer community as well. If you plan to contact Apple, expect to wait months for a response.

After updating the price on one of my apps, it suddenly disappeared from the App Store, and there was no one at Apple whom I could contact about it. A few nerve-wracking hours later, it was on the App Store again, but all I could do for the duration of the problem was wait it out.   **TIP**

Don't take the silence personally and don't let it slow down the progress of your app project. With so many developers and apps on iTunes, even the most communicative of companies wouldn't be able to keep up with all the queries. Instead, connect with other developers, use the abundance of help materials online, and dive into useful books. You'll find your answer much more quickly.

Handling rejection

Apple reviews and approves each app before it goes on to the App Store. The approval team receives more than 700 apps each day requesting the green light; some are new apps and some are updates to existing apps. It's no secret that a good portion of them will be rejected, often for unclear or odd reasons.

> **TIP** An experienced developer can help mitigate the chance of rejection by consulting you about what Apple is looking for when they approve an app. Chapter 4 gives pointers in selecting the best developer and Chapter 5 outlines the app submission process.

It's important to know that if your app is rejected and you make the required changes immediately, it still goes to the back of the line of all the apps waiting for approval. This means you could wait possibly another two to three weeks before Apple gives it the stamp of approval or says more changes are needed, putting you at the back of the line *again*.

The smartest thing you can do is to plan for the extra approval time. If you need your app out for the Christmas download rush, plan to submit it by November. If it gets approved right away but you don't want it released, don't worry. You can tell Apple the exact date to add it to the App Store. (Chapter 5 talks about setting a release date as part of your launch strategy.)

How to grab Apple's attention

It might appear that Apple is on a mission to get everyone and his dog to sign up and create apps, but it isn't. The last thing Apple wants is millions of ugly apps that diminish its glorious devices. It's an effort to recruit *quality* apps that will help Apple sell more iPhones, iPods, and iPads. If your app can lure customers into purchasing a new device just so they can use your program, you're onto something and Apple will notice, turning your single snowflake into an avalanche of success.

Beautifully crafted apps that make the most of the iPhone and iPad features are selected by Apple to be used in their commercials and featured on the App Store. Apple will be your new best friend, skyrocketing your app to the top of the charts. If you scratch Apple's back, it gives you a day at the spa.

You may wonder—what kind of app would lead someone to spend hundreds of dollars on a device? One great example is apps designed especially for people with autism. These apps have revolutionized autistic people's lives, giving some their first chance to communicate. The few hundred bucks for an iPad is a no-brainer investment.

Bobby George, the founder of Montessorium, created an app so he could offer Montessori's unique teaching methods on a grander scale. In August 2010, about a month after launching his first app, he received an email from Steve Jobs himself. At first Bobby thought it was a prank, but in fact it was words of encouragement to keep creating apps. He now has four apps, all of which have been featured by Apple or appear in Apple's advertising (see Figure 1-7).

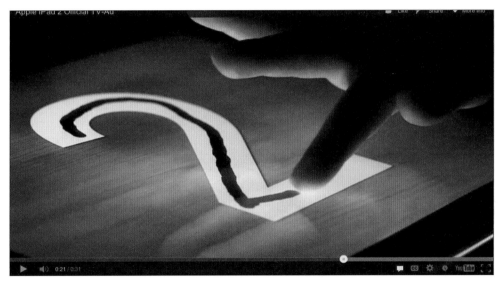

FIGURE 1-7: Intro to Math app created by Montessorium was featured in the "We Believe" Apple Commercial, which was used by Apple to introduce the iPad 2.
Source: Apple Inc.

How iTunes helps (or hurts) sales

If Apple is *Willy Wonka's Chocolate Factory,* then the App Store is the world's largest candy shop, with tiny storefront windows displaying only a few select apps at one time. The App Store appears orderly with its featured apps, categories, and top tens. But underneath, it's a labyrinth of apps clamoring to make it to the top. It has room to highlight only a fraction of apps, and in truth, that's perfect for our flea-like attention spans.

If your app gets the golden ticket and is featured or winds up in the top charts, the App Store's design kills off the competition for you. But if your app loses its spot (or doesn't make it there to begin with), it plummets off a cliff into never-never land with little hope of being discovered. Chapters 5 and 6 include strategies to land your app front and center of the App Store.

Getting paid by Apple

You don't have to be Donald Trump to know that making a profit and getting paid is a pretty big deal. If you're banking on that first check to help pay for your app project, you'd better know a few things first.

- **Apple keeps 30 percent of the revenues.** You pick the sale price of your app, but Apple keeps 30 percent of your app sales (see Figure 1-8). This policy is stated right on the Developer Program web page, so it's not a surprise.

   Apple deals with all downloads, credit card clearing, and refund requests, so be happy to give Apple its cut. In a previous life I managed e-commerce sites and know how much time and effort these tasks take. Letting Apple take care of this headache is worth every penny.

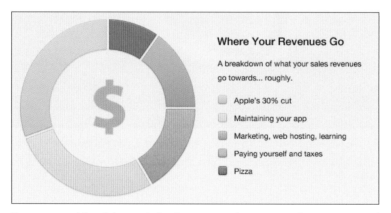

Where Your Revenues Go

A breakdown of what your sales revenues go towards... roughly.

- Apple's 30% cut
- Maintaining your app
- Marketing, web hosting, learning
- Paying yourself and taxes
- Pizza

FIGURE 1-8: A breakdown of what happens to the revenues from your app sales.

- **Apple pays you once a month, after a four-week delay.** Apple sits on your cash for a while before it ends up in your bank account. My first deposit didn't happen until six weeks after the app went live.

   The delay gives Apple time to process any refunds for your app. At any time, people can report a problem about your app and request a refund, and that amount is subtracted from your sales.

This is also smart practice for Apple. It makes a very handsome bonus from the interest on your money during those few weeks. With over $1 million daily sales of apps, the interest adds up quite nicely.

- **You have to earn at least $150 before you get paid.** Apple withholds payment until your payout portion of sales reaches a minimum of $150 per region. If you're like most app developers and price your app at 99 cents, you will need to sell at least 217 downloads to get paid.

  To put this into perspective, if you sold $149 worth of downloads in euros, dollars, or yen, you won't get paid until you have earned one dollar more in that particular currency. Depending on your app's success, you might be better off giving it away because you may never see the earnings anyway. (Chapter 7 uncovers ways you can maximize sales in other countries.)

Getting Organized and Setting Up Shop

Now that you have a good understanding of what's involved, it's time to roll up your sleeves and get started. The beauty of creating mobile apps means your office can be anywhere—the basement, your favorite coffee shop, a library. You just need your laptop, iPhone or iPad, and a decent Internet connection.

Because of all this wonderful mobile technology, your team can live on another continent, working out of the comforts of their favorite hangouts. Later in this chapter, I share some tools to help keep everyone organized. It also helps to plan a couple hours of overlapping office time each day. Ensuring some overlap in your schedules might mean someone has to stay up late and the other gets out of bed early, but it gives you time to talk, pushing your project along *much* faster.

Before we start looking at the hardware and software you'll need, I'll help you understand a few technical terms because like ordering coffee in Paris, speaking a little of the language goes a long way.

Learning how to talk the talk

I'm not about to suddenly flood you with techy-talk, but you should be familiar with the basic terms so you can communicate with your programmer. Understanding these terms will also help you follow along with the steps in this book.

Software programs that run on the iPhone, iPod, and iPad are created with a user interface framework called *Cocoa Touch*, which is built with a computer language called *Objective-C*. Your app will be created with a combination of Cocoa Touch and Objective-C.

Think of it this way: Cocoa Touch is like a LEGO kit. But instead of the blocks being made of plastic, they're made with the Objective-C computer language. Like LEGO blocks, the individual pieces in Cocoa Touch don't do anything, but if you know how to put them together, you can build all sorts of cool stuff.

Instead of creating each block from scratch, Apple has already put together a set of basic building blocks with a nice user interface to make it all easier. The Cocoa Touch framework has blocks for audio, animation, games, address books, maps, and more. Where there isn't a block, or where two blocks need a bit of glue, your programmer will write some Objective-C code.

Here are a few more phrases to help you on your journey in this new culture:

- **iOS**—iOS is short for "operating system." This computer program runs all the other programs on the iPhone, iPad, and iPod Touch. The version of the operating system is the number that follows, for example, iOS6.

- **iOS SDK**—The SDK is the "software development kit" created by Apple that allows you to create apps.

- **Xcode**—Xcode is a set of tools created by Apple for developing apps. You download the toolset to your computer so you can test your app and submit it to Apple. (See Figure 1-9.)

NOTE The "Developer tools" section later in this chapter provides details on downloading the iOS SDK and Xcode.

- **iOS Simulator**—A simulator is a program that runs your app much like it would run on a device, except that it displays on your computer instead. Using a simulator is a great way to quickly test your app, but all final testing must be done on a device. Figure 1-9 shows the Xcode interface and an iPhone simulator.

- **LLVM Compiler**—LLVM stands for "Low Level Virtual Machine." The compiler takes your code, goes through it with a fine-toothed comb looking for errors, and then compresses it into a nice little bundle of code that can be installed on a device. The compiler also allows you and the developer to debug apps and query information while running the apps.

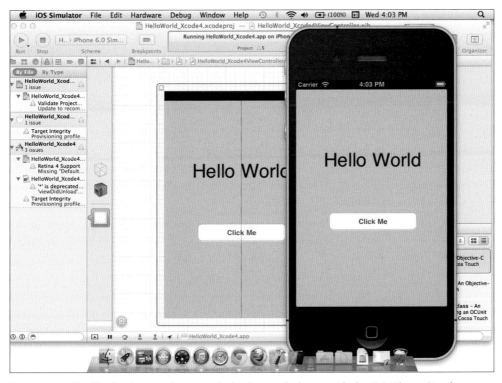

FIGURE 1-9: The Xcode v4.x.interface is in the background, shown with the iOS iPhone Simulator.

Getting the right Mac and iDevice

Just like a plumber needs a wrench and a surgeon needs a scalpel, you also need the right set of tools. In this section, I show you everything you will need to get started, including the right computer and mobile device. Not only will you need a device to test your app, but you also want to study its interface and capabilities. Otherwise, it's like trying to design and build a car when you've never driven one before.

iDevice

If you don't already have an iPhone, iPad, or iPod touch, you need to get one *now*. This might seem obvious, but with the variety of portable devices growing bigger than Starbuck's menu, it's a pretty common mistake. The app you're creating won't run on any portable devices other than Apple's, so you'll need an iDevice for testing your app as well as understanding the multitouch user interface.

You don't need the latest device for your project. Second-hand products from eBay or Craigslist work just as well. Just make sure it's relatively new and kept up-to-date with the latest operating system. If you can't afford the iPhone data plans, get an iPod touch. Unless you need specific features on the iPhone such as GPS, the iPod touch works just as well. If you're unsure whether you should create an app for the iPhone or iPad, you can flip ahead to the section "Which Device Is Right for My App? iPhone, iPad, or Both" in Chapter 2.

Mac computer

For all you PC-lovers and folks with Macs purchased in 1998, I've got some news. To get your app in the iTunes App Store, you must compile it on an Intel-based Mac running Mac OS X. This means you need access to an Apple computer with the latest versions of the Mac operating system—OS X Mountain Lion or OS X Lion.

Macs aren't cheap. The least expensive one available from Apple is the Mac Mini, starting at $599. You can probably pick up a used one on eBay for about half that.

 TIP   If you've never used a Mac computer and aren't familiar with the interface, Apple stores offer free workshops. And when you buy a Mac from one of the Apple stores, you get free one-on-one training.

Downloading the software

Getting all the software tools downloaded and installed on your computer can take longer than watching an entire season of *Mad Men*, so kick off the process as soon as you can. The jumpstart also gives you time to familiarize yourself with everything these tools can do.

Developer tools

The main development tools, iOS SDK and Xcode, come bundled together in one big, fat download. Depending on your Internet connection speed, it can take about a day to download and install everything. The Xcode website has a link that takes you directly to the download: http://developer.apple.com/xcode/.

Apple may upgrade these tools by the time you actually get to the testing phase of your project, which means you'll have to update them later. Don't let that stop you from tucking into them now. While your team is working on the design and development, you can be schooling yourself in Xcode, so when you receive the first bundle of code you know exactly how to install it on your device and test it. That preparation alone can speed up your project dramatically.

NOTE   Check out the section "The absolute beginner's guide to Xcode" in Chapter 4 for more details about getting started with Xcode.

Design tools

Even if you plan to hire someone to do the designs, you will find it helpful to have some design software on your Mac. As with the developer tools, it can take a while to download the software and you'll want some time to become acquainted with the tools, so allow plenty of time to install and learn how to use them. Here are two popular design software tools. (Chapter 3 offers a few more options.)

- **Photoshop** (http://www.photoshop.com/)—Photoshop is the most sophisticated digital image editing software available. At $700, this software is neither cheap nor easy to learn.

  After struggling to find the right designer for my first app, I decided to take the plunge and purchased Photoshop. I found some books at the library, took a course, and spent countless hours trying to replicate sophisticated designs to figure out how they're done. In the end, it was the best investment I made.

- **Gimp** (http://www.gimp.org/)—If you're not quite ready to invest in Photoshop, Gimp is a great option. It's free and does pretty much the same thing but isn't nearly as robust.

Tools to manage your team and project

To keep your project on track, you need to successfully coordinate the ideas and work from everyone on your project team. This step is essential to keeping the app project flowing, regardless if your team is two miles down the road or thousands of miles away on the other side of the ocean.

There are all sorts of tools that empower people to share ideas and resources, bringing teams together, virtual or not. Here is an overview of the tools I use—most of them are free:

- **Google Drive**—(drive.google.com) Formerly Google Docs, this fantastic freebie is simply the best for tracking the project. I use Docs to create my design specification, Spreadsheet to track bugs and issues, and Draw to map out diagrams. You can also set up your email to a Google email account with your domain name.

- **Basecamp**—(basecamp.com) Pretty much the weapon of choice of any software company, design agency, or freelancer, Basecamp is the leading web-based project collaboration tool. It's designed to let everyone on a team plan and exchange information transparently. It costs as little as $20 a month and offers a free 45-day trial so you can see for yourself if it's worth the money.

- **Dropbox**—(dropbox.com) Attaching large files to an email isn't only slow, it's hard to keep track of everything, so I use Dropbox instead. The service is designed to sync files between computers, but you can also use it to share folders with other people. Upload files such as element images and documents and share them with your team by granting access to the folder. Dropbox also offers a free iPhone and iPad app (free up to 2GB).

- **iChat, Skype, and FaceTime**—(skype.com) A real-time communication tool is vital. iChat is standard on the Mac, and because everyone on your team will have Macs, it's a no-brainer. FaceTime lets you connect using your iPhone, Touch, or iPad. My favorite is Skype because it's available on my computer and device; plus, I have a nice history of our texts.

- **Git Version Control**—(git-scm.com) Even if you're a one-person band building the entire app, it's good practice to use source code control, a way for several people to work on the same files and keep all the changes synchronized. Git is a free open-source solution that is fairly easy to learn, but you still want your developer to help get you started so everything is set up correctly for your project.

Registering as an Apple Developer

You'll be pleased to learn that registering as an Apple Developer is free (especially if you just busted out your credit card on a new Mac). All you need to register is an Apple login (Apple ID). You can use the same Apple ID you created when you purchased a Mac or iDevice, or you can register a new one at https://appleid.apple.com.

Once you have an Apple ID, you can register as an Apple developer at https://developer. apple.com/programs/register/. This gives you access to Apple's Member Center website, which is chock full of great materials including the developer tools and iOS SDK, which are distributed together in one download. I'll get into how to do that in a bit.

 TIP Set aside some time to browse through the materials on Apple's Member Center website. This book touches on a few important items offered on the site, but you'll find a lot of useful content.

Purchasing the iOS Development Program membership

Anyone can create an app for free, but to offer it on the App Store, you need the membership in the iOS Development Program. It costs $99 a year and gives you the right to distribute your approved apps through the App Store. You can apply at https://developer.apple.com/programs/ios/.

I strongly recommend that you apply right away because it can take months to process your registration. You have to submit all your details to Apple for review before you're allowed to purchase the program.

After Apple reviews everything, you will receive a series of emails instructing you on the next steps. This process includes verifying your address, signing a license agreement, and receiving an activation code that allows you to purchase the program. In Chapter 5, we step through submitting your bank and tax details using iTunes Connect so that you're all set up to become an app distributor.

Snagging the best domain names

Earlier in this chapter I shared the not-so-hidden secret of success hinges on marketing early. This means that if you don't already have a website for your app, you need to purchase a domain name so you can get a site up and running. You will use it for your "Coming Soon" site to build up hype and collect email addresses. Chapter 2 will get into creating a website and kicking off your marketing campaign.

An obvious choice for a domain name is your app name. If you haven't picked one yet, that's fine (see Chapter 3 for guidance on choosing an app name). You can find a domain name that reflects what the app does. A domain name only costs about $8 a year, so don't worry if it's not the best fit. You can always change it later.

Coming up with a good domain name isn't easy and can take absurd amounts of time. To help you get started, here are a few tools designed to make it faster and easier to find a quality name:

- Domain Hole—http://www.domainhole.com/
- Panabee—http://www.panabee.com/
- Name Station—http://www.namestation.com/

One Small Step to One Giant Leap

Congratulations! If you've just followed the steps in this chapter, you're an official app developer. Perhaps you noticed that once you take that first step, your mind suddenly starts dreaming up all sorts of brilliant and creative ideas. That's good, because now is the time to think big. Up next, we'll mold your idea into a breakthrough app that people want, discover your audience, and get your marketing plan rolling.

Key Points

- You need two things to get your app project rolling: an idea and some ambition. Both of these are free and attainable to anyone. The rest of the talents and tools will come to you as you move forward.

- To hit it big, your app must be understood in 15 seconds or less by anyone, from a five-year-old child to your great aunt.

- If your app helps sell more Apple products, you're on to a hit. Apple will notice and shine a gazillion megawatt spotlight on your app.

- Investing your own talents will save you money, increase your odds for success, and give your app a personal touch, setting it apart from the rest.

- The latest Apple products, expensive PR, and advertising are all a waste of money. Instead, get secondhand equipment, free software, and start your marketing campaign early.

- Dealing with Apple takes time, so you need to set up shop now. Get your Developer Membership, the right gear, and start downloading the software you need.

Shaping Ideas into Apps People Want

"A mind that is stretched to a new idea never returns to its original dimension."

—Oliver Wendell Holmes, Sr.

Ask anyone who successfully landed their app in the top of the charts, and they'll typically tell you the same thing. Some may credit their design while others may say their marketing plan worked. But you know what most of them will agree is the biggest factor? A clever idea. The crazy thing is that most developers spend more time working on their backswing than they do on their app idea.

There are key ingredients that go into turning ideas inspired by your passions into apps that go viral. This chapter unveils methods to mold your idea into an elegant solution that your customers want. You'll explore ways to test your idea and make it even better, shifting it from an uncertain notion into a decidedly confident plan. It will help you select the best device for your app and nail your marketing kickoff. You'll start by discovering how to recognize your audience so you can connect with them, get them fired up about your app, and become their superhero.

Your Target Audience: Finding Your Tribe

Pinpointing a target audience often trips up developers, who find it irresistible to be all things for everyone. But the truth is that before deciding exactly what your app will do, it's important to think clearly about whom you're building it for. It's the first step in creating an app that people *want*.

It's tempting to try to build an app that will appeal to everyone, hoping it rewards you with a huge customer base. It won't. You'll end up overloading your app with too many features in a vain attempt to please everyone, sinking your app to the bottom of the iTunes Store. Not even Coca-Cola sells to everyone.

Your app will be available all over the world, in countries with customs, cultures, social structures, and beliefs far beyond your personal experience. So you need to toss aside the traditional demographics such as age, gender, and income. That too can lead you down the wrong path. There is an entirely different way of looking at app consumers and defining the unique community you plan to serve.

Go tribal

Instead of categorizing and quantifying your audience, think of them as a tribe. We are all members of various tribes connected by our values, goals, interests, and life stages. Your tribe could share a love for the outdoors, a loyalty to a sports team, or a knitting addiction.

Perhaps they're job hunting or trying to shed ten pounds. Figure 2-1 shows how your tribe connects you to a wider network.

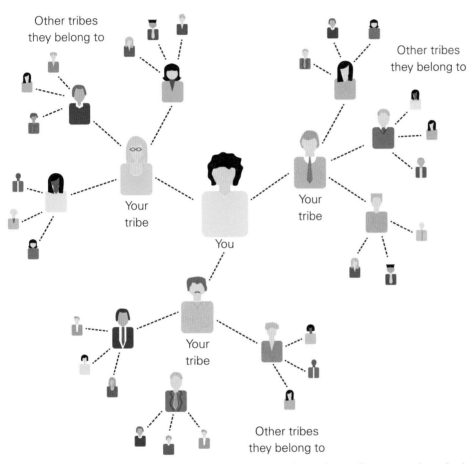

FIGURE 2-1: The beauty of social networking is that your tribe can be small yet its reach can be far.

Becoming a parent, for example, introduced me to the "motherhood" tribe. It completely reshaped me from a globe-trotting-thrill-seeker to a nose-wiping-eat-your-veggies-read-a-book-instead-nut. Mostly, I was suddenly best friends with all moms, even if we had very little else in common. No matter what language we speak, our age, personal beliefs, or cultures we're from, we all want the exact same thing—a happy and healthy family. So we exchange tips about helpful blogs, reliable babysitters, knowledgeable pediatricians and healthy recipes.

To narrow down your tribe, try identifying key characteristics that unite the people you envision using your app, such as a shared passion, stage of life, or desire for change. Remember, your success is inversely proportional to the size of the market you choose to target, so aim to keep it small. Answering this list of questions will help you.

- What are my tribe's shared passions, values, and beliefs? Do they share a common goal?

- Is my tribe at a particular life stage? Puberty? Parenthood? Graduation?

- What is their common identity, sense of belonging, and expression?

- Who do they hang out with? Where do they hang out (both on- and offline)?

- What is my tribe currently talking about? An event? A product? A problem?

- What rituals do they practice?

- What goods and services is my tribe passionate about? How do they link them to others?

- How will my app impact their lives? How does it make their world a better place?

The most important part of our entire process is the beginning—deciding what to build. The first filter an app has to pass for us is relevancy to our own kids because they are a great proxy for the market we serve.

—Christopher Taylor, founder of Playtend (Counting Ants app)

Find your proxy

Once you've established your tribe's shared characteristics, you'll discover it also contains the diversity of a crowded Manhattan sidewalk. The next step is to select a couple of people from your tribe to represent the group as your *tribe proxies*. (You can also call them your *intermediaries*, *key informants*, or *ambassadors*.) They might be your coworkers, friends, or hairdresser. They need to be real people, preferably from outside your app team. You want to select people who feel comfortable being frank with you. It's especially helpful if your proxies are as different from you (and each other) as chalk and cheese, despite your shared interests.

Your proxies will put a human face on your customers, encouraging you to design for real people rather than for a crowd of faceless and homogenous users. You will test your designs on them, watch how they react, and ask them to give you upfront and honest feedback about the features and layout. This will unlock ideas and help you to empathize with your users so you can figure out the features they *really want* and create designs that make perfect sense to them. Even more, it keeps you focused on what matters most to them, rather than diverging and suddenly finding yourself trying to appeal to too broad of an audience.

You can find proxies all around you—at work, the gym, on the seat next to you in the reception area. Get to know them by inviting them to coffee or joining them at their lunchroom so you can see where they work. Go shopping, catch a game together, or try the happy hour martini. Notice where and how they are using their iPhones and iPads, and discover as much as you can about them, from their biggest fear to their favorite foods. Don't try to guess the answers or base them on your own views because that defeats the whole purpose.

Your proxies' opinions and values will be your beacon throughout your project, so it helps to create an outline like the one shown in Figure 2-2 to clearly see their touch points at a glance. You can download a sample proxy summary sheet from the book's companion website at ideatoiphone.com.

FIGURE 2-2: An example of a personality summary created for a travel app.

Post photos of your proxies on your computer to help keep you focused.

TIP

Making the most of your research

The more you get to know your tribe and tribe proxies, the better you'll be at mastering the two critical areas of success: designing a flawless app and reaching your key influencers. The insights they provide will guide you in the following activities:

- Creating an app your tribe wants based on the problems they're trying to solve.

- Selecting features that fit your tribe so your app has viral potential.

- Designing an interface that they can understand in 15 seconds or less.

- Discovering their hangouts both on and offline so you can start tapping into their networks.

- Recognize their key influencers so you can formulate relationships and they can broadcast your message to a wider audience.

You'll start by using your new wisdom to improve your original app idea and make it even stronger. You do this by finding the overlap of your tribe's cares and wants and your own passions and interests.

Creating Apps That People Really Want

Building an app in this competitive market can be scary. It's even tougher if you're uncertain whether your app idea will catch on and people will buy it. An easier and less risky approach is to figure out what they want and give it to them.

The important thing is first building something that people want or need, then word of mouth will take you pretty far.

—Loren Brichter, Founder of atebits (Letterpress app)

Rather than thinking about your app idea as a list of features, consider the *benefits* it brings to your audience. For example, people want apps that give them superpowers, help them solve a problem, or simply let them unwind. If the basis of your app is to give people more of what they want, or less of what they don't want, you're onto a winning idea. To help you along this path, I offer three app strategies. Consider that your app will probably be an overlap of any or all of these options.

The apps that are the easiest to use and most impactful on people's lives are the ones users love to talk about and recommend to their friends.

—Patrick Wetherille, VP of Product Marketing at Lose It! (Lose It! app)

Strategy 1: Fix a problem

If you've done any air travel over the past few years, you would think the industry is striving to create an axis of misery. Now think of all the apps that emerged out of the opportunity to relieve some of the pains of travels. At the time of writing, seven of the top ten travel apps are flight trackers.

The easiest, most straightforward problems to fix are your own. By resolving your own problems, you create an app that *you* desire and want for yourself. Solve your own dilemmas. Humor yourself. Suit your own needs. By using this approach, you create something you already understand because it's your *own* wishes you're fulfilling, not someone else's.

Over the next few months, you'll be making all sorts of decisions about the design, the look and feel, the branding and promotion. Making those decisions is almost impossible if you're trying to solve someone else's needs. But if you're only doing it for yourself, those decisions come easier and quicker.

Eventually you'll find the overlap of solving your own problem while at the same time helping your tribe, too. And soon you'll discover thousands of people who need exactly what you needed.

Think about all your favorite apps and how they made a difference in your world. Now imagine if those apps didn't exist, and consider how your life would be different. Create apps that people would miss if they suddenly disappeared.

My Solution Is Your Solution

I stumbled into the app business by happenstance because I wanted a portable gratitude journal. When I discovered that such a thing didn't exist, I decided to create one myself. It's simply a journal in which you write down five things you're grateful for that day. I had a love affair with my idea because I solved my own problem.

As it turns out, I unearthed a huge market of people who wanted exactly the same app. They became the crux of my success. I originally created the app to indulge myself, but the real key to my fortune is that I'm actually helping *other people* pursue their passions and goals.

Strategy 2: Amuse, charm and captivate

For every app that empowers us do things better, faster and easier, there are two more to help us waste time. But as John Lennon put it, "Time you enjoyed wasting is not wasted time."

These clever apps rescue us from boredom by giving us something to do. They let us briefly escape the world around us so we can unwind and relax. They entertain, challenge, and enchant us like a teenage crush.

These apps flood the iTunes charts and for good reason. They're perfect for mobile devices because they're always with you, ready to save you from any idle moment. The touch screens and motion-detected accelerometer on the iPhone and iPad make these devices perfect entertainment machines.

Games aren't the only apps that fall into this strategy. In fact, all apps can delight, amuse, and engross us enough that we burn our grilled cheese sandwich. In Chapter 3 you'll learn how to design apps that encourage your audience to pause, have fun, and briefly get lost in time.

Strategy 3: Connect us with people and places

Location-based apps geo-tag your information, alert friends when you're nearby, share photos of cool places close to you, and allow you to broadcast your profile everywhere you go so the paparazzi are ready. These apps put a microscope on the vast abundance of information around you, filter it based on your personal details, and pump it out in a useful manner.

Location-based apps are ideal for devices that we carry with us whether we're zipping across town or leap-frogging the planet. More than a "Starbucks finder," these apps take advantage of the iPhone and iPad sensors and any personal information we share to create our very own community of favorite businesses, people, and places. They're a mash-up of maps, camera, and social networking.

All apps can take advantage of the wonderful variety of the sensors available on the iPhone and iPad, not just geo-location specific apps. Sensors like the GPS, camera, and audio make apps more helpful as well as social. For instance, a to-do app can toss up a reminder to pick up your dry cleaning just as you're passing the shop. Later in this chapter you'll learn about adding features like Facebook to personalize your app, making it both useful and viral.

Ingredients for Magnificent App Ideas

If you don't have an app idea yet, stop shopping in the App Store, put away your iPhone, and get some fresh air. Visit a museum. People watch. Flip through some really old books. Go for a nice long walk. Play a round of golf. Learn how to tango. Indulge your curiosities.

Studying the hottest apps might seem like a perfectly fine approach to inspiration, but in truth it's toxic. Nothing will lead you to app death sooner. You will wind up just copying what's already been done, fighting for a sliver of the market with a half-baked idea. The meaning and purpose behind your idea will be lost, as well the ambition you need to see it through. In the end, you'll just hatch out another knock-off that doesn't make iTunes daylight.

Ideas come to us each differently, and we have to be ready for them. If you're preoccupied with the intricacies of other apps, you're not opening yourself to your own unique app idea. Yank yourself away from electronics and the copy-paste world and treat yourself to something fun and different. Your idea is waiting there for you. You just have to show up.

Don't be afraid of crazy ideas

A wickedly clever idea for an app can feel terribly foreign and silly at first, and you might feel it's so far off the beaten path that no one will understand what it's all about. People probably won't even grasp your idea until they finally see it in action on their device.

Don't let this uncertainty stop you. This feeling of unease is what divides you from the mediocrity of apps that get lost on iTunes. Instead, embrace your discomfort as a sign that you are on the right track.

Fresh and new ideas are unnerving because people don't have anything to which to compare them. But when they *do* grasp your idea, they are overwhelmed and it sticks with them.

Let your passions inspire you

Put your passion at the root of your app idea. It can be anything—travel, fitness, food, children, jokes, music, gardening, or dogs. Whatever sparks your interests, gets you excited, or has you daydream while sitting in meetings with your boss. Bollywood movies, yoga, blueberry pancakes. The options are endless.

Having your fabulous Star Wars collection be the heart of your app idea might seem ridiculous. In truth, using your passion gives you a huge advantage because you're already a Han Solo virtuoso. As an old pro, you understand what works and what doesn't. You're not making wild assumptions or using far-fetched ideas.

The enthusiasm you feel for your life's passion will be reflected in your app and branding, giving it a unique pizzazz. And when you're successful, other app developers won't be able to copy your app because it has *your* fingerprints all over it.

Add a dash of personality

As absurd as this may sound, think of your app as a person. It could be anyone—a hero, a character, or your best friend. Think about their personality and the qualities that appeal to you, and tuck those characteristics into the details of your app through sounds, gestures, colors, animations and humorous copy.

For example, the satisfying ascending charms when you check off items in Clear along with the app's warm colors and wise quotes invoke the serenity of the Dalai Lama. Although these tiny details offer little utility to the app, they certainly give the app a personality, shifting it from being a piece of software into a friend that connects with our human qualities and emotional values.

Your app's charisma affects people by stirring up positive emotions. Not only will people want to use your app more, they will also be much more inclined to share their excitement with others, as well as be more forgiving if they experience any difficulty.

To pull this off, explore ways to use small details like the color combinations, screen transitions, copy, and sound to elicit positive emotional responses. For example, sound can be a delicate yet powerful characteristic such as the reassuring "pop" we hear when Twitter is done refreshing. Color combinations can also invoke emotions. Blue and white is associated with inspiration and trust, which might explain why we see it on Facebook, Twitter, LinkedIn and countless other places. Use copy that reflects the emotions you want to evoke and explore ways to use small animations and screen transitions to make your app come to life.

TIP   You can also add personality by thinking about the emotions or attitude you want your app to evoke. Should people feel silly and youthful? Excited and dangerous? Cool and sexy? Plant these characteristics in your app to make it more human and enjoyable.

Also, the way your app responds to touch is another way to give it personality. Gestures are a powerful connection between the interface and user and the app should respond instantly like magic; otherwise we're reminded that we're actually using a computer rather playing with a virtual object.

Tapbots (tapbots.com) has had one hit app after another because it revolutionized mundane tasks by injecting a distinct personality into all five of its apps. Their interfaces act like fun little robots that are friendly, charming, and loyal. Tracking your weight, converting measurements, and doing calculations are now far more enjoyable with these little friends.

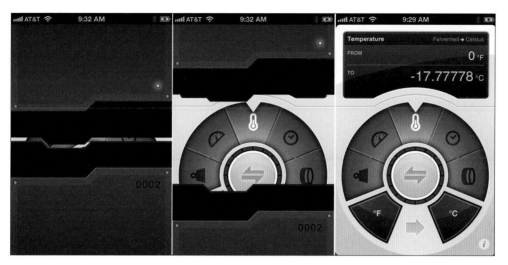

FIGURE 2-3: The app developer Tapbots has created numerous successful apps all reflecting the same warm robot character. The opening animation of Convertbot instantly shows the app's charisma and sophisticated charm.
Source: Convertbot iPhone app

Spice it up with surprises

Great apps constantly flatter and reward us with each tap, twist, and pinch: a laugh, some wisdom, feeling of familiarity, or mission accomplished. Subtle reassurances such as a button changing color give us confidence that we're on the right path. Sweeten that pleasant feeling with some extra goodness by sneaking in a little unexpected surprise—just something simple and fun.

The Dandelion app lets readers advance the story by blowing on their tablet screens to disperse seeds from digital dandelions (see Figure 2-4). The Quip iPad app has little wings that flutter when you update your Twitter list. The Paper Town Friends app uses laughter and a stop-motion animation as the characters come together on the screen. The Clear app treats customers to a free theme when they follow a certain developer's Twitter account. Plant some surprises in your app that your customers can both stumble upon and seek out, and you'll have a definite moneymaker.

The key is to keep the surprise simple and graceful, not to interfere with the main task at hand. The surprise complements your app because it's in keeping with your app's purpose and reflects its personality. They're pleasant hidden prizes tucked into your design. Check out the site Little Big Details (littlebigdetails.com) for inspiration on ways to plant magic in your app.

FIGURE 2-4: Dandelion iPad app lets readers disperse dandelion seeds by blowing on the screen.
Source: Dandelion app

Mix in some viral goodness

Getting an app that will spread faster than celebrity gossip takes a lot more than bolting on Twitter and Facebook buttons. It requires strategizing a world of social interaction inside your app.

First and foremost, your app has to offer something valuable to share. That something can be posting a photo, discovering a great wine, taking turns in a game, reading an article, creating a playlist, or completing a five-mile run. Whatever it happens to be, it's your customer's little pride and joy, *and* it's shareable.

When people share their little gem, they get warm fuzzy feelings of goodness that keeps them checking into the app over and over. The more people check into the app, the more praise and delight they get out of it. And when the app's audience grows, the value just keeps going up.

To help you mix in some viral goodness into your app, ask yourself these few questions:

- Does my app offer something valuable to share?
- How will people be rewarded when they share?
- Why would people want to share?
- Why would they want the contacts in their network to share?
- How will my app motivate people to keep sharing over the long term?

The typical viral flow starts when the user creates something and then shares it, leading to friends discovering the creation and downloading the app so they can get in on the action too (see Figure 2-5). Using this approach, the most obvious way to offer social interaction in your app is to add some buttons so people can share their creations (or actions) on Twitter, Facebook, email, and SMS. For example, the Faces app allows people to design silly faces of friends that can be posted on Facebook, tweeted, and emailed (see Figure 2-6).

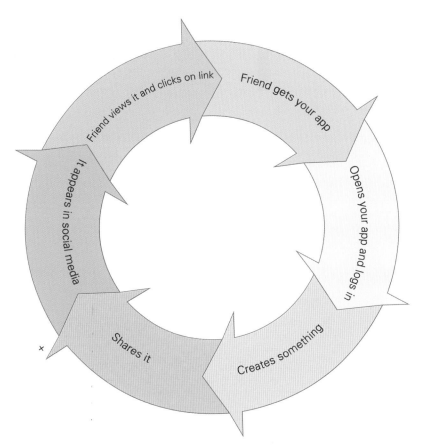

FIGURE 2-5: shows the typical viral flow of sharing.

FIGURE 2-6: Social interaction in the Faces app.
Source: Faces app

Unfortunately this approach misses a lot of opportunity because not every user is going to share and only a small percentage of friends will actually see what is shared, let alone click on the link *and* download the app. To truly go viral, social interaction needs to be about *engaging* your audience. Here are a few examples of how your app can do that:

- Offer one-click sign-on via Facebook or Twitter rather than a username and password.
- Display profile pictures of friends during authentication to increase their audience as well as yours.
- The first screen motivates users to get started.
- Automatically personalize the content displayed by tapping into data about their friends and interests.
- Let users create exclusive groups and invite others to participate, such as a team of supporters in a weight loss or training app.
- Send them useful notifications motivating them to return.

- Offer a limited time promotion to encourage people to opt into the social experience of your app.

- Give users control to filter content, save their favorites, and post to multiple social sites and platforms with one tap.

- Create challenges in your app that users can partake in.

- Promote users with exceptional content or activities and let users promote each other.

Facebook integration is the easiest way to unleash all sorts of social interaction opportunities. With more than 1 billion members, and a team at Facebook dedicated to getting developers to add the network to apps, it's a viral gold mine.

A Brief Introduction to Integrating with Facebook

At the time of writing, nine out of the top ten apps on iTunes are integrated with Facebook. Clearly, there's a reason that everything ranging from real estate to running apps is riding the Facebook wave. It's why we spend more time checking Words With Friends than our email.

Take a look at what a powerhouse Facebook integration can be. *Diamond Dash* initially added in Facebook so its customers could log in to the game using their Facebook accounts and play against their Facebook friends (see Figure 2-7). Then it engaged users by creating weekly tournaments and the app went ballistic. If a player beats a friend's score, the victory is posted to the winner's timeline. When they reach a new level, win a medal, or unlock features, *Diamond Dash* announces it to their entire Facebook crowd. This dynamic created a friendly competition, pulling people back to the game a stunning 18.5 million times in just one month.

You can integrate your app with Facebook in two ways. The first is through Apple's iOS software development kit (SDK). Facebook is included in the SDK like a LEGO block (see Chapter 1), which means you can add in the feature of connecting to Facebook without needing additional code. Your app could connect and post content to the user's wall just like the Faces app does.

The second method is by downloading and including the Facebook SDK for iOS into your app. The Facebook SDK is more robust and has more options than the iOS SDK. For example, people can tag Facebook friends in their creation, such as in a photo, and that photo will then get posted to the friends' wall. You could create a goal for users, such as using the app seven days straight. When a user reaches that goal, a medal or freebie is posted to his or her wall. If two friends have the same app installed, Facebook knows this and connects them. If a friend doesn't have the app, you can suggest it and Facebook will send her a notification with a link directly to your app's iTunes download.

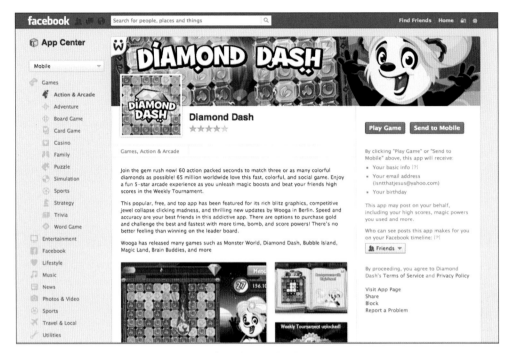

FIGURE 2-7: Diamond Dash app promoted on the Facebook app page.
Source: Facebook

We could fill the rest of this chapter on all that Facebook has to offer. Visit Facebook's developer website at http://developers.facebook.com/ to discover how Facebook integration can profit your app. You might also find the following sites useful:

- Facebook SDK: http://developers.facebook.com/ios/

- List of Facebook SDK experts: http://apps.facebook.com/pmddirectory/

- Facebook app site: www.facebook.com/appcenter/

| TIP | Adding in Facebook's SDK to your app also gets your app listed on Facebook's app site for free. |

Which Device Is Right for My App? iPhone, iPad, or Both

You might not be aware of this, but there are actually three types of apps that you can download. The thing that sets them apart is the device they're designed to run on; the iPhone and iPod touch, the iPad, or all three.

- First are *universal apps,* designed to run on any iDevice. The code recognizes whether it's running on the iPhone or iPad, and displays the right interface.

- Next are apps that run only on the iPad. You can't even install them on the iPhone or iPod touch.

- Last and most common are apps designed to run on the iPhone and iPod touch, but which also scale up for the iPad, although it doesn't look as good (see Figure 2-8). I refer to these as *universal lite*.

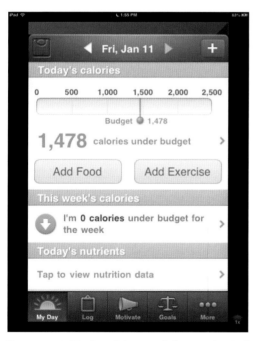

FIGURE 2-8: The Lose It! app scaled up on the iPad. The developers have plans for an iPad version as well.

Source: Lose It! app

Your gut reaction might be to go for a universal app because has the largest market, but there's actually more to it than that. To help you decide which device to go for, take a look at the pros and cons of all three options.

The benefits of targeting both iPhone and iPad

You can think of a universal app like two sides of the same coin. These apps are a single piece of software that recognizes the device it's running on and knows whether to display "heads" or "tails." Each "side" is optimized for the specific device.

For example, if the app is running on the iPad, it will display a different screen layout than on the iPhone because the screen sizes aren't the same and that influences how we navigate the app. The exceptions to this rule are usually game and book apps. The layouts for apps like these work fine on all devices, so they don't need to be optimized for each device type. Figure 2-9 shows the Pandora app on both devices.

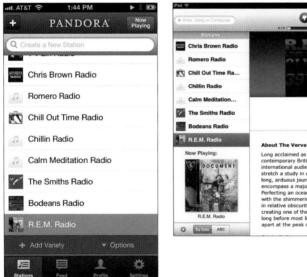

FIGURE 2-9: The Pandora app is a universal app with layouts designed differently for the iPhone (left) and iPad (right).

Source: Pandora Inc

Universal apps have a small plus sign next to them on the iTunes store to help app shoppers spot them (see Figure 2-10). Just like other apps, customers only pay for a universal app once but can download it to as many of their devices as they like. Even though it may look different on the iPad than on the iPhone, it's still the same bundle of code.

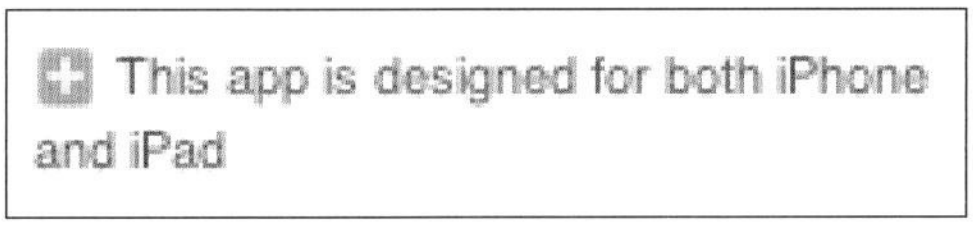

FIGURE 2-10: The plus sign on the App Store indicates that it's a universal app.
Source: Apple iTunes

The advantages to creating a universal app are pretty clear. First, more devices means more sales. Also, you're not isolating anyone from using your app because they don't have the right device, and that makes for a happier audience. And because the app looks stunning on both their iPad and iPhone, customers won't mind paying more for it.

In the long run, you'll only be maintaining a single bundle of code, rather than a bundle for the iPhone and a separate one for the iPad. This means that when you add new features, you can add them to both platforms without having to go through the process of coding it twice and submitting two separate apps for approval.

It's not all roses and sunshine though. For one thing, designing for both devices takes more time and money than if you targeted just one. It might be smarter for you to wait until you can read the reviews (or see if your app even sells) before investing the extra resources.

Another thing to consider is that downloading your app can feel much slower. That's because the size of your app (called the *binary size*) could be much larger if you decide to include images for all the different screen resolutions. (Chapter 5 goes into details about the image size requirements.)

Try to keep the app's binary size no bigger than 50MB so people can download it over a cell
network. You have the option to scale images in your code so you don't need so many versions
of each image. Talk to your developer about the details.   TIP

Unless you install analytics (discussed in Chapter 7), you won't have a clue who's download-ing your app more—iPhone or iPad owners—because the sales reports you get from Apple aren't broken down by device type. The reviews on iTunes aren't separated either, so if your app is having problems on the iPad, for example, those reviews show up to iPhone app shop-pers too. All this can make deciding how to improve your app feel like you're just flying blind.

Both Apple and your customers will vote in favor of a universal app, but the developer com-munity is hotly debating the topic. Because time and money are of the essence, isn't it smarter to target just one device for launch and wait to create a universal app later? Unfortunately, converting the code of a targeted app into a universal app isn't that straight forward (see Chapter 7 for more details on porting your app from one device to another).

You might be better off developing an entirely separate app for the second platform instead. This gives you the freedom to charge a different price for the iPhone version than your iPad version. As you're probably starting to see, all these choices can get confusing, so let's look at the benefits of creating an app just for the iPhone (universal lite).

Why the iPhone's smaller touchscreen might be best

For every iPad in this world, there are at least two iPhones. Top that number off with the millions of iPod touch owners and you'll discover nearly everyone you know has one of these devices. It's by far your biggest market, which means if you're targeting just one device, the iPhone clearly has the biggest sales potential.

You'll get your app to market faster because you're just designing and coding for just one device. It will also lower your cost and your risks. After your app is released, customers will clamor for an iPad version if they want it. By then, your designs, features, and budgets will have all improved. It's okay to make them wait. Facebook made its audience wait nearly two years for an iPad version of its app.

Why the iPad's extended views are the way to go

The iPad was outselling desktop PC's *before* the iPad Mini was even introduced, and that's not something to be sneezed at.

Be careful to remember that the iPad isn't just a big iPhone, and it's far more than a couch potato's companion or an instant babysitter. It's equally useful for parents to read *Dr. Seuss* before bedtime as it is for a pop star to compose her next big hit. Unlike the iPhone, the iPad truly breaks us free from our computers while still giving us the power to edit large documents, share movies, and connect with others.

The most obvious difference between the iPad and iPhone is the screen size and resolution. The iPad is nearly three times bigger, so we hold it differently than the iPhone. We need either both hands or a place to rest it. A larger screen also means we do far less zooming and scrolling than on iPhone apps. This is a serious advantage for games, editing documents, note taking or watching videos. The keypad is also much larger, making it a clear winner over the iPhone's tricky size.

Certain view options, such as popovers and split views, have typically been available only in iPad apps, although popovers have recently been found in iPhone apps as well. A *popover* is a little window that appears "over" the main screen and has an arrow pointing to the spot where the user tapped to open it (see Figure 2-11). It offers additional information, options, or functionality like the ability to email an article.

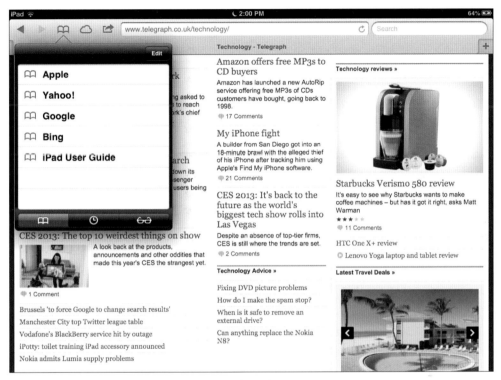

FIGURE 2-11: An example of a popover view in the Safari app.

Source: Safari app

Split view is the popover's trusty sidekick. When people turn the iPad sideways (horizontal mode) a panel of options can appear on the left side of the screen. For example, when the iPad Mail is in horizontal mode, you see two panels at once: accounts, mailboxes, and messages are on the left side and a single message is on the right. When iPad Mail is turned to vertical mode, the left panel disappears and just the panel with the message displays, but you can tap a button at the top left to show a popover of messages (see Figure 2-12).

Teamed together, popovers and split views let users make choices without having the leave the screen they're on. That means a lot less switching between screens in an iPad app than in an iPhone app, making them far more efficient to use.

Some folks have completely dumped their computers in favor of an iPad because it's always on, so accessing apps is a lot faster than waiting for a computer to boot up. Some professionals rely on iPads because they conduct their entire business on the move, like nurses, teachers, builders, and waiters.

FIGURE 2-12: The Mail app in vertical mode (left) and split view (right).
Source: Mail app

Another win for the iPad, from an app seller's perspective, is that the apps are generally priced higher. The research firm Distimo discovered that the average iPad app runs around $5.26 while the average iPhone app is more than a dollar less at $3.84. Lastly, because there are fewer iPad-specific apps, the market isn't quite as saturated.

Doing Your Research

Perhaps you feverishly searched the iTunes App Store as soon as your app idea hit you, investigating to see whether you could find any app remotely similar. If you haven't, you should. Even if you only have a foggy idea of what your app will be, start researching. Don't search just iTunes, but also the entire Internet. You may find teaser sites of similar apps or other consumer products in the same vein.

| TIP | Crowd funding sites like kickstarter.com and indiegogo.com are also great places to investigate for app projects that may possibly rival yours. |

Peel back the iTunes cover and take a really good look at what's inside by becoming an app expert. Set a budget of around $50–$100 and go app crazy, downloading as many as you can. See which apps become popular over the next weeks and which fall in the charts. You might be surprised how quickly they move around. Download apps from the Hall of Fame and ones that are rotten. Get competitor apps and ones completely outside your app's domain.

Even if your app idea already exists, don't get discouraged. There could still be plenty of good reasons to pursue your project. It could be a proven idea that has been done tens of times before but still can be done better. *Instagram* is a perfect example. There are dozens of apps that allow you to take a photo, apply filters, and share the picture with your friends, but *Instagram* designed a unique and better product by simplifying the process, integrating with Facebook, and generally making the picture taking and sharing process as simple and painless as possible.

Remember, you're not searching for your app idea but ways to make your idea even better. Look for features you can sharpen or combine with another feature to make your app even more robust. Read the reviews and feedback, and see what works and what doesn't. Are you about to head down the same dark alley? Or is there a hot fad that will light your app on fire? What are people on Twitter saying about the app? How about their Facebook page?

Go outside your app market space, and explore apps that simply intrigue you. Get a feel for the iPhone's and iPad's limitless capabilities. Maybe you'll discover an entirely new use for the device. Keep your mind open because even ideas that have failed can be shaped into something lucrative.

Making a (Mission) Statement

Taking a wrong turn on your vacation may lead you to a little café you never would have known about otherwise, but in an app project diversions can cost you thousands. To help keep your app project on course, write an app mission statement. This is a single sentence that boils down your idea to its core by saying what your app does and who it's for. (Apple refers to the mission statement as the *Application Definition Statement*.) This statement will be your North Star throughout your project, pointing you in the right direction, and helping you manage scope and stay within budget.

Paste your app mission statement to your wall, computer, or white board—somewhere you will see it every day. **TIP**

Honing your mission statement requires four simple steps:

BRAINSTORM

1. List all the features you can dream up for your app. Go ahead and brainstorm. Include every little feature you can imagine. Fill up your idea board with stars, hearts, and shooting arrows. Write down anything that would possibly set your app apart. Have a ball and don't worry if the list seems too long. You'll narrow it down later.

2. Identify the key feature. Your list of features might fill two walls, but there should be just one feature that stands out as your beloved, essential superstar. This feature is your app's key purpose, and it will be performed first-class with a tap of the button (or a swipe, twist, or shake). That feature will be so simple that it can be described in half of a sentence. For example, "track my flights" or "line up some blocks" or "build a rocket." (for the Flight+ app, Matching with Friends app, and Wee Rockets app, respectively)

3. Describe your target audience (your tribe). Narrow down your tribe to a quiet little niche that will allow you to be the big fish in their pond. A niche market won't diminish your sales, but it will make designing and marketing far easier. It also makes finding your tribe online and elsewhere a whole lot easier.

4. Combine the target audience and key feature. To construct your app mission statement, pull together your app's single key purpose and your audience into one sentence—for example:

   • "view great recipes" + "food lovers" = "A modern recipe collection for food lovers who want to try new and easy meals with ingredients they already have."

   • "search for local yoga classes" + "health-conscious people" = "A location-based yoga class finder for health-conscious people who want to know when and where the nearest class is located."

Keep tweaking your mission statement until you are absolutely certain it captures your app's one key feature and a small audience who will be using it. It's crucial you get it just right because it will be your compass, guiding you through your entire app project.

You will refer to your mission statement to methodically filter and prioritize features. It will help you clearly communicate your idea to your team. It might even help you realize whether your initial decision to create an app is still the right one. You may discover by creating a mission statement that your objective has changed completely.

Avoiding Scope Creep: The $120 Bottle of Shampoo

There is a running joke in my family that whenever I pop down to the shop for a single bottle of shampoo, I wind up coming home with $120 worth of stuff. Admit it, we're all guilty of those quick trips to the store that start innocently with a small basket and end up with a full cart. The same thing can happen to your app, and it's called *scope creep*.

Scope creep is the tendency to just toss one more little thing into your app thinking it will increase its value. The only things it increases are your costs, time, frustration and risk of app failure. Resist the urge to keep adding in more. A complex range of features won't make your app successful. In fact, you'll achieve the opposite. Instead, strip down your app to the purely gorgeous minimum to impress.

Focus on creating an app that does one thing very well. You can always add in features later. **TIP**

Prioritize your features

As tempting as it is to give your tribe everything their hearts could desire, the primary goal is to master the golden 15-second rule; your app must be understood and appreciated in 15 seconds or less to be successful. To achieve this, pluck a pencil from your kid's backpack and scratch out every feature idea that doesn't support your app mission statement, because you really don't need most of your ideas.

> *It's better to launch with a good working app with core features, than a half-working app with loads of features.*

—Alain Hufkins, Co-founder of Wee Taps (WeeRocket app)

Too many features can cause you to lose the focus of your app's real purpose. You could be creating unnecessary screens that only send people down a rabbit's hole of confusion. You might be offering too many choices when people need only one. If you have any question about whether you need a feature, just get rid of it. Then do that again until you trimmed out at least 80 percent of your ideas. Fewer features mean it will cost a lot less to create your app, it will get to market faster, and it will be easier and cheaper to maintain.

Now look at the remaining features and label each one as the primary task or a secondary task. The primary task is your app's single key purpose, as defined by your mission statement. If it's a diary app, the key task might be to add a new entry. If it's a photo app, it might be to edit an image.

Like ice cream on apple pie, secondary features make the primary task even better. After you create your journal entry, for example, you might want to change the font. These features are the bare minimum of what it would take to make your app's key purpose easier and more enjoyable. You might just end up with only a single secondary feature. Remember, less is better.

If you are having problems losing the bulk, go through each feature and ask yourself, "Is it essential to my app's core purpose and [*insert proxies' names here*] goals?" If it's not, set it aside for now.

Limiting the app to the bare essentials makes the app scalable and your project far more manageable. It also makes reaching your niche market easier. So ask yourself...

- Do I really need to offer a selection of themes, or are a couple good enough for now?

- Do people really need to register an email address, or can they get a taste for my app first?

- Do I really need to animate this, or will a simple screen transition do?

| TIP | You might find it helpful to hire an iOS developer to consult on your app features. He can shed light on the technical complexities, costs, and other alternatives. |

Save some killer features for updates

One of the smartest moves you can make for both your budget and your marketing strategy is to purposefully withhold a key feature until *after* your app goes live. Customers will be so delighted to discover the new features in an update; it will be as if someone secretly left a cupcake on their desk (see Figure 2-13).

Saving a few killer features for updates is a winner in so many ways. First off, your audience will applaud that you're investing in the app and be excited that the best is yet to come, leading to positive reviews and more downloads. This also gives them time to tell you exactly what features they *do* want, which can save you from wasting energy and resources on unnecessary ones. Why pay for features up front if no one really wants them?

Secondly, timing is everything, and this strategy gets you to market as fast as possible and for less money. After you bank some coin from your app, you can add requested features, paying for them with your revenues. By reinvesting revenues, you won't need as much to fund your app project upfront. It also buys you time to design and develop features properly. High fives all around!

FIGURE 2-13: Facebook's iPhone app has changed tremendously since it first launched (left) compared to how it looks today (left).
Source: Facebook

Avoiding headaches: Features to leave out

Everything is limited when it comes to the iPhone and iPad—attention spans, pixels, development time, and budget. Your patience will be especially limited once you start developing and testing your app because you'll just want it out there. Spare yourself some future frustrations now by considering whether the following features are truly needed in your first release, or can wait until you know the ropes a little better and have a solid team in place.

Avoid features that require you to own a server

It's best to leave out any features that require owning your own server. Servers introduce all sorts of legal, security, and administrative headaches. You will need to hire someone to maintain the server for you, making sure your customers' data doesn't get hacked or go down. Servers need updating and rebooting, and that's a job for an $80,000-per-year expert.

If you absolutely must store customers' data, there are alternatives to owning your own server. You can store data on other companies' servers using an *application programming interface (API)*, a set of methods for making secure requests to access data from other servers.

Sites such as Amazon and Flickr offer APIs that are designed to let you take content from those sites and put it in your app. Dropbox and Amazon Web Services provide APIs to let you publish content from your app to their servers and platforms.

Here are two other server alternatives:

- **iCloud** (developer.apple.com/icloud)—Apple offers an API service for iCloud so apps can sync in the same way the photo library works. If customers have multiple devices, apps can sync the devices over iCloud so the content on them is the same. iCloud also works as a backup if customers lose or replace their device. The latest improvements in the iOS SDK have made iCloud integration fairly trivial, so it's almost standard for most apps.

- **Parse** (www.parse.com)—This service provides a complete kit with everything you need to get up and running for a data-sharing app like Instagram. It's free for up to a million API pull requests and a million API push requests per month, and $200 a month for more. Parse hosts data for over 35,000 apps, proving it's a great solution for developers.

Avoid features that require moderating

You and I probably wouldn't dream of posting content that would make a sailor blush, but unfortunately others feel differently. Which means that if your app allows people to share content, someone needs to police what is put out there. This is a full-time, 24/7 job. Keeping up can feel harder than running a race in flip-flops. Also, you could be putting yourself and your company in legal jeopardy if questionable or copyrighted content is posted. Apps allowing people to post content should always include a button for users to report inappropriate content, as shown in Figure 2-14.

FIGURE 2-14: Instagram includes a button for users to report inappropriate content.
Source: Instagram

In 2011, the number one selling app, *PostSecret,* was killed off by its creator, Frank Warren, after just three months on the App Store. The app was selling like hotcakes because it allowed anyone to anonymously post a secret and a photo. Unfortunately, a small group of chumps thought it was cool to put out abusive posts, which forced Warren to shut it down. His team had to moderate each piece of content, working 24 hours a day, 7 days a week, prescreening up to 30,000 secrets a day. People complained to him, Apple, and the FBI about the content. Worst of all, threats were made to site moderators and to Warren's family. In the end, even a top-selling app wasn't worth it.

Avoid anything that requires a Terms of Service agreement

Terms of Service (TOS) agreements are rules people must accept to use your app. Try to leave out features that requires them because these agreements are expensive. These huge documents have tons of clauses and paragraphs. They add to your costs because you need to hire a lawyer to come up with the terms.

A good Intellectual Property (IP) attorney charges around $250 an hour, and the average Terms of Service agreement can take several weeks to compile, adding to both your budget and your timeline. That alone can run you more than the app development itself. Instead, try to launch without the need for TOS and use your profits to add it in later.

Keeping Your Idea Confidential and Protected

You might be nervous about putting your app idea out there out of fear that someone might take it. Most people are too busy with other obligations like their jobs, kids, and an overdue oil change to steal your idea. They don't have the time or interest. Unfortunately, "most" still leaves room for "some," and you will need to protect yourself from some of the bad folks out there.

You can have a lawyer draft a *non-disclosure agreement* (*NDA*). This confidentiality agreement is designed to protect your idea. Free templates are available to download online if you can't afford a lawyer. Just be sure to read each word of the dry legalese first.

Ask everyone to sign your NDA first before sharing your ideas with him or her. This includes any prospective freelancers, advisors, and anyone who will test your app.

Will it hurt to skip the NDA? Not if you completely trust the person, which may be the case with your proxies or the helpful neighbor who offered to test the app. Then a friendly reminder is good enough. But if you don't know someone well enough to have complete confidence in his discretion, the chances of him taking your idea are real. I know because I've been there.

I once recruited some beta testers by sending out an email to my newsletter distribution list requesting volunteers. The slots filled in the first hour and I was tickled pink with my success of enlisting generous people who went on to find all sorts of bugs in the app.

Fast-forward a couple of months, and I noticed another app just hit iTunes vaguely similar to mine. I recognized the developer's name immediately from my beta testers list. He was one of the first to offer his service. I had only myself to blame for failing to do my homework and making everyone sign an NDA before getting involved with the project.

Testing Your Idea's Pull Power in Three Easy Steps

Now that your idea has evolved from a nebulous notion into something more solid, you probably want to see if anyone would buy it. You could run it past a few insightful friends who will most likely applaud your brilliance, or you could ask your trusty eight-ball.

If you want something more scientific, there are ways to micro-test your idea to see if people would even consider using your app. These tests are designed to gauge your idea's appeal based on hard data, so your decision to press ahead hinges on more than your intuition or a few well-meaning friends.

This basic three-step test won't tell you how much you'll make from your app, but you will see whether complete strangers think your idea is worth a minute of their time. All for a fraction of what it costs to create an app. Not a bad gamble.

Step 1: Create a site for your app

Even though your app doesn't even exist yet, you'll create a website advertising it to potential buyers. This site helps you determine how many people might actually buy your app by tracking the number of visitors to the site and how many people try to purchase your app.

You can build your one page site (also called a *landing page*) as if your app is already for sale, with fake screen shots, a few key features, and a "download from the App Store" button. The buying experience won't be anything like the App Store, but it will give you an idea whether people are interested in your app.

Services such as Unbounce (www.unbounce.com) make it possible for you to create a landing page in minutes. Unbounce offers a few predesigned iPhone app templates that you can easily edit through its drag-and-drop dashboard. Another option is to build a landing page using a template from Themeforest (www.themeforest.net). A template costs about $10, and you'll need some basic coding knowledge. Chapter 6 offers more details about creating websites.

You can reuse your landing page when you start marketing your app. The promotion message will change, but some of the graphics and text can be reused, kicking off your promotion faster. | NOTE

Step 2: Run an ad campaign

After your web page is up and running, the next step is to send some web traffic to it. If you already have a decent online audience, you can share the link to your page on your social websites. Otherwise, plan to invest about $50 to run an ad campaign using a service such as

Google AdMob or Facebook. Both of these services allow you to set a maximum daily budget so you can control how much you spend. Plan to spend $10 a day for three to five days.

Google AdMob (www.google.com/ads/admob/) is a service designed specifically to promote mobile apps within other mobile apps so potential customers will view your ad on a mobile phone. The downside is that they will also see your landing page on their phone, which might not look as good as it would on a full-screen device.

Facebook ads (www.facebook.com/advertising/) display your ad only on the Facebook website. The ad won't show in any other websites or in the Facebook mobile app. The upside is that people typically view the Facebook site from a computer, so when viewers click the ad, your landing page will look far better than if they viewed it through an iPhone or iPod Touch.

Step 3: Watch it for a week

Once you start sending traffic to your web page, you can track how many viewed your page and how many clicked the download button. Watch it for a week and see what happens.

Stats are included in Unbounce's web page solution and can be viewed right on its site. If you're building a custom landing page or using a template like the one shown in Figure 2-15, you can include Google Analytics (http://www.google.com/analytics/) to track visitors and clicks.

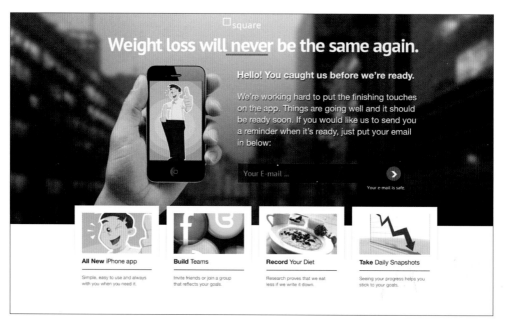

FIGURE 2-15: An example of a landing page for a fictitious app.

What to make of the test results

Frankly speaking, this test isn't 100 percent accurate. For starters, not everyone who clicks on your iTunes button will necessarily buy your app. Users may just want to read more about it. Another issue with this type of test is the outcome hinges on your ability to create good copy. Both writing and creating fake screen shots take time. Lastly, not everyone is comfortable with the idea of creating a fake web page. If that's true of you, switching out the iTunes button with an email form might be a better option, as in Figure 2-15.

If you would rather not deceive people with a fake web page, you can still run a test using a "coming soon" page instead. I discuss creating this page later in the chapter when we kick off your marketing campaign. NOTE

The flip side is that a micro-test can cost you as little as $50 and possibly save you thousands. If it validates your original gut feeling, that's better than relying on your trusty eight-ball. Also, you can reuse the landing page and its content right away when you kick off your marketing campaign.

> *We've had good luck using our kids as a way of determining whether there is demand for an idea. If our kids like a given app, many other kids seem to like it as well. We've gotten close to 2 million downloads using this approach, so something is working.*

—Christopher Taylor, Co-founder at Playtend (Counting Ants app)

Kicking Off Your Marketing Campaign

Say the words *marketing plan* in a room of developers and you might get three suggestions: build a website, email the popular blogs, and pray like crazy. The fact is, you need a much better plan than that if you want to hit it big.

Don't make the mistake of all the other app developers who start thinking about marketing after the app is developed. It will feel like you're trying to win the Tour de France on a tricycle. You'll be desperately trying to keep up rather than riding the wave of excitement in your shiny new app. You need to start your marketing *before* anything else.

As soon as you have a good notion about your app idea and features, get the word out and crank up the buzz machine. Sure, you haven't designed anything yet. You might not even know what you will call your app, but you can start connecting with your tribe, share your passions, ignite the excitement, and make some new friends.

You're not just creating an app; you're putting on a show

We're so inundated with information these days that we tune it out better than a kid being told it's bedtime. The best way to break through the clutter and connect to your audience is with a gripping story. A good tale targets the heart and most importantly, makes the person telling it appear interesting. We all want a good story to tell, so give us one.

A good story can teach us, influence us, and motivate us to take action. It makes us compelling and gives us an edge. At the very least, it can make us sound smart hanging around the water cooler. So don't just think of yourself as just an app creator; you're also a storyteller. (Chapter 6 gives examples of the type of stories that go viral.)

Your tribe already loves you; they just don't know it yet

For some folks, dreaming up riveting stories might sound dreadful and awkward. Perhaps you're more accustomed to your work speaking for you. Don't worry. You don't need to be a narcissist or a world-class hustler, and you're not bragging to get noticed. Don't think of sharing so much as talking about yourself, but as talking about your shared passions.

Tribes are constantly looking for leaders who will introduce them to a new product, service, or message that speak to their passions. Before they promote you to leader, your tribe has to know you exist. Here are some tips on how to introduce yourself without coming across as a pushy salesperson in a bad polyester suit.

- **Brag about others.** If talking about yourself seems dreadful, brag about someone else. Did someone in your tribe launch a new website, create a new product, or score tickets to a Madonna concert? Publicly praise him or her. Not only will the karma gods smile on you, but you're empowering your tribe to tell more stories about themselves.

- **Ask for help and thank people.** People actually want to help others succeed because it makes them feel valued, so speak up and ask your tribe for a lending hand. Show how grateful you are by praising the generous people who stepped forward and boasting about their amazing talents.

- **Create a common goal.** Successful leaders inspire us to rally around a common goal. Be the driver of change and create a goal for people to pursue, such as dropping ten pounds or improving their backhand. Don't fret about having all the answers because part of the fun is letting your tribe share their wisdom.

- **Help others.** We all have bills to pay and a family to feed, so offering your services for free might seem out of the question. But giving away a couple of hours of your time costs far less than hiring a PR firm. If you have a special talent, give it away. Write a guest post for a blog, offer some free consulting, or just answer a few help requests found on Twitter.

■ **Fess up to your failures.** Share your setbacks as much as your wins. Being vulnerable is not easy, but exposing your kryptonite creates a more profound and worthwhile connection. Don't dwell on the negative; rather, reveal a glimpse into your more unguarded self and find the humor.

Jumping on the social media bus

Even your grandma knows that the best way to stay in touch these days is through Facebook. Social media sites not only help you quickly connect and share with your tribe, but they give fans an easy way to follow progress and mention your app. The following list points to some of the top social sites so you can decide which ones are the best for you.

If you can, try to post something each day to at least one of your social media sites. They all offer mobile apps, so daily posting is a pretty easy target. Most of them link to each other so you can create a photo on Instagram and have it automatically posted to both Facebook and Twitter.

■ **Facebook Fan Page** (www.facebook.com/pages/create.php)—Facebook pages are like normal profile pages but are designed as a tool to promote your business or brand. Fans who "like" your page will see the photos and updates you share on their wall. You can personalize the page with a cover photo, add contact details, and highlight any major events.

■ **Twitter** (http://www.twitter.com)—Unless you've been living on Mars, you've probably heard about Twitter. If you've never used it before, Twitter is a microblogging site that allows you to send out a text of 140 characters. Tweeting is like people hanging around the water cooler injecting little bits of conversation. Some people are there all day just chatting away, and some only stop by with a burst of exciting news.

■ **Pinterest** (www.pinterest.com)—Pinterest is a social networking site that lets you publish photos from interesting links around the web. Members have a collection of theme boards where they "pin" images from cool stuff they discovered. You can create a board for each of your interests and hobbies, letting it reflect your personality and your app.

■ **Instagram** (www.instagram.com)—Instagram can make even the worst photograph look great. Because this service is free and so viral, it's a great way to share your personal side with photos of your pet hamster, your neighborhood, and your Friday night shenanigans.

■ **WordPress blog** (www.wordpress.com)—You don't have to be a prolific writer to have a blog, and you don't have to write every day. Just write about what interests you most and your experiences creating and promoting your app. Your tribe will eventually gravitate toward your blog, giving you an audience to share your story. WordPress lets you create a blog that's quick to set up, easy to use, and free.

- **Tumblr blog** (www.tumblr.com)—Another blogging option for your online face and personality is Tumblr. It's a free microblogging and social network site. You can post text and multimedia from your browser, phone, desktop, or email. Other Tumblr users can follow your posts. Think of it as an easy way to create an online scrapbook of what interests and intrigues you.

- **Flickr** (www.flickr.com)—Flickr is an online photo site that is worth checking out if you want to post teaser photos of your app or any other creative images. You can also upload photos to Flickr and then embed them in your blog.

Don't be discouraged if the only people following you right now on Twitter are your roommate and your girlfriend. The point is not the size of your current audience. You want to start creating content and sharing your story, passion, and personality so when the fans and media start flooding in, they have something to entertain them. The last thing you want is to feverishly be creating an online image the week before your app goes live.

Concocting an enticing teaser video

Since most of us don't personally know any celebrities, star athletes, or billionaires we can convince to brag about our app, the best way to make your message viral is good video. You can wait until your app is designed to create a video (Chapter 5 has more details), or jump the gun with a clever teaser video to attract an audience.

Either way, start thinking about the marketing potential for your app. For example, instead of thinking about how cool the features in your app will be, consider how cool the YouTube video selling your app will be. Then mold your app to fit that video. This might sound crazy, but your advertising will cost you peanuts and could sell an insane number of apps.

If you have the budget for a video producer, hiring one would be a wise investment, but you certainly don't need one. All you need is a clever story, a camera, and some video editing software. You could get by with using your iPhone and the iMovie app for only $4.99. (The popular movie *Apple of My Eye* (http://youtu.be/6amrKRmI1bI) was shot with iPhone 4 and edited with iMovie app in just 48 hours.)

Images and demos of your app aren't required for a teaser because you're creating a small, somewhat cryptic message to entice people without revealing too much. For example, videos like *Jotly—Rate Everything* (http://youtu.be/QIWpbfZHHzc), shown in Figure 2-16, and *Om Nom Stories* (http://youtu.be/bj3cbCE56wQ) have view counts larger than the population of New York City and yet show little or none of the app. In fact, Jotly started out as a parody video making fun of the abundance of rating apps. It proved it to be such a hit that the creators decided to make the Jotly app after all. All you need is a short story—less than 30 seconds—designed to build anticipation for the main event. Let's take a look at a few more ideas for your video.

FIGURE 2-16: The video *Jotly—Rate Everything* started as a joke but became so popular the makers decided to go ahead and create the app.
Source: YouTube.com

Try for some humor

If you find yourself staring into your cereal bowl, with no inspiration for a good video idea, try exaggerating with humor. For example, a video for a recipe app can have a college student zapping a bowl of ramen magically transform into Julia Childs whipping up the ultimate rack of lamb. If it's an app to protect private data, create a seductive bodyguard willing to risk life and limb to keep your data safe. Maybe you're creating something completely unknown. You can have two people in the middle of nowhere talking in a foreign language about all the things they can't wait to get back to—a cheeseburger, their pillow, a good shower—and mostly, your app. The subtitles can add even more humor.

There are plenty of ways to create a funny, off-the-wall story about your app with the basics around the house. Just think about your app idea differently, objectively, and humorously.

Keep it clean and simple

Of course, exaggerated humor doesn't work for all app ideas. Another approach is to mimic Apple's advertisements with simplicity and subtle music. Apple has figured out a formula that works for its market, which is also your market, so go with it. Keep the video lighthearted, clean, and convincing. You don't even have to say anything in the video. The images and text can speak for themselves.

If your app is a social network, show how it ripples to a friend, then a stranger, across the city and around the globe, returning to your back yard. If your app has a character, show that character in his natural environment, brushing his teeth and getting ready for a day on the iPhone.

When friends refuse to be actors

Not everyone dreams of staring in a viral video, so if you or your friends aren't up for going Gangnam style, you could try to use video already available online. Sites such as VideoHive (www.videohive.net) offer high-quality video for around $4 that can be used for your entire story or just a portion, giving it a more polished look.

You can also try posting an ad at your local college's drama department where you might discover a few volunteers happy to perform for a free lunch. Also check out local theater groups for your potential star. Some folks might love the chance to flaunt their talents. Another option is the Art Institutes (www.artinstitutes.edu), which has locations all over the U.S. and students itching to get started in video production and editing.

Where to share your masterpiece

Pretty much every video on the Internet has its home in YouTube (www.youtube.com) or Vimeo (www.vimeo.com), and so should yours. That's because these services are free, have a massive audience, can handle millions of visitors, and they make sharing videos to other social sites a cinch.

After uploading your video, share the link on all your social media sites. Tweet it every now and again. Post it to your Facebook page, your Tumblr site, and share some screen shots on Instagram. Most of all, include it on the "coming soon" web page you're about to create.

Keep floating the video on the social networks, and if it's not gaining traction, ask your proxies what is wrong with it. They will be more than happy to share their two cents. Don't be offended if you don't hear the joyous praise you were waiting for. This might be the first video you ever created, so cut yourself some slack. Listen because your proxies are giving you precious insight that could help you improve your message.

Growing your audience with a teaser site

A good teaser site can make all the difference in your launch, which is why getting a domain name early is key. You can reuse the landing page you built for your micro-test or create a new one. A simple one-page site is all you're after right now.

The main purpose of your site is to collect email addresses. They will be like gold when your app launches. Building a strong distribution list takes time, so you need to get started right away. A teaser site also motivates you to get your app done; once email addresses start rolling in and you see how much interest there is for your app, you'll feel a new spark to get it done.

> Even if you already have a website or blog, you should also create a separate web page designed specifically for your app. The web address will be easier for people to remember and pass along to their friends. **TIP**

Sites such as Onepagelove.com are filled with inspirational ideas for your teaser page. Gorgeous mockups of your app can wait for now. You just need to intrigue visitors enough to gain their trust, hopefully share their email, and come back again after you launch.

The site gosillk.com doesn't reveal anything about what the company is creating but speaks directly to the people who could benefit from its invention. The site themurtaughlist.com shows an iPhone app with a stock photo image, and it is more than enough to spark the imagination (see Figure 2-17).

This could be the first time visitors ever "meet" you, so make your page a friendly welcome as well as an invitation to return again. Be sure to include links to your social media pages to help build your network and include your teaser video.

You can hire a freelance web developer to customize an inexpensive template for you. Or if you have the budget, create one from scratch. (Chapter 6 goes into the details about creating websites.) If you chose to create a unique site rather than use a template, you can submit it to design galleries to create an avalanche of traffic and fans. Do a search for "web design gallery" to find dozens of sites like Onepagelove.com. Most have a way to directly submit your site. If it gets selected, all sorts of new fans will pay you a visit.

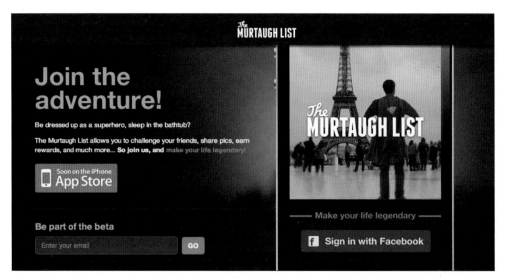

FIGURE 2-17: The teaser website for themurtaughlist.com shows just enough for visitors to gain interest so they sign up to learn more.
Source: themurtaughlist.com

This might be the first website you've ever created. Don't start hyperventilating, because that's actually a very good thing. You're picking up all sorts of new skills that will help you glide through the rest your app project, such as working with developers, managing your time, and discovering the thrill of creating something new. Mostly, you're starting to think about designs that work, which is the next vital step in evolving your ideas into a flawless app.

Key Points

- Think of your target audience as a tribe connected by common values, interests, life stage, goals, or beliefs. Share stories to strengthen the bonds of your tribe, and in return, your tribe will spread your message and app like wildfire.

- Make your life's passion the foundation of your app idea. Create something you want to use yourself every day. Aim to build something that makes people happy—if your app suddenly disappeared, people would notice.

- Make your app more human by giving it personality. Charisma connects with people and gets them talking about your app. Stir up positive emotions with subtle surprises. Integrate social networking to hit the viral hot button.

- Draft an app mission statement to keep you focused and help you make critical design decisions. Plan to strip 80 percent of the features on your wish list for your launch version.

- Plan to add in a killer feature after your app goes live. This gets your app to market faster and gets people excited knowing better is yet to come.

- Launch your marketing campaign before you even design your app. It takes a long time to build the social snowball, so start it rolling now.

CHAPTER 3

Designing Luxurious and Stunning Apps

"He who works with his hands and his head and his heart is an artist."

—St. Francis of Assisi

When we think about design, the first thing that comes to mind tends to be the interface; squishy buttons, realistic switches, and just the right balance of colors. While the "packaging" is important, it is only half of the design equation. An app's interface can rival a Monet, but if it's confusing and burdensome to use, people simply won't get it. Designing for function is just as important as designing for aesthetics.

Although you may think it's best to leave your design work to a professional, there's actually quite a bit you can do yourself. That's because as developers learn more about what makes apps easy to use, they're also discovering easier ways to design them.

The methods you are about to learn are based on the same principles used by elite design firms. They're affordable, agile, and straightforward. Best of all, anyone can do them.

This chapter walks you through every step of the design process, from pencil sketches to final production. It explains the various navigation models and design elements on the iPhone and iPad. You'll learn how to whip up quick mockups and evolve them into interactive proto-types without writing a single line of code. You'll discover how to get quality feedback and build on the ideas of others to help you fine-tune your designs into stunning works of art. Finally, the chapter explains how to hire a designer or, if you're up for the job, create the final production yourself.

TIP	Set aside time to read the iOS Human Interface Guidelines (HIG) from Apple (http://bit.ly/g3TbaY). It includes critical details that aren't repeated in this chapter.

Getting the Ballpoint Rolling

If you're wishing you had paid more attention in art class right about now, you'll be pleased to know that what you learned in first grade is good enough. That's because exquisite design is about making an app easy and enjoyable to use, not just composing something worthy of a spot in the Louvre.

Just as there's a process to distilling your ideas, there's a process to pulling them together into designs that are easy to understand *and* easy on the eyes. So before contacting a designer or hunkering down at your computer to whip up the layouts yourself, put down the mouse and pull up a chair.

Creating computer layouts at this point is the biggest mistake you could make. Even if you're just trying to capture some vague ideas, you're actually cementing the design because things as simple as the colors and fonts you select can unconsciously lure you in the wrong direction.

Instead, you'll create your initial designs using the same tools you had in first grade—pencils and paper. You'll test these designs on your proxies, who will help you make them even better, and then gradually work your way up to creating everything on the computer.

As an independent developer, you may be thinking that these steps are unnecessary, or perhaps you're planning to outsource the design, so you feel it's the freelancer's job. Skipping these steps or expecting someone else to do them for you won't shortcut the process or save you any money. Hand over heart; it's just the opposite. This process *is* the shortcut. You will be thanking yourself down the road.

Design problems are worse than software bugs and they hide in the details. Even the hottest designers don't have elegant creations magically appear to them over a cup of Earl Grey. They encounter the same design dilemmas that you do and use the same tactics to discover what works best. If you plan to hire a designer, there are still some incredibly productive activities that you can do to both save money and help your designer create the masterpiece you're aiming for.

A carefully thought out design is the cornerstone of quick and affordable development because developers know exactly what to create and aren't guessing, filling in the gaps with their own ideas. Development will be faster because you'll have fewer code changes and bug fixes. The time and cost estimates you receive will be far more accurate because just like your plumber, developers pad estimates to account for unknowns. But if you show developers a well thought out design first they won't have to guess, so comparing bids will be comparing apples to apples.

It all pays off at the selling stage. Your app will sell more because it's easy to use and stunning. Plus, you'll have a competitive edge over the other apps whose creators mistakenly thought the design process could be shortened or cut out altogether. Sales will be hot because your customers love your app and are telling friends and family about it. They will leave priceless feedback on iTunes, send you fan mail, and when you create another app, they'll automatically buy it because your design reputation precedes you. Best of all, Apple will feature your app, making you a global blockbuster and opening doors to all sorts of new opportunities.

If for some reason you're still not convinced, rest assured that these steps are actually entertaining and don't take that much time. You'll progress from pencils to the computer soon enough. For now, close your design tools as you learn about the components of an app. Because before you can build your rocket, you need to understand the nuts and bolts.

I always start every design process by sketching out a ton of different ideas before touching the computer. Putting a pen to paper is a fantastic way of exploring as many crazy thoughts as possible. When you're on a computer it's difficult to concentrate on more than one thing at a time, but sketching enables your creativity to jump around and hit on original ideas that you'd never find otherwise.

—Paddy Donnelly, co-founder and designer at WeeTaps (Wee Rocket app)

Understanding the Navigation Models

There are all sorts of navigation schemes you can use to get around in an app. The first apps on the market closely mimicked the layout, style, and navigation of the apps preinstalled on devices created by Apple. There were very loyal to Apple's Human Interface Guidelines because people instantly recognized the designs. But recently trends have shifted, and designs are heading in all sorts of fascinating new directions. They're making better use of the space, gestures, and how we get from screen to screen.

Apple's standards are still the best blueprint for your design. People will immediately recognize the flow because it's used in most apps. This section dives into some of the most common "out of the box" navigation models such as nested dolls and tabbed navigation; plus, it outlines some newer trends such as the bento box and slide-out models. It also gives examples of when to use each one.

> **NOTE**   Most apps use a combination of navigation models as appropriate for various features of the app. Even apps that boldly experiment with new interfaces may go back to the basic Apple navigation approach for certain features.

Nested dolls

The *nested doll* model lets you drill down into layers of information, like opening a series of Russian matryoshka dolls to reveal a smaller doll inside each one. Also referred to as *tree view*, it's the standard model for funneling information. A basic example is the Settings app. The main screen shows a list of options; after you select an option a related menu is displayed on the next screen, offering more specific options. Nested doll navigation allows you to drill down into layers and layers of other screens.

> **NOTE**   The nested doll model and the bento box model discussed shortly are adapted from Rachel Hinman's coverage in *The Mobile Frontier,* Rosenfeld Media (2012).

FIGURE 3-1: The unfolding series of Twitter screens use the nested dolls navigation, seen here in the iPhone version of the app.

Source: Twitter

The nested doll model is normally teamed up with a navigation bar so people can quickly surface back to the main screen. The bar also displays the current screen name so we know which screen we are on in the hierarchy.

Nested doll navigation works great as the main navigation for apps with content that has a large number of categories or items, such as news, recipes, and tasks apps. It's also smart for apps with extended features and settings, like a banking app.

A major inconvenience in layering information is getting back to the top level. In some cases, people may have to back up quite a few screens just to select another option, which is frustrating. An advantage of the extra space on iPads is that the main selections can be docked to the left side of the screen so people can just flip between screens as with a tab bar (coming up next).

Tab bar

Another oldie but goodie, *tab bar* navigation is a tidy way to quickly jump back and forth among popular screens. The tab bar docks at the bottom of the screen and has a maximum of five options on the iPhone (see Figure 3-2) and seven on the iPad. When you tap on a tab, the content in the main section of the screen changes, but the tabs at the bottom of the screen remain the same.

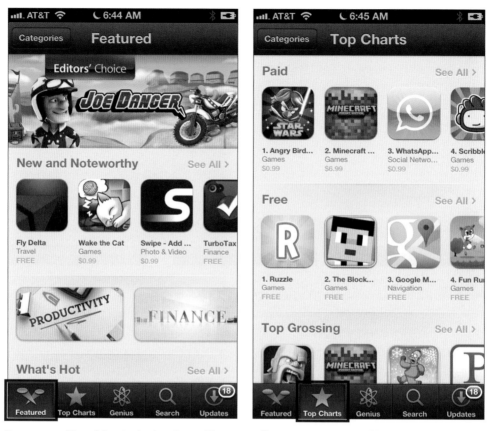

FIGURE 3-2: The tab bar in the App Store iPhone app allows you to jump quickly from featured apps to top selling apps.

Source: App Store iPhone app

Tab bars are ideal for displaying different perspectives of the same information. For example, the Weather Channel app lets you quickly switch to different views of the current local weather. Tabs also work well for apps with a very specific purpose, such as sharing a photo. The ever-present "share" button on the center of every screen continually broadcasts a reminder that the apps are about getting in on the action as much as being a spectator.

A popular feature is to fade tab bars and the screen header out of view while the user plays with an app. This trick opens more space for the app's content. The tab bar and header appear again when the user scrolls to the top of a list again or taps on the screen.

Breaking the tab bar ceiling

The downside of tab navigation is that you're restricted to a five-button limit on the iPhone. You can assign one of the buttons to be a "more" button for additional screens. This leaves you with four screens for your app, with the rest bundled into the "more" screen, as in the iTunes iPhone app. Apps have slowly drifted away from this solution, for good reason. You're not only forcing more taps but also hiding screens. A couple of custom designs, swiping tabs and slide-out navigation, follow a similar principle as tab bar navigation but allow you to offer more options.

Swiping tabs

Swiping tabs are swipeable button bars that allow for more choices than a traditional tab bar. Placing an arrow on the current selection or fading buttons on both sides of the swipeable menu lets people know that there are more choices beyond what they can see on the screen, as shown in Figure 3-3.

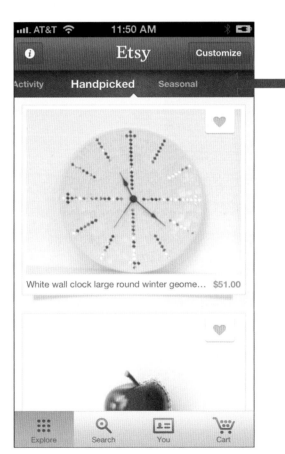

FIGURE 3-3: Swiping tabs found in the Etsy app lets you select between categories such as "handpicked" and "seasonal."
Source: Etsy iPhone app

Slide-out navigation

If you use Facebook you're probably already familiar with slide-out navigation, which is becoming the standard for social networking apps on both the iPhone and iPad (see Figure 3-4). A button reveals a scrolling panel that slides out from the side of the screen with a list of options while the main screen is nicely tucked to the right, just a tap away from full view. It's a great solution for apps with content that can quickly mushroom. If you plan to use this design, make sure the main panel is at least 44 pixels wide when it's "hidden" on an iPhone layout.

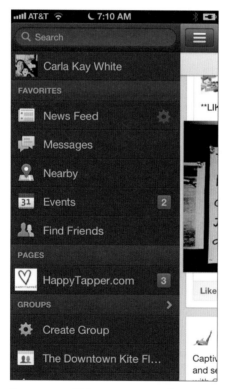
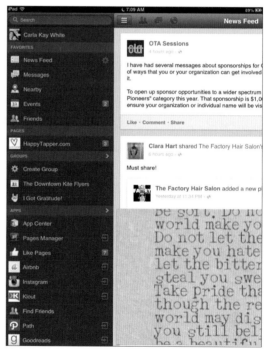

FIGURE 3-4: Slide-out navigation became popular with the *Facebook* iPhone (left) and iPad (right) apps can now be found in most social apps.

Source: Facebook iPhone and iPad apps

Bento box

Another trending new model, also presented in Hinman's *The Mobile Frontier*, is bento box navigation. Just like the bento boxes used to serve meals in a Japanese restaurant, this model carves up the screen into tappable blocks, each one leading the user to a unique experience.

Commonly used in gallery apps, this model has expanded its reach into content-heavy apps as well. You can find examples of this in Flipboard and Pulse, both news apps, as well as Snapguide, an app that lets people share and view step-by-step guides. Emphasizing the images rather than the text is a smart move because people are more drawn to pictures than words. Figure 3-5 shows Flipboard on an iPhone and Snapguide on an iPad.

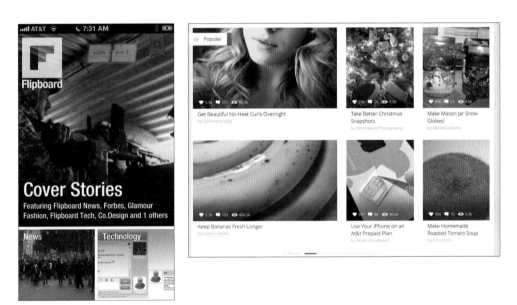

FIGURE 3-5: The bento box navigation model shown in Flipboard (left) and Snapguide (right).
Source: Flipboard iPhone and Snapguide iPad apps

The bento box approach takes the grid view navigation seen in apps such as Goop to the next level. That app uses grid icons on a dashboard to navigate through the app (see Figure 3-6). The downside of this flow is that we have to peddle backward to select other areas of the app.

FIGURE 3-6: The traditional grid screen navigation in the *Goop* app.
Source: Goop iPhone app

Bento box navigation is an interesting alternative for apps with groups of content that are closely related to each other. For example, the weather app Solar uses bento box navigation to quickly select among cities, and Pulse uses it to display a selection of articles, as shown in Figure 3-7. The Statnut app uses it to add new social network accounts.

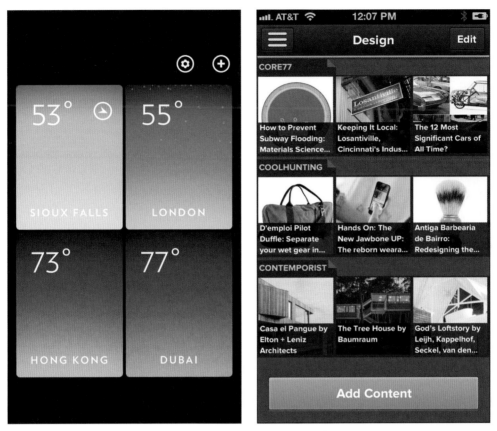

FIGURE 3-7: The Solar (left) and Pulse (right) apps both use bento boxes successfully.
Source: Solar and Pulse iPhone apps

The sliding cards

Like flipping through your kid's multiplication flashcards, sliding cards navigation lets people swipe through screens, card by card. It often includes small dots at the bottom to indicate which card they're currently viewing.

This type of navigation lets you concentrate all your attention on a single nugget of content at a time. Unlike nested dolls, this type of navigation is flat. There is no drilling down to sub-menus. If related details are available, users can tap on the "front" of the card and flip it over to look at the "back" of the card and see more information.

Sliding cards navigation works best with highly appealing visual content. It's an elegant approach to laying out instructions when an app launches (see the Calcbot example in Figure 3-8). It also is wonderful for browsing and discovering content, such as in the BBC News and Nigela Quick apps. Both of these apps let users slide through the content, taking it in with a glance.

FIGURE 3-8: Sliding card navigation used in the Calcbot app instruction screens.
Source: Calcbot iPhone app

Immersive designs

We all have seen apps that don't follow any of the standard conventions, but instead blaze their own navigational path. Apple refers to them as "immersive" apps. Immersive apps are full screen, graphically rich, yet understood at a glance. They are barren of tab bars, back buttons, and headers and make the most of gestures such as swiping and pinching.

Games, books and entertainment apps usually wave off the standard conventions, taking over the whole screen and engrossing us in a virtual world, as with the Counting Ants game shown in Figure 3-9. Immersive design lets us set the scene and have full control over the adventure.

FIGURE 3-9: The Playtend Counting Ants app uses the full immersive model.
Source: Counting Ants iPad app

A popular trend with immersive apps is to create navigation models that are metaphors of real-life objects. These apps are intuitive because their interfaces are based on day-to-day gadgets that we instantly recognize—spinning dials, knobs, buttons, switches, and levers. I discuss this design tactic more later in this chapter.

The immersive model means that the entire interface is created from scratch, and pulling off successful designs requires additional attention to details. Unique navigation isn't exclusive to games, children's apps, books, and entertainment apps. The tasking app Clear invented its own navigation model. The key is to have the navigation support the task at hand, not distract from it and gradually become annoying. Each transition must be quick, subtle, and natural.

Navigation found on the iPad

Just like a Hollywood mansion offers more layout possibilities than a New York studio apartment, the iPad has more navigational opportunities than the iPhone. In Chapter 2 we touched on the popover and split view combination. Here are a few more different navigational solutions that work well for an iPad app.

Layered navigation

Layered navigation is a lot like nested dolls, but as you open each doll it's stacked on top of the previous one. Just like nested dolls, this model lets people drill down through layers of information, but as they progress through the screens, a portion of each of the previous screens is still shown underneath, with the main screen at the very bottom. For example, when another screen opens in the Pinterest app, it falls on top of the first one (see Figure 3-10).

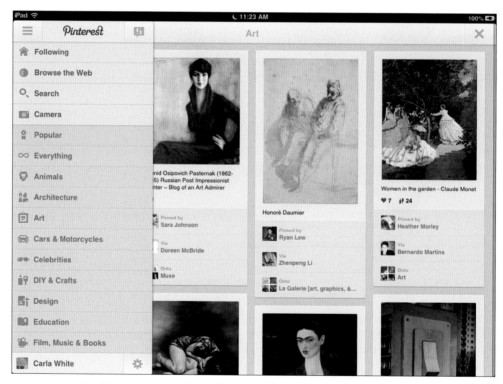

FIGURE 3-10: The Pinterest app uses layered navigation as a way to help people understand how many layers of screens they have drilled down to.
Source: Pinterest iPad app

Sidebar navigation

Sidebar navigation is similar to the slide-out navigation describer earlier, except the side panel is always present, rather than tucked behind the screen. Some apps such as Snapguide and Flipboard collapse the sidebar by default and open it when users tap a button. Then the main screen darkens so focus is on the sidebar. See Figure 3-11.

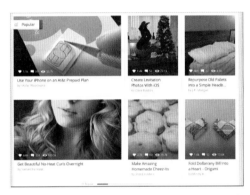 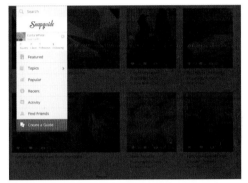

FIGURE 3-11: The Snapguide iPad app open with the sidebar collapsed by default (left).Users tap a button to open the sidebar (right).

Source: Snapguide iPad app

Button and Tab Combo Navigation

Earlier you learned that the downside of using tabs on the iPhone is the five-button limit. On the iPad seven buttons is the cut-off point. Sure, there's room for more, but too many buttons and it starts to get overwhelming. Instead, the extra space on the iPad means there's room for buttons at the top to let users quickly flip between screens or perform a function like signing in.

This approach works best with content heavy apps like news apps, and can be accomplished in a variety of ways. For example, the tabs in MOMA's iPad app open a submenu, or people can scroll through artist's names at the top (see Figure 3-12).

I could easily fill the rest of this chapter with the wide variety of navigation models, but I just highlighted the most common ones. Next, you'll dissect apps even more by looking at some of the standard controls.

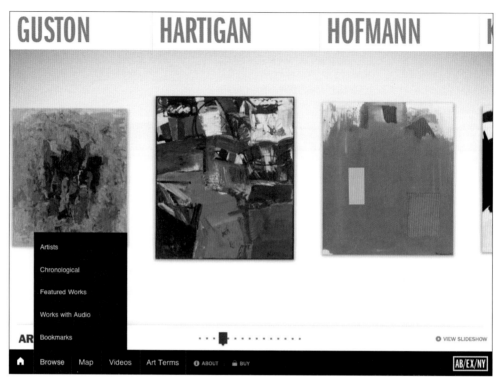

FIGURE 3-12: The MOMA iPad app offers users alternative ways to browse the app's content.
Source: MOMA iPad app

Taking a Peek at the Standard Controls

Just like an IKEA dresser comes with everything you need to put it together, the iOS SDK comes with buttons, text fields, list views, keyboards, and icons, saving you the time to create them and making app development a lot easier. Best of all, if you use these standard elements in your app, they will automatically be updated anytime Apple makes a change to them. Just like you can add your own knobs to an IKEA dresser, you can also create your own custom elements to give your app a distinct appearance, as I explain later in this chapter.

The bars

The iOS SDK has several types of bars with one thing in common; they're located either at the top or bottom of the screen, framing the content. Let's take a look at the three most important bars.

The status bar

Always located at the top of the screen, the status bar (Figure 3-13) shows important information such as network connection, time of day, and battery charge status. On the iPhone, the status bar can be gray, black, or transparent black. On the iPad, it's always black. You cannot customize the look of the status bar.

FIGURE 3-13: The status bars for the iPad and iPhone look nearly identical.

It's a good idea to display the status bar in your app because if you don't, you force people to exit the app to see any of this information. Instead of removing it, create a full view mode of your app so that customers can hide it themselves if they prefer.

The navigation bar

The navigation bar rests just below the status bar. Its main purpose is to navigate between screens, but it can also include controls for managing content on the screen. The screen name is always located in the middle of the bar, but some apps also use this space for buttons. Truly, the navigation bar should contain no more than the title, a back button that is always on the left, and one control for managing content (see Figure 3-14).

Keep in mind with iPhone apps:

- Don't fill the navigation bar with lots of controls. Use a toolbar instead (see the following section).

- When a user gets to a new level, two things need to happen to the navigation bar:

  - The title on the bar should change to the new screen's name.

  - A back button should be displayed on the left side, labeled with the previous screen's name.

- Navigation bars help people from getting lost. If you add one to a page but would like people to focus more on the content, make it slip it out of view (and return) with a tap on the screen.

FIGURE 3-14: The Pastebot iPhone app navigation bar in this figure includes the screen name Clipboard and buttons to go to the Dashboard or edit the items on the screen.

Source: Pastebot iPhone app

The toolbar

On the standard iPhone layout, toolbars rest at the bottom of the screen, with buttons that let people manipulate, share, and edit content (see Figure 3-15). They're located at the top of the screen on the iPad. Be careful not to confuse toolbars with the tab bar that helps you navigate around the entire app. Toolbars let you do something with the content of the current screen, such as change the font, or forward the content via e-mail.

FIGURE 3-15: The toolbar on the Safari iPhone app is anchored at the bottom of the screen (left) whereas the iPad version places it at the top (right).

Source: Safari iPhone app

The combination of buttons, icons, and controls you create is purely up to you. Apple supplies a standard collection of icons, but plenty are available on the web for download, as we'll explore a little later in this chapter.

Keep in mind:

- Hit target areas should be 44 × 44 points for each toolbar item.

- Toolbars always appear at the bottom on an iPhone, whereas on the iPad they should appear at the top.

- Don't overload your toolbar with too many options. Jamming buttons together is a recipe for tap disaster, especially on the iPhone.

The table view

Tables are the most versatile element of the standard interface, and this section is just a short introduction to their superpowers. Boiled down, they're really more lists, rather than what is typically considered a "table" with rows and columns. But you can beef them up and mold them into extremely powerful screens where users flick, drag, and tap to navigate, delete, or move items around. Some of the most cutting-edge apps are based on table views.

Traditional table views grace most apps with long list of scrollable information, as in Contacts and Mail apps. They're also used in more graphic- and animation-centric apps such as Drinkspiration and Path. Figure 3-16 shows two examples.

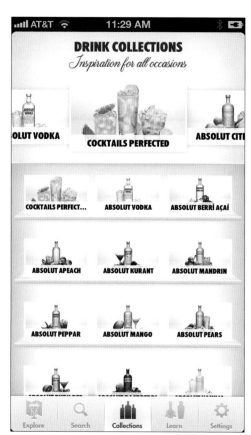

FIGURE 3-16: A traditional table view used in the Contacts iPhone app (left) and a more complicated table view used in Drinkspiration iPhone app (right).

Source: Contacts iPhone app and Drinkspiration iPhone app

There are two styles of table views, called *plain* and *grouped*. A plain table view lays out data in rows and can be divided by sections, as in the Contacts app. A group table view displays data grouped together, as in the Settings app. With both styles, you can tap an item in a table to do things like add or remove rows, select multiple rows, open more information, or reveal another table view.

Keep in mind:

- Always provide feedback when someone selects an item in a list.

- Animate changes the user makes to a list to provide instant feedback and to strengthen his understanding of editing powers.

- If your app displays real time information, as with Facebook, don't wait until all the data is available before displaying anything. Instead, fill rows with text immediately and show the more complicated things such as images when they're available. Waiting until all the content is available before displaying it is commonly called "blocking" the user and Apple doesn't allow it.

- If your app's content changes infrequently, display "stale" content while new content is downloading.

- If the content is slow to load or complex, display a spinning activity indicator and a message such as "Loading. . . ."

- Keep row heights the same. The standard is 44 pixels.

Inputs and outputs

The last things we'll go through are the standard controls that let users enter information into an app, and a couple of ways the app can display information back to them. Some of the most common input and output interface elements are listed in the following table. The limits to how you use them are capped only by your imagination. This is just a glimpse of what is available.

Input elements

Element Name	Image	Purpose
Text field		Lets the user enter small bits of information.
Text view		Lets the user enter longer text.
Action sheet		Displays at least two options for the user to select from.
Picker		Lets the user set the date and time or set a timer.
Detailed disclosure button		Lets the user reveal additional details or functionality for an item, usually in a new window.

Element Name	Image	Purpose
Button	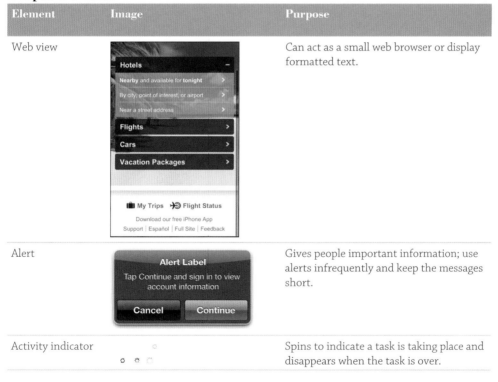	Performs an app-specific action.
Slider		Lets the user define a point between two values on a spectrum. Can display vertically or horizontally.
Switch		Presents two mutually exclusive choices such as on/off or yes/no.

Output elements

Element	Image	Purpose
Web view		Can act as a small web browser or display formatted text.
Alert		Gives people important information; use alerts infrequently and keep the messages short.
Activity indicator		Spins to indicate a task is taking place and disappears when the task is over.

Once you have an educated eye and know what to look for, playing around with apps takes on a whole new level of interest. Up next: finding inspiration and stealing navigation ideas.

Stealing Good Stuff

WHO WHAT WHAT HOW
DISCOVERY

When you spot a particularly noteworthy app, an alarm goes off and you marvel at how the app's creator came up with such a clever design. It might surprise you to learn that the most amazing apps are not purely original. They're actually the offspring of another idea, even though we might not be aware of what the original idea might be. For example, did you know that Tapbot's apps are based on the lovable characters in the movie *WALL-E*? Notice the resemblance? The tasking app, *Clear*, has a novel interface, but the pull-down-for-new-content feature was first seen in the *Twitter* app. These examples aren't outright copies of ideas, but transformations of them.

To help unleash your imagination, spend some time studying other designs. Examine clever interfaces, pick out great features, and think about ways to transform and remix them. You aren't searching for a style for your app, but rather becoming an expert in app layouts and flow. Think of it as getting your MBA (Master in Beautiful Apps).

Go through every feature in your app and see how other apps execute the same concepts. You'll discover that something as simple and common as a search feature can be designed all sorts of ways. Notice where other apps place the search button, what happens to the screen when you tap it, and how the results are displayed. These subtle details are what separate the successful apps from the mediocre ones that fail to get noticed.

Don't plagiarize or create an exact imitation of an existing app. That is simply a waste of time (not to mention, a breach of your agreement with Apple, and an ethical and possibly legal violation). To make your app design uniquely yours, take ideas to the next level. As Jean-Luc Godard said, "It's not where you take things from—it's where you take them to."

Finding design inspiration

With so many apps available, discovering the most innovative can as overwhelming as selecting the best *Idol* contestant. Fortunately, there are several online design galleries with great collections of clever and stunning interfaces to help get you started. Here are a few of my favorites:

iPhone Designs

    Mobile Patterns (mobile-patterns.com)

    pttns (pttrns.com)

    TapFancy (tapfancy.com)

    TappGala (tappgala.com)

iPad Designs

    Landing Pad (landingpad.org)

iPhone, iPad, and Icon Designs

Apple Inspires Me (appleinspires.me)

lovely ui (lovelyui.com)

iOSpirations (iospirations.com)

Patterns of Design (patternsofdesign.co.uk)

Dribbble (dribbble.com/tags/ios)

Behance (behance.net)

Blogs about Great Designs

Beautiful Pixels (beautifulpixels.com)

iOS App Designs (iosappdesigns.tumblr.com)

Building your collection

Soon you'll be stockpiling design ideas faster than Adele does Grammys, so it's smart to organize everything to make it easier to refer back to ideas again later. Keep all of your favorite ideas in one place. You can store them in a file on your computer, on a Pinterest board, or you can use an app like Screenshot Journal. Be sure to note what strikes you most about a design because you may not remember when you come back to it later. Having your ideas pulled together in one place makes it easier to share them with someone else, like your designer.

By now, you probably have a good notion of what your app will do, how it will do it, and what it will look like. Up next: how to engage, capture, and occupy your user's complete attention.

Creating Natural Flow in Your App

The best apps appear so effortless; the design fades to the background, making the task at hand surprisingly easy. This is *flow*, and it has nothing to do with processes or charts. It's about being completely absorbed in doing something you love and not being distracted by confusing or burdensome steps. You lose your sense of time and self, and become completely immersed. It's why your kids won't stop playing Minecraft and why your friend just spent three hours on Pinterest.

flow & story

Most app creators fall into the trap of designing individual screens rather than focusing on the big picture. The result is an app with broken flow. Instead, step back and think about how people will be absorbed in your app (what flows are you trying to create), and let that drive the design process.

Map out the flow with boxes and arrows

To figure out your app's flows, think about the main goal of your app such as "book a flight" or "find new music." I'll give you a hint; it's on your app mission statement. This tells you exactly what activity you want people to get absorbed in when using your app. When people are trying to achieve this goal, don't throw up any barriers, hurdles, or distractions to stand in their way. You also don't want people to get bored, so you need to offer some secondary goals too. You guessed it. That's your features list.

Next, create a diagram so you can visually see how people can reach their goal using the different screens in your app. A *flow diagram* outlines how each screen links to each of the others with boxes and arrows. Creating a diagram forces you to think about your app's natural flow. It also gives you an idea about how complicated or confusing the navigation is because it visually displays the sequence of actions people take to navigate through your app and reach their goal.

For example, Figure 3-17 is the original flow diagram for my journaling app, which you see is extremely simple. You quickly grasp that there are only a few screens and how they link together. An app like this is fairly quick to design and inexpensive to code.

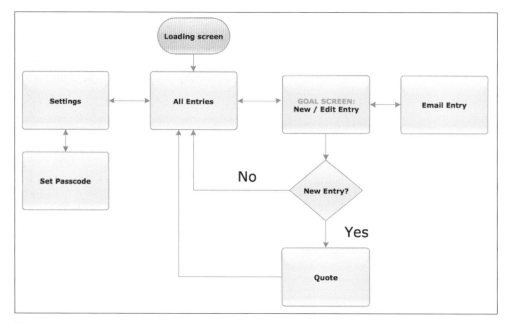

FIGURE 3-17: The flow diagram created for my first app was kept very simple.

To create a flow diagram, think about your app's main purpose (the thing that completely absorbs people) and secondary purposes (functionality that helps them get absorbed). Then map out how a person would navigate through your app to accomplish the main purpose. Secondary tasks support the main one, so they should branch off. If your diagram starts to get as complicated as the Tokyo subway system, you have too many features and screens for an app.

Your flow will constantly be revised as you design your app, so stick with pencil and paper so it's quick to create and easy to edit. You can just use boxes or arrows, or if you want to give your diagram more details, use shapes similar to those shown in Figure 3-18.

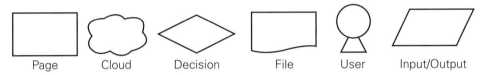

| Page | Cloud | Decision | File | User | Input/Output |

FIGURE 3-18: These basic shapes can be used to sketch a flow diagram.

Even if you have only a few screens, this diagram confirms you designed a logical and practical navigation. It will also save you a lot of explaining in your specification. Pictures are always far more powerful than paragraphs and translate well into any language.

> *When I get an idea for an app the first place I go is paper. I have a notebook where I write down all the things that I want the app to do. From there, I organize the way the app will flow. I use an app called MindNode Pro for this; they have a Mac version as well as an iPhone app and they work great together. This gives me a good idea of how the app will work and what screens and buttons I will need.*

—Shelby Meinzer, founder of MindTapp (Photonest iPhone app)

Try tools such as Omnigraffle, PowerPoint, and Google Presentation to create your flow diagram on a computer. NOTE

Turn the flow into a story

The flow diagram answers the questions of *how* people will accomplish their goal. Creating a story tells you *why* they want to use your app. It breathes life into your app idea, putting the spotlight on your customers and helping you empathize.

First, identify *who* is the main character. Your tribe proxy is an easy choice. Now add in the other elements of the story. *Where* are people using your app? *When* are they using it? And most importantly, *why* are they using it?

A short paragraph unraveling the plot is all it takes. The key is to keep it real and plausible. Stirring people into your app idea gives it a heartbeat, and that spurs ideas. Also, a story about your app helps the team you hire gain a better understanding of your customers' concerns, wants, and goals before plodding into a solution.

Shifting Your Ideas into a Killer Design

Believe it or not, you're already at the 50-yard-line of the design process. The next step, creating a *prototype* or basic model of your idea, is the most exciting part because you get to see your ideas gradually come to life. It's also the most important because you will test your ideas to make them even better. As indispensable as prototyping is, most app developers mistakenly leapfrog over this process, diving right into the Photoshop waters instead.

They rush ahead because they can't wait to see the final production, believing any flaws in their design can be fixed after the app is in development. There is nothing worse than discovering a design flaw after hours have been sunk into development. It's a costly gamble no app creator can afford to take, wasting months of development. I know because I've made the same foolish mistake myself.

Sure, you can press ahead, hand over your ideas to a designer, and hope for the best. They could lead you to a slightly better app. But it means you have already decided to settle for a suboptimal product, so don't be surprised if your designers and developers follow your lead with sloppy work. Or you can set yourself apart from the majority of other developers, test your ideas, and confidently know that you'll have a *significantly* better app.

How anyone can design like a pro

One unfortunate trait most of us have in common is falling in love with our initial ideas and clinging to them for dear life. We let our egos dictate our designs. To design like a pro means you have to become selfless and dump your mental baggage of assumptions, prejudices, and beliefs. There is actually a process to quieting your ego so incredible design ideas can transpire.

This process doesn't involve yoga mats or chanting monks but rather pencil, paper, and all your best ideas. You'll learn how to quickly transform your ideas into prototypes, share them with your proxies, and build on *their* viewpoints. These steps aren't about polishing your design; it's about building on other people's ideas and exploring the best interface and screens layouts so people "get it" in 15 seconds. Figure 3-19 lays out the path.

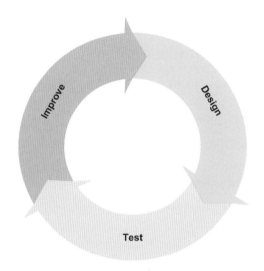

FIGURE 3-19: The iterative design process.

Why prototyping is the best thing since sliced bread

If you're digging your heels in as I drag you to a sketchpad, let me ask you this. Would you be a reluctant artist if I told you that each prototype you created was worth $50? No, you're not about to sell your mockups on eBay (just yet), but rather think of that number as your return in investment.

You see, the only way to discover what people really want is by watching them, and prototypes give you that power. Just a few minutes invested in floating around a mockup of your screen lets you get inside peoples' heads and get the feedback you desperately need *before* your app is on iTunes. The ripple effect is a far better design that sells more and costs you a lot less to develop. Prototypes let you create a caviar app on a hotdog budget, easily paying for themselves in the end.

Start by sketching

Not to sound like a broken record, but the best advice I can give you, dear first-time-designer friend, is to start with pen and paper, *not* a computer. This gives you artistic freedom design software could never deliver. Computer mockups tempt you to spend too much time on unnecessary details before you've even grasped the basic concepts of what you're creating. So steal a notebook out of your kid's room, maybe a highlighter, some markers, and a few crayons, and dive in.

Don't worry if you can't draw. Sketching has nothing to do with artistic talents. In fact, some of the best designs I've ever seen were created by people who claimed they couldn't draw. If you can draw basic shapes, arrows, and stick figures, you're set.

Paper prototyping costs peanuts and can be done in minutes. Because it's so cheap and easy, you can experiment with as many versions of your designs as you like without wasting hours of work. Also, people will know you didn't invest a lot of time creating the mockup so they'll be more comfortable with giving you honest feedback. Another vote for paper is that it's a great way to document everything so you can go back to ideas you may have otherwise deleted on a computer.

Our apps always start out with a pencil and paper. Once we get a basic design and functionality worked out, there are probably three to four iterations done in Photoshop.

—Mark Jardine, co-founder and designer at TapBots (Tweetbot app)

BRAINSTORM

Creating paper prototypes in a flash

To create a paper prototype, select a screen from your flow diagram and draw it out as fast as you can. Don't aim for perfection because the purpose of paper prototypes is not to produce "oohs" and "aahs," but to explore concepts and ideas (see Figure 3-20). You're also not evaluating any ideas or trying to identify the solution. Just get everything out of your head and into your notebook, making your ideas visible.

If you're having some designers block, start with a skeleton outline of its most common elements such as the header, screen name, and navigation buttons, and then fill in the rest. Use your research and collection of ideas to inspire you. Remember, you're just experimenting with layouts, so quick doodles are all you need.

FIGURE 3-20: This is a quick sketch of a layout idea that I was able to test with my proxies.

If you want something more sophisticated than a crayon, there are tools like the nifty stencil and paper kits available for purchase from uistencils.com (see Figure 3-21). You can also get sketchpads from appsketchbook.com and pixelpads.com, but there are plenty of free versions available for both iPhone and iPad layouts that you can download and print out.

If you're struggling with your layouts, try sketching some of your favorite apps instead. You'll start to notice small details like the buttons included and where they are located. Remember, nothing in great app design is by chance, it's always well thought out.   `TIP`

Test, edit, repeat...

After sketching out your ideas, lock your ego in a vault and bravely share your paper prototypes with a few people for feedback. This is called *user testing* and it's the best way to gauge if your ideas are any good. Feel free to jump ahead to the section "Putting Your Designs to the Test" to learn more about ways to test ideas. Each time you test a design, you'll learn ways to improve it. So plan to sketch and test a few iterations of paper prototypes before moving on your computer to create everything.

FIGURE 3-21: A stencil kit from uistencils.com can make the process easier.
Source: UI Stencils

Creating working prototypes: No coding required

The next step, wireframing, is seriously mind-blowing because you can suddenly see your app in action without having to contact (or pay) a designer or programmer. Better yet, you gain a whole new level of insight in user tests, *and* you will be way ahead of the 90 percent of app developers who skip this step.

Creating a *click-through* or *wireframe*, which is an interactive version of your design, is kind of like putting together a jigsaw puzzle. You'll use your sketches and flow diagram as your guide to laying out the screen and linking them together. Then you'll fill in the rest of the puzzle pieces with transitions between screens and screen elements, like swiping right, fading, or revealing more content.

A simple web search for "wireframing tool" pours out a plethora of products all claiming to be faster, easier, and more powerful. So which one do you choose? Unfortunately, there isn't a clear winner. The one you choose is a personal preference based on what you're most comfortable using.

I personally like a free tool called Cacoo (cacoo.com) because I can quickly lay out black-and-white prototypes using the design elements that come with the tool. It has a drag-and-drop editor so I can create a basic layout in minutes, as shown in Figure 3-22. I can then link screens together to transform my prototype into an interactive version of my app.

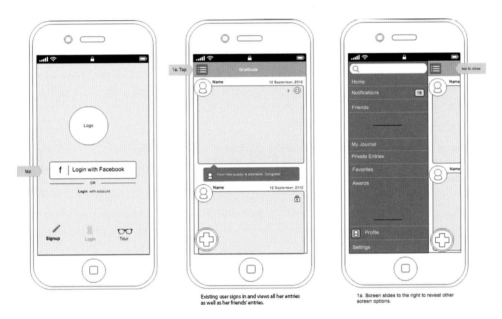

Existing user signs in and views all her entries
as well as her friends' entries.

1a. Screen slides to the right to reveal other
screen options.

FIGURE 3-22: Basic wireframe screens can be put together in minutes using an online program like Cacoo or Proto.io.

Another tool I discovered is proto.io (proto.io), which claims to be "silly fast" prototyping. The wireframe can emulate anything an app can do, including touch gestures, screen transitions, animations, and orientation changes. You don't have to write a single line of code to create an interactive version of your app. Now here's the kicker. You can share designs directly on devices for testing (using a free 15-day trial).

Most of these products offer a basic plan for free so you can road test them first. Try creating a very simple screen to see if you're comfortable with the interface and understand the help materials. Be sure the tool already has the iPhone and iPad elements so you can get started quickly. You can also upload your own elements if the standard ones aren't enough. Here are a few other tips to keep in mind:

- **Be consistent.** Use the same colors and fonts everywhere. Stick to black and white and only a few shades of gray, and only two different fonts. Nothing more. The wireframes might be boring, but it's a sure-fire way to make them consistent and therefore easier to understand. Even a small change in font weight make someone wonder, "Is this label bigger because it's more important?"

- **Use real examples.** Dummy data never works. Use real examples of what the content will be to make sure that images fit, text wraps correctly, and photos are the right orientation.

- **Make sure all hit points (the screen hot spots where people can click) are 44 × 44 pixels.** The default elements that come with most prototyping tools should all be within the correct tap size. If you create any of your own elements, make sure they are at least 44 pixels high and/or wide.

- **Don't be worried about the details.** The purpose of these designs is to help you lay out your ideas in a cleaner fashion than when using paper and pencil. Adding on the sugar and spice is what you'll do next.

I never begin the design phase of a project without having some solid wireframes worked out beforehand. Just as sketching allows you to pursue a variety of ideas, wireframing allows you to realize those ideas. Wireframes and prototypes allow you to quickly see what's working and what's not working, where there are dead-ends in your app and how it 'feels' to use. Exploring every aspect of your project with a good set of wireframes will save you a mountain of time when it comes to the pixel-perfect design phase.

—Paddy Donnelly, co-founder and designer at WeeTaps (Wee Rocket app)

> **NOTE**   To view designs on your iPhone or iPad, email an image of your prototypes to yourself, save it to your photo library, and then open it on your device. You can also use a free tool called LiveView (www.zambetti.com/projects/liveview/). It lets you view the designs on your computer directly on your device at the same time.

Putting Your Designs to the Test

If you've ever helped your dear grandma figure out how to use a webcam, you know that it's a recipe for a bad sitcom (or a hit YouTube video). To you it might be the easiest thing in the world, but to her it's akin to flying a spaceship. That's because not everyone thinks the way you do and knows what you know, meaning they won't use your app as you do either.

To make sure people understand how to use your app, you need to test each of your layouts by showing them to people and watching their reactions. If they grimace, you know that you need to fix something. Do this with each layout you create in the design process, starting with your paper prototypes right on up to your interactive designs and final productions (you'll learn how to create those in a bit).

This testing process will unearth powerful discoveries you can't find any other way. Even if you only manage to get the pizza guy as he's dropping off dinner, you are still better off than if you didn't ask anyone.

> *Getting your app out there in the hands of real users is invaluable. It's very easy to get too close to a project when you're focusing on the pixel-perfect details, and this makes it more difficult for you to see the wood for the trees. In particular with our apps for children, as much as we like to think of ourselves as big kids, there's only so far our grown up imaginations will take us and sometimes we just don't know what kids will find fun and what they won't.*

—Paddy Donnelly, co-founder and designer at WeeTaps (Wee Rocket app)

Capture useful feedback

Getting quality feedback on your designs can be harder than getting an honest answer out of a salesperson when trying on jeans. No matter what, people will just say it looks fantastic so as not to hurt your feelings. But how does that improve your designs?

The secret to getting genuine and useful feedback is to zip your lip and keep your eyes and ears on your testers. If they wince, furl their brow, or let out a "huh?", you know you have to fix something. If all you get is a stone cold poker face, you can prod them along with some questions (examples are coming up next).

If your tester has never heard about your app idea before, avoid discussing it beforehand because you want his first impression to be genuine. You also want to discover if he can figure out what your app does without any hints. When you're ready, pull out your design layouts (paper, wireframes, or final production) and try the following tests. Each test should take only a few minutes.

The "Get it?" test

Best for testing: paper prototypes, wireframes, and final production designs

"Get it" testing is just what it sounds like. You show testers the app and see if they understand what your app does without your explaining it to them. Ask them to think out loud and be sure to keep your opinions to yourself. It's important that you hear their opinions *without* your influence. To prod them along you can ask them:

- What they think the app does.

- Why they think that.

- What they think about the flow of the app.

- What the purpose of a certain button is.

As a bonus, you can give the testers a photocopy or printout of your design and have them write suggestions directly on it.

The key task test
Best for testing: wireframes

Good for testing: computer-generated prototypes and final production designs

With "Key task" testing you ask the person to do something specific with your app design and see if they can do it. For example, with an alarm clock app you can see if they can set the wake time. The purpose of this test is to discover if people use your app the way you intended.

The test is even more effective if you let people decide for themselves what tasks they would like to do with your app. When people are doing assigned tasks, they have no emotional investment so the feedback isn't as revealing. After they establish what the app does, ask them what type of task they think they can perform with the app and then ask them to perform it. Don't prompt them or help them out, because that will defeat the purpose of your testing. You want to see whether they can figure it out for themselves. Ask them to think out loud while you keep quiet and take notes:

- Are they able to do the task without asking for help?

- Are they doing what you expected them to do?

- Did they become confused before being able to finish the task?

- Did they spend time thinking through all the possible options?

- Did they have a preferred way of doing something?

- Were some functions and screens not used?

- Were some methods used in ways you didn't intend them to be?

Five-second test

Best for testing: final production designs

Good for testing: paper prototypes, and wireframes

This next test is so quick and wonderful that it's almost sinful. You simply show someone your design for five seconds and then hide it out of sight. Ask that person to try to recall everything he can about the design and see what he remembers. For example:

- What do you think the app does?

- What caught your attention first?

- What was most helpful? What was least helpful?

- Where would you tap first?

- What do you remember most?

- What do you like most about the design? What do you like least?

This simple test reveals what about your design stands out the most, what people are instantly drawn to, and what turns them off. And most importantly, it proves whether they "get it" within that golden 15 seconds.

Edit, edit, and edit again

As painful as it can be to have people blast apart your designs, they're doing you a favor. Consider all you learned, go back to your original mock-ups, wireframes, or Photoshop layouts, and make them better. Seeing your handiwork through someone else's eyes may suggest entirely new app solutions or may let you see an old idea in a new light.

Resist the impulse to add things. Instead, take out any unnecessary features and consider changing the navigation to make it more usable. Stick with a simple, clean, uncomplicated design and focus on easy wins. Even a minor change can have a major impact.

> *Keep it simple. It takes discipline and restraint to keep an application focused on the task it was designed to do. Don't add features just because customers demand it.*

—Mark Jardine, co-founder and designer at Tapbots (Tweetbot app)

From Mockup to Masterpiece

It's no secret that beautiful apps sell better because they appear more valuable and are more enjoyable to use. That's why most app developers, myself included, want their app to look unique and smashing. But before we get into how to polish up your masterpiece, let me make it clear that not every app needs its own style. The number one selling app at the time of writing, WhatsApp Messenger, is proof that using Apple's standard controls can work just fine.

In either case, creating a beautiful design is far quicker, easier and cheaper when you have a few tested prototypes under your belt because you (or your designer) can easily copy the layouts while focusing on the finer details like color combinations, gradients, shading and patterns. So go ahead and pat yourself on the back because your earlier efforts will give you a leg up.

Next, you'll learn even more shortcuts to transforming your mockups into finely tuned layouts using tools such as Photoshop, Gimp, or Illustrator. First, you need to understand the different resolution requirements for the various devices because it dictates the size of your image files in your app. Eventually you'll hand over all your designs to your developer and you want to make sure she gets the correct size for each images.

Preparing your designs for Retina Display

About two years after apps first hit the market, Apple threw developers a curve ball and introduced Retina Display. The screen resolution of devices suddenly got very important. The iPhone and iPad pixel density of screens went through the roof, and is now double what it was originally. These devices squeeze four pixels into a space where there used to be just one. That is why everything looks so crisp (see Figure 3-23).

> **NOTE** The first iPhones (iPhone 1, 3G and 3GS) had a resolution of 163 pixels per inch, but the retina display versions (iPhone 4 and 5) are 326 pixels per inch, twice the size of their predecessors. The first iPad resolution was 132 pixels (iPad 1 and 2, and iPad Mini is 163 pixels), while the latest versions (iPad 3 and 4) are double that at 264 pixels per inch.

To accommodate both the old and new screen displays, apps have two copies of each image: one for the lower resolution and another for the higher resolution (Figure 3-24). All images are the PNG file type and are named according to their sizes. The regular-size image only has the filename (for example, `image.png`) and the retina display version has `@2x` added to the name (for example, `image@2x.png`).

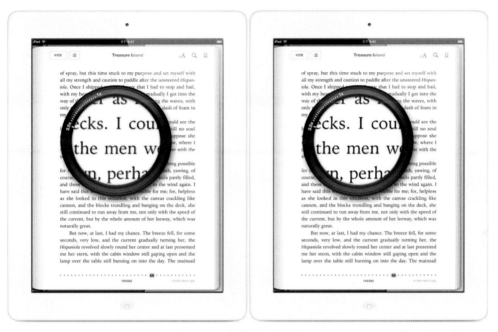

FIGURE 3-23: The normal display is shown on the left, while the Retina version on the right is far clearer because it shows more pixels.

FIGURE 3-24: An example of the two sizes and their corresponding filenames.

The following table shows the differences in the image resolutions, sizes, and names for all the various devices.

Screen size and image name by device type

Device	Image name	Resolution	Screen size
iPhone 3G	imagename@png	163 ppi	480 × 320
iPhone 4	imagename@2x.png	326 ppi	960 × 640
iPhone 5	imagename@2x.png	326 ppi	1,136 × 640
iPad 1 and 2	imagename-ipad@png	132 ppi	1,024 × 768
iPad Mini	imagename-ipad.png	163 ppi	1,024 x 768
iPad 3 and 4	imagename-ipad@2x.png	264 ppi	2,048 × 1,563

Building designs that scale using Photoshop

To make sure your app displays perfectly on older devices as well as new ones, you must either scale up or scale down your custom designs. In other words, you can create all your layouts on the 960 × 640 pixel screen (2x retina) or on the 480 × 320 pixel screen (1x normal), as illustrated in Figure 3-25. If you start with retina design (2x), you must scale down a copy of each image to be half as big (you'll learn how to do that in a bit). If you start with normal display (1x), you must scale up a copy of each image to twice as big. There are good reasons for choosing either method, but personally I don't think the choice matters. I'll explain a bit more.

Your developer will put together each screen in your app using a tool called *Interface Builder* (this is called a *.nib* file). These layouts are a bit like the drag-and-drop prototypes you created, and include any custom images using the smaller "1x" version of the image. Every element snaps to a grid, including your "1x" custom image. When the app runs on a device with retina display, that grid automatically doubles, but uses the "2x" version of the image instead. To keep everything correctly aligned on the grid, its best that the height and width of "2x" version are even numbers. If they aren't, they may not display properly, leaving a blurry edge (see Figure 3-26).

NOTE   The iPhone 5 screen is 176 pixels longer than the iPhone 4. "Stretching" layouts to fit the iPhone 5 screen size is mostly done with code, but if you are creating images that are the full size of the screen (a background, for example) you will need to produce a copy that is scaled to iPhone 5 screen size. Be sure to ask your developer for details.

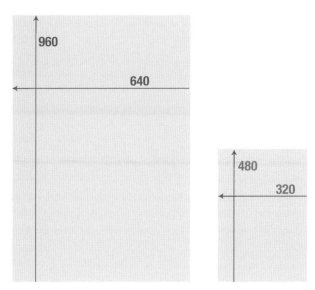

FIGURE 3-25: The 2x retina screen dimensions are shown on the left, and the 1x normal dimensions are on the right.

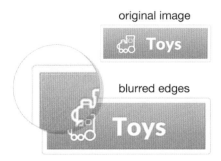

FIGURE 3-26: Example of blurred edge on the 2x retina version of the image.

Creating your layout

Just as there are all sorts of tools to help you build prototypes faster, there are also tools to help you create the final designs. This section suggests some basic tools and tips to shortcut the process of creating a custom interface. I mainly use Photoshop for my designs, so the tools I suggest are based on that software. Similar solutions for other design tools are also available if you have another you're more comfortable using.

> **NOTE** Some more affordable alternatives to Photoshop include Pixelmator ($15, pixelmator.com), GIMP (free, gimp.org), and Sketch 2 ($30, bohemiancoding.com/sketch/).

Shortcuts to layouts

Creating custom layouts got a whole lot easier and faster after UI Parade released a Photoshop plug-in called DevRocket (devrocket.uiparade.com). For $10, this plug-in lets you design for both resolutions with one document. With a tap of the button, it creates the layout for you in the correct sizes. It also applies the @2x at the end of the filename when you save your retina display graphics. The plug-in is easy to use and definitely worth a try for anyone who uses Photoshop to design app interfaces.

Stealing some templates

There is no shortage of iPhone and iPad templates and elements that can save you hours of work creating everything from scratch. My personal favorites are the Photoshop PSD files created by Teehan & Lax for the retina display (www.teehanlax.com). Rock star app designers use them, and best of all, they're free, making them a great place to start.

The number of free and inexpensive toolbar icons available to personalize designs is mushrooming like crazy as well. A search for "iPhone or iPad elements" or "toolbar icons" will get you started. I also keep a collection on Pinterest (pinterest.com/carlakaywhite/).

Making each image

When it comes time to pass along everything to your developer, you won't hand over your Photoshop layouts, but rather images of each element. This means that your custom designs must be taken apart, and every graphic element created as a separate image in *.png* file format. You can use the DevRocket plug-in to shortcut this mind-numbing and tedious process, or follow the steps outlined here (these steps are for Photoshop but other programs might be very similar):

1. Create a new file in your design software with a transparent background and dimensions larger than the element you are going to export.

2. Drag that element layer from your layout onto the blank new document. Trim off any excess space (Image⇨Trim).

3. Select File⇨Save for Web and Device and name the file name@2x.png (see the following section, "Name Files").

4. Open the file you just created and decrease the image size by 50 percent (Image⇨Image Size).

5. Select File⇨Save as and name the file **name.png**.

Naming files

Most of us are pretty bad at remembering names, and developers are no different. Recalling names for all sorts of images isn't easy, so make them more obvious by using the naming conventions in the following table. If you hire a designer, pass this list onto her and request that she use it.

Filename conventions

Filename	Example	Usage
btn-	btn-back.png	All button images
tab-	tab-home.png	All tab bar images
bkg-	bkg-main.png	All background images
-up	btn-facebook-up.png	Inactive state buttons
-down	btn-facebook-down.png	Active state buttons
-hover	btn-facebook-hover.png	Hover state buttons
@2x	btn-back@2x.png	This is a standard suffix required for all retina display graphics.

Creating Designs That Really Stand Out

With more than a million apps available, the best way grab people's attention is with an elegant design that not only behaves as we expect it to but also pays attention to finer attributes. With apps, it's the use of subtle details like color combinations, textures, and space that attract our attention. Just the right mix of these fine ingredients makes the difference between an app that is overly fussy and unnatural and one that is uncomplicated, classy, and striking.

In this section, you'll learn about the basic principles of design and how to apply them, as well as some popular design trends. I start by explaining how important it is to make the most of every pixel in your designs.

The importance of pixel perfect design

Designing for a small screen means our eyes have a limited space to roam, so there's a greater chance of any design errors standing out. Because the smaller screen means few buttons and less content to look at, every pixel and every word counts. Everything must be precise, perfectly aligned, and centered. Edges must be razor sharp. Images can't bleed or be blurry. This isn't easy, but pixel perfect design is the difference between a sloppy app and an exquisite one.

Make it *subtly* real

Some of you may have chugged an iBeer or two, maybe because it was the only beer you could legally drink at the time. The app, designed to look like a genuine pouring and frothing beer, was a huge hit because it cleverly played on something that almost every college student is already familiar with.

Apps like iBeer set the first big trend of designing interfaces that look and behave like everyday objects around us. Other common examples are spinning a virtual wheel or turning a digital page that feels like a real book. This is known as *skeuomorphic* design. Apple has been using this approach for years (see Figure 3-27), going back to the use of folders and the email icon in early interface design, but lately it's been going a bit overboard.

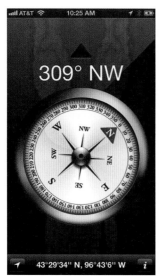  

FIGURE 3-27: Apps created by Apple that mimic real-life objects (*Compass, Calculator,* and *Find Friends*).
Source: Compass app, Calculator app, and Find Friends app

The best reason to design your app to resemble real-world objects is so that people will instantly be comfortable and familiar with the interface. It looks like the real thing, so it will be easy to use, right? That builds people's confidence. The attention to detail in skeuomorphic designs makes them visually rich and engaging, and designers love creating the details of this type of look.

The problem with designing your app like a real-world object is that it can hinder usability. If not done right, the design gets in the way because it's too confusing or distracting. The extra decoration can be a poor use of space. And no matter how cool the design looks, it can date your app quickly. The key to using wood grain and marble veneer successfully is to simply make a *reference*, not slather it on. For example, the hit word game Letterpress only shows its namesake printing style on the app icon, not in the game. The banking app by Simple has a background resembling plain chipboard to reflect the name and brand (see Figure 3-28).

FIGURE 3-28: The Letterpress app icon (left) and Simple iPhone app interface (right) only make reference to real-life objects, creating a nice balance.
Source: Letterpress app and Simple app

Make it easy and effortless: The ABC's of design

There's another way to give people confidence through familiarity, and that's building off the knowledge they have from using other apps. Some of what we instantly recognize is based on apps using the standard interface guidelines, but some is based on design principles like *grouping* and *emphasizing*.

This next section will introduce you to some design principles, and give you examples of when best to use them. So pull out your trendy glasses, put on that skinny tie, and get ready for a crash course in design. If you want to learn more about basic design principles, *The Non-Designer's Design Book* by Robin Williams (Peachpit Press 2003) is a great start.

The power of contrast

Contrast is one of the most important principles in design. You can use contrast to guide the eye directly to an element by making it strikingly different from everything else, indicating its importance. Contrast isn't limited to a brighter color. The text can be larger, or shape of the object different. Secondary elements are more subtle and maybe a different size.

The SoundCloud app (Figure 3-29) lets you share recordings on your social networks. Its minimalist design makes it incredibly easy to use. The main purpose of the app is to create a recording, and the big orange Rec button in the middle of the toolbar emphasizes this point. The other buttons all fade to the background with a standard look and feel.

FIGURE 3-29: The SoundCloud app uses contrast to make a button stand out.
Source: SoundCloud app

An easy way to test whether the contrast in your design is effective is to turn off all the color and bring it right down to grayscale (Figure 3-30). Do the main buttons still stand out? Is the text easy to read?

FIGURE 3-30: The same tab bar in grayscale; the main button still stands out.

Repetition and grouping

On the opposite end of the spectrum from contrast is making similar elements look the same so people quickly grasp the relationships among them. Repeat the same style in any related elements in your apps. This makes it's easy to understand their meaning and significance. Their look, feel, and behavior should all be akin.

Group related items together to help people quickly scan sets of items, letting them move through your app faster (see Figure 3-31). Arrange groups by hierarchy so users can identify their relationship quickly.

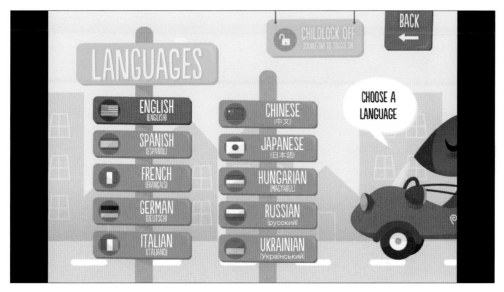

FIGURE 3-31: The Counting Ants app groups all the language choices together on two signs while the other buttons are separate.

Source: Counting Ants app

Give it some space

Just as important as what you can see is what you *don't* see. The invisible element of space directs the eye across the layout. Small screens can quickly feel cramped if elements aren't given enough breathing room. Space gives the eye a chance to rest between the options, controls, functions, and lists.

Controlling and shaping space in designs create rhythm, direction, and motion. Space can be used to both separate and connect elements. It makes the entire design easier to read and follow (see Figure 3-32).

Consistent use of space on screen layouts connects the screens and creates flow. Using space as a template keeps people from getting lost in a design. Navigation stays in the same places across the different screens.

FIGURE 3-32: The Letterpress app uses space to create a clean look that feels easy to use.
Source: Letterpress app

Same, same, same

Imagine if stop signs were all different—rather than using the common red color and octagonal shape, each stop sign had its own color and shape combination. Any fool knows that would be a recipe for fender benders and pileups. Repeating design elements, navigation, language, screen layouts, and graphic styles shows the users where to go and helps them drive safely through your app, as demonstrated in Figure 3-33.

FIGURE 3-33: The PopBooth app uses bright pink for all the main buttons, making it easy to navigate.
Source: PopBooth app

Make it delightful

Even apps designed to help us through the pains of tax time can be a joy to use if they're designed with feel-good factors that boost our self-esteem. Simple things like offering clear choices make us feel empowered and in control, even if tax time doesn't.

This next section offers some suggestions on how to give people confidence and make them feel good when using your app. As the taxman will tell you, it's the little things that count.

Tuck it away

The touch, swipe, and pinch gestures of the device interface make it easy to tuck unnecessary elements out of sight so the main focus can remain on the screen (see Figure 3-34). Help people discover hidden elements by piggybacking the gestures they're already familiar with, such as swiping a list item right to left to reveal a Delete button. Pull down on a list to refresh or reveal a search field. Tab bars, navigation bars, and toolbars can slide out of view when the user starts scrolling content on the main screen, and then slide back into place with a just a familiar tap. Hiding elements doesn't make them less important; it just clears the way for the content to flow.

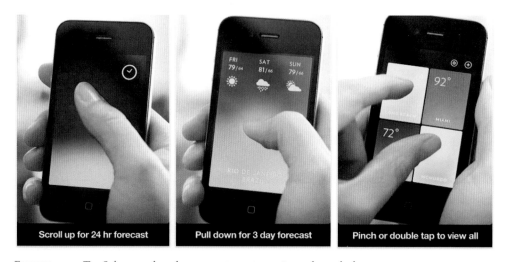

FIGURE 3-34: The Solar app cleverly uses gestures to navigate through the app.
Source: Solar app

Be careful with the interruptions

Any time your app throws up an alert or notification, it's interrupting flow, killing the blissful feelings your customers were engulfed in at that moment. If you're going to bother people with a message, be sure it's a friendly one that makes life easier and happier.

A couple of ways to grab attention is with alerts or notifications. *Alerts* pop up while people are using an app. They halt everything to share some urgent information related to the app and people must close them to continue using your app. *Notifications*, on the other hand, are messages that bob up on the screen when the related app isn't right in front of you, like text messages and calendar alarms. They can surface at the top of the screen as a banner or in the middle like an alert.

Good alerts let people know the app can't complete a task, for example, because there is no network connection. Or the app needs permission from the user to proceed, like requesting their location. *Bad alerts* interrupt people to ask them to rate your app or to buy another app you created. Like any other advertising, these alerts feel like annoying spam.

Good notifications are useful reminders, such as a message to pick up the dry cleaning when someone happens to be passing by the shop, or a notice about a gate change for a flight. *Bad notifications* are unwanted, excessive, or unnecessary announcements. Throw up a notification on the screen every time a person receives a message, a "like," or a friend request, and no doubt you'll see the word "annoying" in the reviews on iTunes. If you plan to add notifications in your app, design a settings screen so your customers can decide if and when they'll be alerted.

Making That Critical First Impression Count

In just one quick glance people will form an opinion about your app based on just the icon and name. This first impression can be almost impossible to reverse, and sets the course for the flood of opinions that follow; ultimately leading to the decision to download the app. To make that first impression count, you need to understand what makes an app icon notable, the app name memorable, and introductory screens welcoming.

What you need to know about icon design

Few properties are as in demand as the little half-inch square space on iDevices occupied by app icons. To make the grade of the coveted plot, this tiny picture has a big job portraying an intuitive representation of what the app is all about (see Figure 3-35). Some designers choose to keep it as simple as possible, whereas others prefer to stretch the limits of creativity with ambitious attention to detail.

FIGURE 3-35: The Classics app wowed people with its finely detailed icon. Just as impressive is the simple style of the Solar app icon.
Source: Classics app and Solar app

A polished and intricate icon suggests customers will find the same attention to detail in the app itself. On the other hand, apps like Solar have been equally successful without the fine level of detail. To help you, here are a few approaches to designing your icon:

- **Use your mascot.** This approach works well for games or book apps with a central character. For children's apps, it's pretty much essential because children remember the mascot easily so they return to the app more often. I used a mascot for a diary app because I wanted a happy face to convey a warm and friendly feel. Figure 3-36 shows some examples.

FIGURE 3-36: I used mascots in all of my apps (Gratitude and Vision Board). The children's app Counting Ants also uses a mascot.
Source: Gratitude Journal app, Vision Board app, and Counting Ants app

- **Use your app design.** Apps with a very distinctive and unique design can pluck a piece of that design for the icon, making it a preview of the app interface (see Figure 3-37). The repetition of the design makes it easy to recognize the app on both iTunes and the device.

FIGURE 3-37: The Paper app and Toybox app icons reflect the design inside the app itself.
Source: Paper app and Toybox app

- **Use a metaphor.** Some of the best icons are colorful, fun, and clever, using metaphors instead of words, and sometimes re-creating mundane objects into recognizable brands. To successfully pull this off, the metaphor must be *obvious*, as in Figure 3-38. If it's too cryptic, people quickly become confused about the purpose of the app, won't bother to take the time to find out, and aren't tempted to download it. Even if that means a dull icon, it must be literal.

FIGURE 3-38: The weight-loss app Lose It! has an icon that uses a clever metaphor.
Source: Lose It! app

Shortcuts to creating an icon

Icon templates can be found all over the web, taking some of the guesswork out of creating icons because they include all the various sizes you may need. Some icon templates have quite a high level of detail and don't need much customization. Sites like graphicsriver.net offer "template generators" for the bargain price of about $7. These are Photoshop files of highly detailed icons that you can easily customize by turning on or off layers in the image. If you feel fairly confident with using a design tool these templates shortcut the process considerably.

Another option is to hire someone to design the icon. This could prove to be a wise investment. I found a couple of really amazing designers on Dribbble.com who charged me $400–$700 for very detailed custom icons.

Apple will automatically adjust your icon to make it consistent with the others. It rounds the corners on all icons, so create a square graphic and leave the carving to Apple. Otherwise, you might end up with empty and ugly spaces if you try to do the work yourself. Apple also adds the gloss effect, but you can turn that off using Xcode and instead create your own lighting to fit better with the details of your icon (ask your developer to do this). Lastly, Apple places a drop shadow below each icon, so you don't need to create one in your icon image.

The icon image you see on the App Store is a larger version of what is displayed on an iPhone. And the icon on the iPad is a different size than what is on the phone. Just to add to the fun, the sizes vary depending on the device and whether it has retina display. Making heads or tails of what you need to create can produce a dust storm of comments on help forums. Figure 3-39 provides an overview of the sizes you need to create and the related file-naming conventions.

It's all in the name

We all suffer bouts of forgetfulness, some of us more often than others, and some simply because they had too much fun at happy hour. That's why the name of your app has to be memorable, so people can recall it when they want to talk about it.

The name determines how easily people can find your app when they search iTunes. It's also a reflection of the app's personality. It adds nothing to the user experience, but everything to marketing your app. Here are some basic rules to naming an app:

- **Stick to 11 or fewer characters.** That is how much space is allowed below the icon on the device screen. If the name doesn't fit, Apple chops out the middle of it, making it impossible to read and sounding like something you'd find in a Petri dish. For example, *Finding Friends* becomes "Findi...nds." A solution can be to use an abbreviated version of your name. For example, the app *Good Night Safari* shows up with "G'night Safari" on the device.

- **You can have a slightly longer name on iTunes.** The name displayed on iTunes can be longer than the one that is shown on the device, so you can add a couple of extra descriptive words to that name. Keep it to 22 or fewer characters; otherwise, you run into the same problem where Apple lops off the end of it, adding confusion, not clarity.

- **Use your app's main function.** There are more than 100 voice-recording apps on iTunes, and the number-one selling one is simply called *Recorder*. It's successful because it is easy to find. If that's a little too vanilla for you, try teaming your app's main function with a word that enhances it. For example, *Wunderlist* or *Awesome Note*. You could also add in a short verb such as "go" or "hit." Think of *Cut the Rope*. Keeping the main function in the name helps people find your app, understand instantly what it does, and remember it.

- **Make sure it's pronounceable.** Taking the vowels out of a word isn't a trend you want to follow with your app. It doesn't make the name any more memorable or easy to find. The same holds true with inventing an all-new word, for example, *Choggy*. Stick with what your audience is already familiar with so they instantly get it.

- **Do some research.** Make sure the name you choose isn't trademarked. Apple might still approve your app, but it could pull the app from iTunes as soon as it gets wind of a trademark issue. Also, do some web searches of the name you select. This will give some indication of how searchable it will be on iTunes, and help you to include common words your audience uses to describe the product.

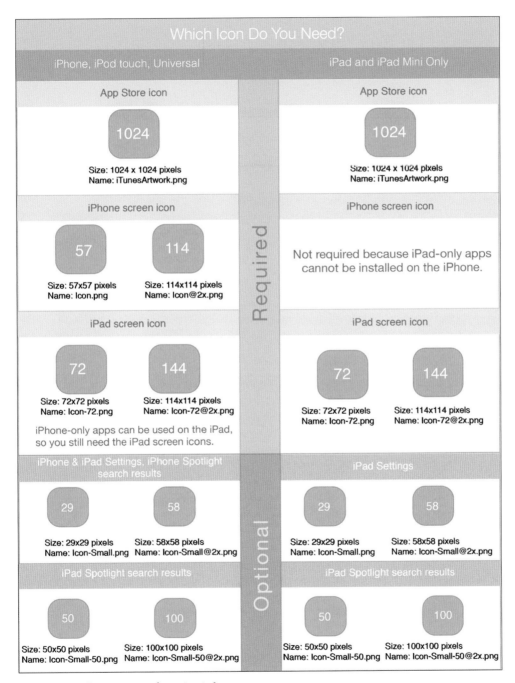

FIGURE 3-39: Icon sizing and naming info.

A Rose by Any Other Name

It took me weeks to name my first app. When I searched all my ideas in Google, "gratitude journal" came back with umpteen more results than my other choices. It is the most common phrase my tribe uses to describe this product. This result is what told me that customers would instantly understand what the "Gratitude Journal" app is without having to read the description.

I wanted to call it *Gratitude Journal,* but those two words wouldn't fit under the application icon on the screen. So I came up with shorter names like "Soul Journal" and just "Journal." It wasn't until much later that I discovered the name on the App Store could be different than what is displayed on the phone. So on the App Store the name is "Gratitude Journal" and on the phone it says "Gratitude!"

Your app's name not only helps with searches and instant product recognition, but also says that you understand your tribe. You speak their language and you are one of them. Choose wisely because your app's name has a huge impact on your sales.

Launch screens of love

Thanks to Carly Simon, we can't help but sing each syllable of the word "anticipation." It's how a teenager feels about getting a driver's license, and your dog feels about you coming home after a long day. And as people patiently wait for your app to download onto their device, it's how they'll feel about using it. That's why the first screens they see must carefully thought out.

While your app is loading, a launch image (named *Default.png*) fills the screen for a few seconds and is the first thing people see when they open your app. The trick is to make the launch screen almost invisible so customers don't feel as though they're being kept waiting even longer before they can step inside.

A launch image that looks like an empty shell of your app's first screen (see Figure 3-40) will create the illusion that your customers are already in the door. They instantly see the interface and know the app is busy in the background working to load the content. This type of welcome tells your audience that you respect their time and space and that you care about them.

FIGURE 3-40: Can you tell what app is about to launch? It's the Twitter launch screen, and it works perfectly because it will be viewed dozens of times a day by a typical user.
Source: Twitter app

On the other end of the spectrum, creating a pretty splash screen with a giant logo or promoting your other apps feels like a meaningless delay. You're vainly keeping people waiting while you talk about yourself for a few seconds. It's like making them watch a commercial before the app loads. This delay only draws attention to how long it is taking for your app to load, losing you points before people even get to see your app. Figure 3-41 provides an overview of the screen sizes you need to create and the related file-naming conventions.

Which Launch Screen Size Do You Need?	
iPhone and iPod touch apps	iPad and iPad Mini apps
Non-retina display (portrait)	Non-retina display (portrait)
Size: 320 x 480 pixels Name: Default.png	Size: 768 x 1004 pixels Name: Default-Portrait.png
Retina display (portrait)	Retina display (portrait)
Size: 640 x 960 pixels Name: Default@2x.png	Size: 1536 x 2008 pixels Name: Default-Portrait@2x.png
iPhone 5 retina display (portrait)	Non-retina display (landscape)
Size: 640 x 1136 pixels Name: Default-568h@2x.png	Size: 1024 x 748 pixels Name: Default-Landscape.png
Non-retina and retina display (landscape)	Retina display (landscape)
Not supported.	Size: 2048 x 1496 pixels Name: Default-Landscape@2x.png

FIGURE 3-41: This table outlines the various launch screen sizes and required names.

Once they're inside the door, a simple guide can help quickly help people get their bearings. It should appear only the first time someone opens the app, and then is quietly tucked away in a "help" section of the app. Here are some common formats for guides to get you started:

■ **Dialog box**—A dialog box is the easiest format to program, making it the most popular option. It's also the most likely one to get ignored because nobody wants to be forced to read something first. Customers will just tap OK without soaking in one word, so you might as well forget it.

■ **Tips**—Tips are little pop-ups that can be placed anywhere on the screen, as shown in Figure 3-42. Place them close to the feature, keep the text short, and have them fade into place. The users can tap anywhere outside the tip to close it.

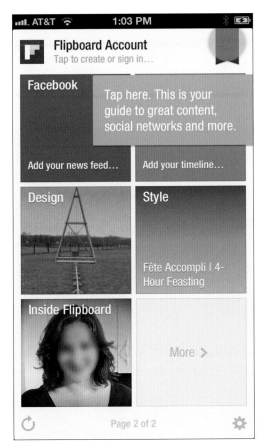

FIGURE 3-42: The Flipboard app briefly places a tip on the screen to help users navigate.

Source: Flipboard app

- **Carousel**—A carousel is a little tour of the app using sliding cards, like the one from the Solar app shown in Figure 3-43. Solar's tour starts with a thank you for purchasing the app; then the next few images offer hints on how best to use it. Keep the messages short and sweet, use page indicators at the bottom, and place a Close button on the screen to give people the power to end it anytime.

- **Transparency**—A transparency is a see-through layer of small helpful diagrams located just above the screen's content, as in Figure 3-44. With apps taking more bleeding-edge navigation models, this format is becoming increasingly popular but shouldn't be a compensation for poor design.

FIGURE 3-43: The Solar app greets users with a carousel of helpful cards.

Source: Solar app

FIGURE 3-44: Transparencies appear above the screen as shown here in the Burst app.

Source: Burst app

Outsourcing to a Professional

If you passed the limits of your design skills quite a few pages ago, it's probably time to pass the baton to a professional. Knowing who to hire is easier if you first attempt to do part of the job yourself. That's because you'll have a better understanding of what skills are needed and what quality work looks like (or at least what sub-standard work looks like). So if you even attempted to create some prototypes and screen flows, not only will it make your designer's job easier, it will also make finding the right designer a whole lot simpler.

Finding a ~~good~~ *great* designer

Elite app designers can be incredibly hard to find and even harder to hire. The combination of design skills topped with iOS savvy makes them a hot commodity that all the big players are after. Don't even think of trying to compete with those shops. You'll have far more success if you look outside the world of celebrity mobile designers.

I'm not a big fan of posting design projects to typical freelance sites. This approach is okay for hard technical skills such as coding, but design is an altogether different ball game, and getting the right player is critical.

Two highly regarded, exclusive online sites that showcase good designers are Dribbble.com (with three b's) and scoutzie.com. To be listed on either of these sites, designers must be proven professionals with a quality portfolio as proof. You're more likely to find highly qualified designers on these sites than on many other freelance sites.

Another site worth checking out is behance.net. Anyone can join, so it's not as exclusive. **TIP**

Another option, and perhaps a more affordable one, is to contact the career center at your local colleges and art schools. Let them know you're hiring and ask to be put in touch with the graduating art students. Hundreds of seriously talented designers are about to graduate and are desperate to get a job. Give them a springboard into becoming the next designer rock star.

You want to confirm their design style melds with the personality you're aiming for in your app, so dig through their portfolio as well as contact a few references. You could also test the waters first by having them design only one screen of your app before jumping into a contract.

Web design skills don't necessarily transfer to the world of mobile. Be sure your designer has mobile apps in her portfolio. **IMPORTANT**

Most importantly, you need to gauge whether your candidate can talk to humans and is not a shy turtle who retreats into his shell at the first hint of changes. Talk to him a few times and share some emails back and forth. Some friendly banter sheds light on his communication style and whether he can commit to schedules, appointments, and deadlines. It will also give you time to discuss your app and see whether that initial excitement in his eye has already faded after a week or so.

NOTE   Have a copy of your non-disclosure agreement (NDA) available for your potential designers to sign at your first meeting.

What the designer needs from you

After you've chosen your designer, signed the NDA, and agreed on a price and payment schedule, give her a detailed specification that clearly defines exactly what you want. I use Google Docs for all my specs. Your spec isn't a long-winded document that will receive the same love as an instruction manual—just something that tells the story of your app with all the labor-of-love work you did. Your spec should include:

- Your app mission statement

- Your user stories and personas

- Any mockups you created

- Your final wireframe designs

- Your user test findings

- Any artwork (such as logos and fonts) and copy you want included

- A list of features

- Your navigation flow diagram

- A clear delivery schedule

- Your collection of apps that you like most

Your designer will bear hug you as if she won the lottery if you hand over all of this without her having to beg for it. She will still have plenty of questions, however. Be sure to include your answers in the spec so everything is documented in one place.

TIP   Create a free account on Dropbox.com to upload and share all your materials. Your designer can also use it to hand over her work.

What you need from your designer

Every designer has his own methods for creating a masterpiece. Some may first create a mockup of your app based on everything you provided. Don't be alarmed if it doesn't glimmer with the sparkle of final-touch glory. It could be a quick production to initiate ideas and get things going. On the other hand, your designer could very well surprise you with something nearly perfect for production.

After all the changes have been made and the final layouts are produced, make sure your designer provides all the following files:

- **Original copies of all the screens**—Most likely they will be Photoshop PSD files, but they could be Illustrator or Fireworks. They will include all the screen layouts with each custom element. Depending on your designer's preference, they would be done in normal display (1x) or retina display (2x) size.

- **Regular and high-resolution PNGs of each unique element**—Your designer should create PNG images of all unique design elements in the correct sizes for all devices (1x and 2x sizes for each element). Have him use the naming convention listed earlier in this chapter.

- **Regular and high-resolution PNGs of your loading screen**—If your app uses both landscape and portrait orientations, you will need a loading screen for both views. These must be named `Default.png` and Default@2x.png, as discussed earlier in this chapter.

- **Original copies of your app icon**—If your designer also is creating your icon, be sure you get the original file. This could be a Photoshop PSD file, but might be Illustrator or Fireworks.

- **Copies of your icon in all the required sizes**—Request copies of your icon in PNG format. You will need one copy of each size according to the icon size chart presented earlier in this chapter.

Signing the contract

Even if you plan to hire your favorite cousin, the one who always remembers your birthday, write up a contract for both of you to sign. Don't make the mistake of skipping this process out of fear of offending someone. A contract is actually a friendly way to make certain that you both are on the same page about deliverables, schedules, and responsibilities. You may have discussed all these things already, but nothing is clearer than seeing everything in black and white.

You can download contracts from the web, but they aren't preprint documents where you simply fill in the blanks. Take the time to read them carefully and customize the terms and conditions based on your project needs. Be sure to include the following items:

■ A friendly welcome thanking the designer for working with you.

■ A list of services and deliverables that will be rendered by the designer.

■ Fees, bonuses, and time schedules.

■ Who is responsible for any additional costs (normally you, the client).

■ The agreement start and end dates.

■ An out clause so either of you can quit the contract given sufficient notice.

■ Signatures and dates.

Doing without the designer

It goes without saying that if you got this far in the design process; you might be up for doing the final production yourself. Maybe you've been using Photoshop for years, or perhaps you just played around with it enough to erase wrinkles from photos (not yours, of course). That's enough to get you started.

Maybe you've shopped around and designer estimates are killing your budget, or aren't providing the quality you expect. That's exactly what happened to me. If you find yourself in the same rickety boat, and have never used a design tool, be prepared to make one such as Photoshop your new best friend.

I've used Photoshop for years but still have plenty to learn. It took a few weeks of practice, but I managed to create the same level of quality you'd expect from an Apple product. Here are a few shortcuts to jump-start your design skills:

■ **Learn from the best.** The web is littered with incredibly simple online tutorials outlining exactly how to create shiny buttons, gradients, and the latest design effects. The site mobile.tutplus.com is a great place to start. Another nifty trick is to download every app that you think has a great design. Scrutinize each pixel and try to re-create their styles in Photoshop to learn how to produce the same quality of art. Of course, don't copy.

■ **Take a few Photoshop courses.** A simple one-day Photoshop course could be enough to clear the fog. If you can't afford to attend a training course in person, plenty of great Photoshop courses are available online. Lynda.com has dozens of courses and costs only $25.00 per month ($37.50 for the premium plan that comes with all the exercise files).

- **Use your library card.** Check out every current book you can find about Photoshop. You don't need to devour them cover to cover. Reading *War and Peace* would be easier. Just study the sections that reflect what you want to accomplish most with your design. Using a book might be easier than flipping back and forth from a website to your design software.

- **Go on some field trips.** If your app represents a true-to-life object, get out to the shops and study as many varieties of it as you can. Pick it up, take photos of it, move it around in different lights, and see how the shadows and gradients change. Study it backwards, upside down, and inside out.

- **Invest in one professionally done element.** If you can't afford a designer for your entire app, try getting one unique item done professionally. Your app icon is a great choice, or you might want to have a character created for your app.

Marketing Ideas Checklist

At the same time that you're consumed with pixels and fonts, you can be growing your audience and interest in your app by sharing your adventure with your tribe. Here are a few activities that will give your marketing a boost during the design phase of your app project.

PROMOTE

- **Update your website with sneak peeks.** Put some sneak-peek shots of your app on your teaser site. The preview doesn't have to look like the final thing. You just want to give your audience a taste of the greatness about to come. Include your icon if that is done, too.

- **Send out a newsletter to your first fans.** Did a few people sign up for your newsletter distribution list? Reach out to them with an email. Show them a couple of "exclusive" previews only they are privileged to see. Share a story about something funny, particularly challenging, or completely unrelated to your app project. Keep it short—something they can glance at in just a few seconds.

- **Share your ups and downs on your social media sites.** Creating your designs is so much more fun when you share it with your audience. Give them a sneak peek of your sketches. Share stories about your discoveries. Just a shot of the corner of a screen or a particular design element is all you have to reveal, not the whole enchilada. Creating apps is seriously exciting and cool, so share your adventures!

Key Points

- Always sketch out your designs on paper first. On a computer we tend to get absorbed in the details of the app design and lose focus on creating flow.

- Create a simple flow diagram to see how all your screens link together. This will also give you a good indication on how complicated your app is as well as how much it will cost to develop. Write a story about your app to give it life.

- Test your designs on real people, starting with your paper prototypes. Testing takes only a few minutes and is the bridge to designing an app that can be fully understood in 15 seconds or less.

- Don't leave your icon and launch screens as afterthoughts. First impressions are hard to change, so make sure you get it right with an icon and name that make it easy to discover your app and tell people exactly what it does.

- Forget trying to hire the rock star designers and instead build your own superstar. Check out local colleges and art schools to find good candidates. Meet with them a few times because knowing whether they can communicate and finish the job is just as critical as knowing whether they have the right design skills.

- If you can't afford a designer, get online and to the library to teach yourself to use Photoshop or Gimp. If you can, try to hire a professional to do at least one element of your design, such as the icon or mascot. That might be all you need.

Developing and Testing Your App

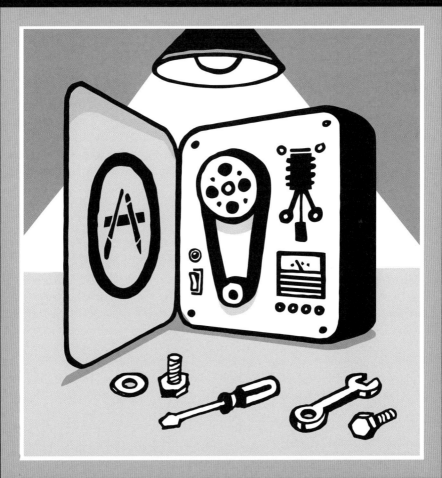

"Quality means doing it right when nobody is looking."

—Henry Ford

Without a doubt, picking your developer can be the most overwhelming and difficult part of the project. If you don't understand a *framework* from a *factory*, how will you know the developer is someone you can trust to do a quality job for a reasonable price? Here's the catch. You can pay someone thousands to build your app and it ends up being riddled with bugs, or you could pay someone half that and your app does even more than you expected. That's because it's not about the costs, it's about the *quality*. In other words, you can hire a developer who might be charging you less, but it could take him ten times longer to finish your project and in the end actually costs you more because the code isn't up to par. Rather than pouring money down the drain, this chapter clears up a lot of the confusion about finding a seasoned developer you can trust.

It explains where to look for qualified and affordable developers and how to determine whether they are truly the crème de la crème they claim to be. It walks you through any challenging technical hurdles, shows you how to create a design specification that is both impressive and effective, and explains how to win over your developers so they're rooting for your success. It also lays out a practical plan for testing your app, resolving issues quickly, and determining the best point to go live.

Finding Dependable and Talented Developers

DEVELOP

It used to be that there were very few iOS developers on the planet, and most of them were pretty mediocre because iPhone apps were so new and they had little experience with the iOS platform. Although the language used to code iPhone apps, Objective C, was a relatively mature language, the frameworks and libraries were brand new. Fast-forward five years to today and the Internet is littered with countless iOS developers, most claiming to be experts.

With hundreds of companies peddling iOS development skills, it might be hard to believe that finding a decent developer can be almost as difficult as scoring backstage passes to a Rolling Stones concert. The truth is that there simply aren't enough *experienced* developers to meet the market demand.

Just as politicians tend to be the target of jokes, iOS developers also find themselves getting a bad rap. That's because the increasing demand for these rare talents is pushing unqualified or barely qualified developers onto the scene, hoping for a slice of the pie. These unskilled developers are like politicians at election time; they'll make all sorts of wonderful promises they simply can't keep.

If you're like me and have the programming skills of a fish, you not only need to find someone to build your app, but also a couple of iOS-savvy friends whom you can turn to in a pinch with a question or for advice. Otherwise you're gambling way too much on one person or development shop.

The following section explains how to expand your network of technically talented friends so you not only have some helpful iOS buddies that you can trust, but also so you can locate and select the best developer to build your app.

Consider hiring a second developer to advise you through your app project. This person won't build your app but will be available to consult with you when you need him. If you happen to find a developer you really like but can't afford to hire him for the entire project, consulting might be good option.   **TIP**

Reaching out to the iOS community

As hotly competitive as the app market is today, you might find it surprising to learn that the iOS developer community is actually, in my experience, an incredibly helpful, friendly, and supportive group. What's the reason for this? My theory is that when this community first coalesced in 2008, there were zero resources available besides the Apple Developer Portal. Like explorers trying to climb Mt. Everest without a map, developers had to rely on each other for guidance, setting the tone for how the community interacts today.

The good news for you is that when you're in a bind, there's plenty of firsthand advice available from experts all over the world. It could be from a seasoned professional who has been doing this for years, one hit app after another, or a guy just trying to keep his app afloat hoping someone will throw him a life vest.

Numerous forums exist where you can discuss any design or code problems you're facing. But to find a talented developer to help you on your project, you need to reach out to them in the places where they hang out.

Where to scout out the talent

You probably already searched the Internet for iPhone developers and came across dozens of developer sites with impressive portfolios, enticing offers, and proven track records, so you have a pretty good idea what kind of jungle it is out there.

To help you machete through the weeds, this list offers some of the most common places to find developers both online as well as in your own community. Remember, you're not just looking for someone to code your app. You also want to build your developer network and find friends with some iOS knowhow.

- **Check out oDesk, Elance, Freelancer, Guru**—These freelance job-posting sites are great for quickly finding some developer talent. Later in this chapter, I explain a bit more about the pros and cons of these sites and how to get the most out of them.

- **Visit filtered freelance sites**—Sites like theymakeapps.com and grouptalent.com are similar to the previous freelance sites with the exception that the talent available is pre-filtered, taking out some of the guesswork for you.

- **Post on social networks**—Post that you're talent hunting on Facebook, LinkedIn, and Twitter and you might make a few new friends. You can also search for Facebook pages, look for Twitter hashtags, or find iOS groups on LinkedIn that you can join.

- **Go to meetups**—Check out meetup.com to find iOS developer groups in your area. If there isn't one, start one yourself. You can also check out other professional and technical clubs. Chances are there is at least one developer or entrepreneur club in your town.

- **Stop by a code camp**—These weekend-long cramming sessions are for developers. You don't need to sign up for the entire course, but stop by during the lunch break and mingle with the attendees to see whom you discover. One of the most popular is Big Nerd Ranch (bignerdranch.com).

- **Phone your local tech or startup center**—The people running these businesses are incredibly well connected. Ask them if they know anyone developing mobile apps and ask to be put in touch. Their jobs are all about networking, so they should be more than happy to help you out.

- **Visit a Hack-a-Thon**—Check out hackatopia.com to see if an event is scheduled in your area. These events are designed for technical and nontechnical attendees to network, code, and most importantly, learn.

- **Ask everyone you know**—Let anyone and everyone know you would like to meet iOS developers. Talk about it family reunions, church, your kid's ballgames, and when you run into your neighbor while walking the dog.

- **Check the App Store**—Look up your favorite apps and contact the developers who created them. Let them know that you are fans of their app, hoping to create your own, and would appreciate being in touch with any developers they may know.

- **Post to Craigslist**—I'm constantly amazed at what people discover on this site. A good friend landed an app project there, started her own business, and in less than a month handed her old boss her notice.

The cool thing about this business is that you do not have to be a developer to be in it. There are a lot of developers out there who are looking for good ideas to work on. If you have an idea, roll with it! Search Elance and other freelance sites to find people. It really is amazing the opportunities that are out there if you go look.

—Shelby Meinzer, founder of MindTapp (Photonest iPhone app)

Throughout your app project, all sorts of people will generously lend you a hand, perhaps by giving you feedback on your ideas, offering technical advice, or introducing you to new contacts. If someone helps you out, make it a point to say thank you with a gesture of appreciation.

For example, Amazon has gift cards for as little as $5. It probably won't get much, but at least it tells that person you value her time and are respectful of her profession. If you create any type of product, give the person a free sample. Better yet, old fashion snail-mail her a gift so it's a nice surprise tucked among the bills and junk.

NOTE

Making the most of Elance.com and other sites

In the last five years, I've probably hired over a dozen developers; some were overseas shops I found online, while others were freelancers I met through the iOS community. I discovered my first developer through an online marketplace called Elance.com, and the relationship worked like a charm. That was back in 2008, and Elance was the only place I knew to look for coders, and to be honest, not many other sites existed.

Today sites like Elance, oDesk, Freelancer, and Guru are just a handful of the many online communities and marketplaces where you can find and hire "undiscovered" freelancers all around the world. By "undiscovered," I mean "cheap." And "all over the world" includes the United States as well as elsewhere. Regardless of where you discover developers, the key to hiring one who won't cripple your project and leave you out of pocket is to take the time to do your due diligence.

Qualified developers might charge between $125 and $200 per hour. I'm sure they're worth every penny, and if you can afford those rates, by all means go for it. But if you can't, don't haggle with them because they probably have other top-dollar opportunities waiting.

IMPORTANT

Bargain shops charge as little as $10 to $40 per hour, which seems like a far better option on the face of it. Go this route only if you are 110 percent confident that developers in these shops are completely qualified to do the job.

If you did all your homework up front, you will know. If you have any doubt, either ask more questions or just walk away, because if you hire them and they can't deliver, you will wind up back with the higher rate developers asking them to fix everything. In the end, it will cost you more to develop your app, not to mention all the revenues you missed out on because it took so long to get it on iTunes.

Even if you don't find or hire your developer from Elance, this site is packed with advice about outsourcing; plus, it offers free downloads of some of the contracts you'll need. Turning to Elance or similar sites for your developer provides additional benefits:

- **Ease of use for beginners**—These sites give you access to developers all over the world, saving you from having to shop around to various sites.

- **Affordability**—The cost of living where many of the developers are located is much less than in the Western world, so contractors can afford to offer lower hourly rates.

- **Easy payments**—The site takes care of all the payments for you. You enter your credit card details into the system, specify when and how much the contractor should be paid, and the site takes care of the rest.

- **Opportunities to stay informed**—oDesk has a visual timecard called the Work Diary. It's an overview of the work the developers performed so you know the contractor is actually logging time on your project.

- **Reviews and feedback**—Clients can review the freelancers they hired after each milestone and at the completion of the project. You want a developer with a recent track record of happy clients. If you notice a lot of projects with no reviews, this could be a red flag that projects are running over schedule because they haven't hit their milestone review yet.

- **Proficiency testing**—Most sites test developers as a way to see whether they are as good as they claimed. You can try to take one of the tests yourself to gauge what is involved. It's worth noting, however, that if a shop tested well, it doesn't necessarily mean the developer who took the exam will be the same one working on your project.

Your first instinct might be to quickly post your project to these sites just to see who bites. But before you do that, study other iPhone and iPad app job postings. This will give you an idea of the types of projects attracting the most developers and the average costs. So instead of posting your job, first approach the site as a freelancer would and select the link "Find Work," and then do a search for "iPhone app" or "iPad app" or "iOS app". You'll see well over a thousand projects that you can sort by "Proposal Counts" to see which are the hottest.

In the following sections, I suggest a couple of ways to scope out quality talent on these freelance sites. In the first scenario, you approach the developers directly by narrowing down all the possible candidates and then contacting your top choices. In the second, you let developers come to you by posting the initial outline of your project for developers to bid on.

Search for the developer you want

At first glance, it might appear that projects with the highest number of bids have the pick of the litter and will have no problem finding a qualified developer. But the truth is that sifting through a plethora of bids is as fun as trying to find a diamond at the dump. Screening all those applicants is tedious, time-consuming, and it stinks. Instead, hunt for the talent you want rather than hoping developers will come to you.

Of course, posting your project may very well may lead to some great contractors, but try this method, and you'll most likely enjoy far better success:

- Step 1: Go to at least two sites. I usually start with Elance.com and then check out odesk.com.

- Step 2: Register with the site. This gives you more search options than those available to nonregistered users.

- Step 3: Log in to the site and select the link to "search" or "hire" contractors. Figure 4-1 shows a portion of the page on oDesk where you can select your search criteria.

- Step 4: Try to narrow down the results to find the upper 10 percent of the contractors. The criteria to narrow down search results will be different for each site, but will include items similar to the following:

  - Mobile Developer

  - iOS Developer

  - Reviews and feedback 4.5–5 stars

  - Minimum 100 hours billed or two jobs

  - Tested in the top 10 percent in English speaking and writing and iOS development skills

  - English level is 5 stars (oDesk)

  - Belongs to the iPhone Developer Expert group (Elance)

  - Last activity 0–15 days (oDesk)

If there still are too many profiles for you to thumb through, trim down the list by entering keywords about your app. When you get a digestible number of developers, you can begin reviewing the portfolios (the next section explains what to look for in the profiles). Once you boil down the candidates to the very best ones, contact them with your job description and an exclusive offer to bid on your project. This will initiate conversations and move the screening process forward.

FIGURE 4-1: Some of the search options on the ODesk website.

Post your project and let the developer find you

The beauty of posting your job to these sites is it doesn't cost you a cent. You can tap into a skilled talent pool of more than 100,000 tested and rated freelance contractors and get a rough idea of how much your project will cost before you even start designing it. The downside of posting your project so early is that the bids you receive won't be a true reflection of what your app will actually cost to build.

You might notice that most of the job descriptions on these sites barely have a paragraph describing the work. This vagueness protects the idea but means developer estimates will be all over the place. Most developers will request more details before placing a bid, and that's an administrative headache. Some will bid extremely low hoping to win the job. Others will pad in thousands of dollars of wiggle room. Or you might get the standard cut-and-paste response the sales rep puts on every single project that hits the site.

To avoid this, I use job descriptions that are a little longer. They still don't have enough details to get accurate estimates of the costs involved, but this approach narrows the gap enough to start a dialogue with prospective candidates. Here is an example of one of my job postings. Feel free to copy and edit this for your own use.

Title: iPhone notes app development—Experienced developers only

What I Need Done:

I'm looking for an experienced developer or company who understands the iPhone SDK inside and out. I need an Objective C developer to create Notepad-like iPhone application (3 screens). The program is fully designed and does not require any complicated functionality.

What I Will Provide:

All screen designs are complete, as well as the loading page and icon. I will provide all designs, content, and images, final QA testing as well as full project management.

Other Context/Requirements That Providers Will Need to Know:

Although the application is basic, I definitely want to work with someone who has excellent iPhone application development experience. If I find a developer whom I work well with, I have other projects coming over the next 3–6 months.

Specific Expertise That I Am Seeking:

iPhone application development experience is key. Ability to speak fluent English and communication skills are also critical. Must have proven examples of work on iTunes.

Find other places to circulate your job description

Think of your job description as your project's business card. It opens the door to conversations without your having to sign a non-disclosure agreement (NDA) first. Share it with anyone you might be interested in bringing onto your project.

- If you are using a freelance site like Elance, send the description to the candidates in your search results short list.

- Send it to any developers you have met through networking events. If they aren't available to do your project, ask them if they know of anyone who might be.

- Email it to local universities, tech groups, and startup centers. Let them know you are hiring an iOS developer.

- Share it on your website and social network sites. Nothing says you're growing like a "We're hiring" sign.

- Send it to your favorite web shops. A lot of web agencies are branching into app development and will welcome the chance to have a good app in their portfolio.

- Give it to everyone you know. Pass it along to relatives, friends, and the pizza guy who just generously tested your designs.

Selecting the Best Developer for Your App Project

Just as an electrician's handiwork is concealed behind plaster and paint, most of the developer's work is hidden behind the app's interface, making it hard to gauge if they're as good as they claim. The app may look incredible and function just fine, but the coding underneath could be a horrible mess and a disaster waiting to happen.

This next section helps you filter out the posers and rookies from the experienced and truly talented by showing you exactly what to look for. It offers a checklist of developer qualifications, interview questions (and suitable answers), tips on how to review their work, and advice on checking their references. Remember, you cannot rush the task of hiring your developer because a superb developer will go on to do amazing things for your app while a terrible one will crush it.

The developer review checklist

Some shops toss around terms like "award winning" and "on budget" as if those are the most important qualities for a developer to have. While that's certainly a good start, it's more involved than that. For one thing, there's just too much included in the iOS SDK for a single person to know every framework or library. To get you started, here's the must-have list of what to look for in a developer to determine if he's qualified to build your app.

> **NOTE** All developers should have experience with iOS development and the iOS SDK, as well as with C programming (Objective C and C++) and Cocoa. They should also have at least one app in the App Store.

- **Apps similar to yours in their portfolio.** Promising candidates will have already created apps with functionality like the one you're creating. For example, if you have social networking integrated, make sure they have already done that in a previous app and are not teaching themselves how to do it on your dime.

- **Fluency in your native language.** It's hard enough ordering a coffee in a foreign language, let alone discussing the intricacies of latest software technologies. A Skype call is the only way to truly establish a developer's fluency. If you're interviewing a software shop, make sure you talk with the actual developer and not the sales rep.

- **Overlapping working hours.** If you can manage to have 2 or 3 hours that overlap each day, your project will go a whole lot faster. Waiting 24 hours for an answer that only brings more questions can drag weeks into months; a few minutes on Skype every few days could be all you need to keep things moving.

■ **Legitimate work.** Look for at least three fully working apps in their portfolio. Download every single app they created, and then contact the owner of each one to ask about their experience with the developers. This might surprise you, but more than once I've had developers put my apps in their portfolios and I had never even heard of them, let alone done business with them. I found out from people contacting me as part of their due diligence interviewing the developers (and no, they didn't get hired).

■ **Integrity in their work.** Contact every one of their references. It's easy to skip this step, thinking that everyone lists only references that will be positive. Some shops and developers list bogus references thinking no one will bother calling them. Also, if any of the apps they created are subpar, don't hire them. If they created a sloppy app for someone else, they'll do it for you, too.

■ **Responsiveness to questions and emails.** They should respond to emails and queries within 24 hours. You also want to set expectations up front by requesting they commit to replying to all questions and requests within 24 hours during your project. Let them know that you'll also commit to the same quick turnaround.

■ **Attention to details.** They should answer every question line by line and be consistent and easy to understand. Steer clear of developers or shops that give canned responses to your job listing. Anyone that refers to me as "Sir" gets the boot, no matter how enticing the shop might be.

■ **Sample code available on request.** Simple programs are okay. Don't let your lack of programming knowledge stand in your way of requesting some sample code. If you can, ask an iOS buddy to help you review the sample. I nearly skipped this step once because I wasn't sure what to look for. Thankfully, a friend said he'd help, and it turns out the developer I nearly hired sent code that doesn't even run on the iPhone. My app was going to be his first project. Also, if a shop or a developer doesn't want to share any examples, thank them for their time and move on.

■ **Willingness to teach and offer assistance.** The developers should willingly suggest their own ideas for your app. Don't be shy to ask plenty of questions. Everyone was a newbie at some point, including your developers. They should happily take the time to explain everything to you, including confusing terminology and technical details.

■ **Time to commit to your project.** Ask how many other projects they are currently engaged in and how many programmers are working on each project. The sales reps are often paid on getting projects in the door, not on actually completing them. Make sure they have the time to commit to your project and will give it the attention it deserves.

■ **Confirmation that you own the source code.** You paid for it, so you should own it, but unless you state this fact up front, they may think they own it and can do what they please with it—including making a variation of your app and selling it off.

Interviewing prospective developers

Most of us had to sit through at least one job interview to find employment, so you're familiar with the drill. It's a good idea to interview each candidate at least once. You're not so much interested in discovering where they "see themselves in five years," but rather what your project will cost, how long it will take, and most importantly, if they have what it takes to do the job.

It goes without saying that plenty of candidates will exaggerate qualifications that are vaguely accurate and sometimes impossible to verify. Pay attention to what they say directly and personally to you, instead of relying on long bulleted lists or copy-and-paste responses. If your first correspondence isn't so hot, the next ones will probably never make up for it. Just move on quickly if you sense the relationship won't work out, but if your gut tells you there might be a match, set up an interview to move things forward.

It's not the most loving gesture to ask for a signed NDA from your candidates before sitting down with them for a discuss your project, but make sure you do it *before* sharing any more details, especially the detailed design specification. (You will learn how to create this spec later in this chapter.) It's a tedious legality, but nothing is more infuriating than having your work stolen. If developers refuse to sign, scratch them from the list and move on, plain and simple.

Buying local isn't just a campaign to boost your town's economy; it can also boost your confidence in a candidate because you can meet in person at least a couple of times. But if schedules make that impossible or candidates live too far away, set up a Skype conversation for the interview. Even if you happen to discover a developer through a friend who only speaks highly of him, you need at least one conversation to find out if you get along.

If words like *class* and *subclass* sound like slang terms for who's hip or not, try inviting a "techie" friend who is familiar with software development to join you. Even if your friend doesn't know iOS programming, she will be able to sniff out dubious programmers quickly.

Questions to ask

Your shortlist of candidates might include independent freelancers as well as agencies that offer a team of developers. If you're considering an agency, your initial correspondence most likely will be with a salesperson, but when it comes to the interview, you want to talk to the developer who will be creating your app, not a sales rep. If a shop won't let you talk to the developer, scratch that shop from the list. The sales rep can join you on the call, but you want to talk to the person actually building the app.

Planning the call will give you an idea of whether your hours overlap and if it's a convenient time for you. If it's at 4 a.m., be prepared to drag yourself out of bed and be available at that time during your project. This call also gives you a chance to hear how well the developer speaks your native language. You're not looking for a great personality, but you should verify that language barriers aren't going to cause communication problems and delays during your project.

You can ask some of the following questions in your email correspondence, and then go through them again in your interview to verify whether the answers are consistent.

- **What is the developer's history developing in Objective C?** How long has he been creating iOS apps? What were his biggest learning curves? What was the hardest feature he developed? What other developer languages does he know?

Remember that iPhone apps have been around only since 2008, so anyone who claims to have been creating them longer than that is fibbing.   `TIP`

- **How frequently will he send builds to test on your device?** After the initial framework of the app is programmed, you want weekly or bi-weekly builds made available to you to evaluate the user interface, start testing, and track bugs. We get into testing and bug tracking later in this chapter.

- **What support does he offer?** Will the developer help you install the app for testing? Will he help you submit it to iTunes? When the app is complete, how will he follow up on any bugs that are later found? Will there be a cost? If so, how much? The developer should offer to fix any bugs found even after your app goes live.

- **What is his experience working with any specific technologies in your app?** If you are creating a game, ask him about his experience developing other game apps. If the app has a special feature, such as in-app purchases, see whether he has worked with it before.

- **What other platforms has he worked on?** Does he have experience creating websites? Desktop applications? Other mobile platforms? This will give you an indication of how seasoned of a programmer he is and whether he put in the time as a developer to see projects through to the finish.

- **Does he work with an in-house artist?** Some shops just go ahead and create any missing design elements themselves, and developers seldom know enough about design tools to do this correctly. You can later fix any design elements created, but sometimes the developer plows down a path pretty far before you're made aware of the design work the shop created, and fixing it almost can't be undone.

- **Has he attended WWDC?** This is the developer conference sponsored by Apple. It sells out in minutes after tickets go on sale and is incredibly expensive, so it's an added bonus to you if your developer did attend.

- **What devices does he own?** He doesn't need to own all the latest gear from Apple, but you want to make sure he's developing on the products that are going to be used by the majority of your market.

If you really want to drill developers, you can go through this next section of technical questions. You might not have a clue what they're talking about and that's okay. If the candidate doesn't understand these questions either, he's probably about as capable as coding your app as you are. Again, having a code-savvy friend join the interview can be helpful.

- What is XCode? Explain its debugging tools.

- How do you use Interface Builder?

- Talk me through submitting apps to the App Store and everything that is involved (certificates, App IDs, and so on).

- Tell me about Objective-C and using properties.

- Tell me about Objective-C and using delegates.

- What do you know about networking with ASIHttpRequest, AsyncSockets, GameKit, and Bonjour?

- Explain subclassing to me.

- What do you know about CoreAnimation and CoreData?

- Can you list all the usual interfaces on iOS like UITableView?

- Tell me everything you know about memory management. (Someone good at memory management is usually good at everything iPhone, so if you ask just one question, pick this one!)

How to review the developer's prior work

An interview reveals only so much, and how *long* a developer has been doing projects doesn't matter as much as how *well* he can do them. To truly assess a developer's skills you need to peel back the cover and look under the hood.

First, download every app the developer created and test them as much as you can. If the shop has hundreds of apps, request just the ones exclusively created by the developer who will be working on your project.

You also want a copy of sample code from the developer who will be building your app. You don't need an entire app, just a couple of screens (`.xib` files) and the supporting files (`.m` and `.h` files). Open the files in Xcode and look for good documentation inside the code. These lines are shown in green with `/*` at the start and `*/` at the end. While well-documented code doesn't affect your users, it certainly impacts your ability to push out updates. It also makes it easier for other developers to quickly come up to speed on the app's architecture and code so you aren't entirely dependent on one person the rest of your app's life. If you're unsure of how to open a file in Xcode, there's an introduction to the tool later in this chapter.

Lastly, send the files to an iOS developer friend, or to a consultant if you hired one and ask if she would take a couple of minutes and look at the code too. She should be able to tell you if it's any good, or if it raises any red flags.

Where to find honest feedback on a developer's skills

It would be nice if all your correspondence, interviews, and code examples painted the whole picture of your candidate and not just their best side. The only way to find out if they are as good as they seem is to ask people who have worked with them before. This means contacting each reference and every app owner listed in the developer's portfolio. This might be taxing and time consuming, but don't leave anything to chance by skipping this step. The costs of a bad hire more than justify taking the extra time to try to hire the right person.

To keep track of who said what, put together a spreadsheet of all your prospective candidates, their apps, and the names of everyone you plan to contact. Then shoot off a copy of the following email to each contact.

Dear _____,

I'm writing to you about your app _____. I'm an app developer and was considering hiring _____ to do the development on my app. I noticed they created your _____ app so I was hoping you could answer a few questions about your experience working with them.

When did you work with them?

Were you happy with your experience and would you recommend them?

Did they deliver on schedule and budget?

If you're not working with them now, why not?

Would you hire them again?

Is there anything I should know that will make working with them a better experience?

I realize you're very busy, so I thank you for your time. Best of luck with your app!

Regards,

_____

If you get enthusiastic and positive feedback, that's great! You are finding good candidates. If not, even better. You just saved yourself from hiring a lemon.

Understanding that cheap can be expensive in the long run

As tempting as a good bargain might be, never select a developer shop only because it has the lowest bid. Low bids mean the shop is putting a novice on the project and that person is learning as she goes. This shop might end up building an app that doesn't even look like your designs, and it won't care. Typically it just wants to bank the first payments so it has some cash while its newbie learns the ropes. You'll get ripped off, and your project will fall way behind. Then you'll wind up hiring an expensive developer to fix it all, costing you twice as much in the end.

IMPORTANT   Don't go with the agency that claims it can build your app the fastest, either.

Comparing apples to apples

Later in this chapter, you'll learn how to create a design specification so detailed that prospects can easily envision your app by glancing through the document. You need to go through your design spec page by page with your short-listed candidates (after the NDA is signed) so they can calculate a fairly accurate time and cost schedule. A "rough guesstimate" isn't good enough. You want to know *precisely* what it will cost, how long it will take, and most importantly, if the developer can actually deliver.

Also, developers love projects that can be turned around quickly. If they can easily envision your app, their motivation to take on your project is fueled by the buzz of seeing the end result. More importantly, seasoned developers can calculate fairly accurately how many hours your app will take to develop as well as any specialty skills your developer may need. This will help you sort out the time-wasting novices from the real McCoys. You may not be able to afford this rock star in the end, but her input can certainly point your project in the right direction.

After each candidate has walked through your spec and had a chance to study it, request a bid proposal on your project. The bid proposal is a document that outlines the following items:

- **Scope**—A recap of the work the candidate will provide preferably broken down into milestones. For example, the document will break down the app features the candidate will develop, including any testing she will do, assistance with installing the app or submitting it to iTunes, and so on.

- **Deliverables**—A list of everything the candidate will give you, including the source code, technical consulting, or artwork she creates.

- **Schedules**—Dates for delivery of each phase of the project as well as to complete the project.

- **Costs**—A breakdown of what everything will cost. Some developers might do the project for a fixed fee, whereas others charge an hourly rate. Be sure the bid notes who is responsible for any sundry costs such as outside consulting, artwork, or future bug fixes.

- **Payment terms**—Details as to when the candidate expects each payment. A general rule of thumb is four lots of 25 percent, with the final 25 percent being paid upon project completion and the remaining three being spread out across milestones during the project.

- **How the candidate works**—This is a nice little bonus if it's included. It describes things like the development process, how the candidate keeps the client informed, and how she handles problems.

Independent freelancer and boutique shops often just send a one-page document, and that's fine. Putting together proposals takes a lot of time, but the more details you can get, the easier it is for you to make a confident decision. If the shop doesn't put the details in writing up front, confirm them in your correspondence and then add the information to your contract.

Shops that offer discount incentives for signing a contract in a week should be put at the bottom of the pile, or better yet, in the garbage can. Also, toss anyone who wants payment in full up front. The following sections cover a few other important considerations to bear in mind when comparing your bids.

When can work start?

Make sure the developer or shop can start a week after all contracts and agreements are finalized. Because like New Year resolutions in February, the initial excitement for a new project slowly starts to fade. You want to tap into it as early as possible and keep the momentum going.

You also want to find out how many projects the shop currently has on the table. The sales rep may not be completely honest, but you have to ask. You don't want your project to be neglected because it's not the highest earning project for the shop or gets lost in a sea of other work.

The size of the team dictates the number of projects a shop will be working on at one time. If there's just one developer, two or three projects tops is the most you want her engaged in at once. Any more than that, and you are looking at long delays.

When will I get my app?

Let's face it, we're all terrible estimators. If your project is expected to take more than six months, pad in 50 percent more time (another three months) to be safe. Shops promising to deliver in an incredibly short time frame compared to the other estimates you get should be thrown out. It's difficult for anyone to predict the future, so expect estimates to be off to some degree, but don't go with Speedy (a.k.a. Sloppy) Gonzales.

To make your guesses a bit more realistic, break the project into smaller steps. The smaller it is, the easier it is to estimate. The time estimate may still be off, but it will be a lot less of a guess than if the developer estimated a big project. If something takes longer than expected, it's better to be a couple of weeks late rather than months overdue. Interim dates also allow you to check on whether progress is going according to schedule.

Just to be clear, delivery time depends as much on you as it does on your developer. You must commit to making time each week to properly test and document each build. The quicker you can turn around your results, the faster your developer will be able to address the bugs and fix them. Remember, developers want the project done as quickly as you do.

Test-drive with a mini project

If you really want to see how a developer or a shop's team works, hire them for a short project. Even if it is only 10 or 20 hours, you learn how they communicate, make decisions, and whether you get along. This is a regular consulting project with an hourly rate and real-world work that needs to be done on your app. Most importantly, a test drive gives you the chance to evaluate them based on their actions rather than just their words.

> **NOTE**   Large projects that involve a lot of time and money should be broken down into smaller projects. Use one of these mini-projects to audition your developer. Some people break up their projects and divvy up the work to two or three different freelancers so work can get done faster; in so doing, they also lower their risks.

Learning to trust your gut

Above all else, you have to believe that you can trust your developers, that they have integrity and won't take your designs and run. After a few email exchanges with my first developer, I knew that I could trust him. He was open and answered all my questions with as much information as he could. My gut told me I could trust him, and sure enough, he proved it. This is an email he sent me after the app he helped me create, *Gratitude Journal*, went live:

A couple of weeks after Gratitude was out, we got a bid invitation on Elance for a new project. This was a project listing posted just to us.

They wanted to make an application titled "Ingratitude," basically to record the things that didn't go well that day. It is exactly the same as Gratitude but for recording the opposite events. All we had to do was change the application name, icon and graphics. No code change and quickly make the money.

Of course we decided not to work on this application in principle, I mean after working on Gratitude how can we do an app like that? We believe in the power of positive thinking.

Sarat

Signing the contract

We invest in insurance for our cars, our houses, and our health and hope that we never have to use it. Likewise, a legally enforceable contract is your insurance to protect your project. A contract clearly spells out every detail about the deliverables, milestones, costs, responsibilities, and most importantly, ways to exit the project and cancel the agreement. If the developer refuses to sign one, go with your second choice developer and don't worry about passing on what might seem like a good deal.

Your developer might send you a contract to sign, but you can still draw one up yourself or request to amend the copy she gives you. Sample contracts are free to download from sites such as Elance. They are also called Statements of Work and Engagement Letters. Take the time to read them line by line and customize the terms and conditions based on your project needs. Be sure to include the following items:

- Both party contact details

- Project details, services to be rendered, and deliverables

- Payment terms and schedules

- Change control policies

- Property rights and who owns the source code

- Termination of agreement

- The agreement start and end dates

- Confidentiality

- Signatures and dates

Working with Developers

Unlike the Twinkies you stockpiled in the pantry, the enthusiasm developers have for a new project has limited shelf life. When it fades, the motivation is gone, and the project slowly goes as sour as two-week-old milk. But when developers are high on inspiration, their productivity goes through the roof.

During my career, I've worked on both sides of the table—as a contractor being managed and as a client managing the contractor. The biggest lesson I learned is that you need to do everything you can to keep the developers happy and to make their life easier. That's the only way to bottle the new project motivation.

The secrets to keeping your developers happy

Here are my seven secrets to a prosperous and happy relationship with developers.

1. Listen to them.

Developers are creators, not machines, so respect and consider their ideas even if you have no clue on earth what they're talking about when they're tossing out confusing technical terms. Don't know the difference between this and that *subclass*? Ask. It's an opportunity to learn.

2. Don't keep changing your mind.

Throughout your project people will constantly be giving you feedback, and you'll see features in other apps that spark ideas. It's really easy to throw these ideas back at your developers. Don't do this to them.

If you are going to change the scope of your app project, take something out so you can get your app on iTunes quicker. Then you can add in new features later with the profits you made. Commit to a code freeze so your app can get out the door.

3. Be specific.

Your meticulously laid-out design spec sets the stage for the level of detail that you will continue to provide to your developers throughout the project. Developers work in a world of absolutes and don't like to guess. If you provide vague or sloppy input, expect sloppy output.

4. Have realistic deadlines.

The truth is deadlines don't work. Things inevitably break, and even freakishly genius developers don't know how long it will take to fix the problem. If there is a feature that is holding up the release of your app, pull it and move on. You can add it in later after your app is on iTunes.

5. Check in but don't micro-manage.

Be available enough so you can prevent the project from going down the wrong path, but don't be a helicopter client hovering over them. Give them space to think creatively and to get in their zone so they focus on what they're doing. Every email, instant message, and meeting interrupts their flow, and getting back into the groove can take hours. Be available, but give them alone time so they can get stuff done.

6. Make decisions quickly.

Putting off decisions until you find a perfect answer is toxic. If every choice you make means you have to hold a meeting or check with a stakeholder, your decisions are going to pile up into a massive roadblock. Developers will be infuriated. Your choice will likely be as good today as it will be tomorrow, so just make a decision and move forward.

7. Don't use any four-letter words.

Go ahead and swear if you must, but some four-letter words offend developers, such as *just*, *easy*, *fast*, *need*, *must*, and *only*. These words indicate that you don't value the developers' time and skill, and are red flags that communication is suffering and the project is going to run over.

Be nice and be boring

Despite the rumors, nice people don't finish last, and boring doesn't mean stupid or uninteresting. It means narrow and focused. You pay attention to detail; you are predictable and steady. That's the type of client all developers love. They didn't take your project in hopes to find a new best friend, so don't try to be the charismatic salesperson trying to win them over. Just be boring and nice.

Money as a motivator

Some might call it bribery and others prefer to call it rewarding good behavior. Either way, it works. To really keep your developer motivated, offer a bonus at the end of each milestone, enough to celebrate the small win. Also, offer them a bonus for completing the project on time and even more if they complete ahead of schedule.

Also, don't be shy about surprising them with little presents along the way as well. You don't need to give much. A fun pair of socks or some movie tickets goes a long way. These gifts can make the difference between pushing your project to the front of the line, shortening development time, and getting on iTunes faster or holding it back in favor of other, more enticing projects.

TIP Search Pinterest for small gift ideas and see all the clever ideas you get.

It's more than a short courtship

You might think that your relationship with your developer ends when your app ships, but it doesn't. You'll be dreaming up new features, wanting to fix bugs, and trying to keep up with Apple's iOS updates. All these things require technical expertise.

It's a whole lot easier to go back to the person who created your app than to find someone new. If your relationship with your developer is solid, updating your app will be much easier, affordable, and quicker because you won't have to go through the lengthy talent hunt again.

Also, passing your code from shop to shop isn't good. A different developer may not understand how the app was written. It will take time (and your money) for him to get up to speed on its structure and code. In the end, the new developer might be better off writing the app over completely from scratch.

Kicking Off Development

Whenever we hire a professional to do a job, it tends to be the unsaid specifics that lead to quarrels, headaches, and high blood pressure. And because we want things faster, better, and simpler, important details can easily fall between the cracks. To save your project's bacon, you need to set expectations upfront with a plan tighter than a pair of skinny jeans. And to make sure everyone is on the same page, you need the right tools in place *now* because communicating and sharing files should be as easy as possible. (Chapter 1 lists some of the best tools for this task, such as Google Drive and Basecamp.)

This section explains how to create a specification that clearly outlines your plan. Your spec document paints the big picture of your app and how you'll get there. You'll also learn what to expect on your journey with your developers, so you can kick off your project with all the excitement and glory of the World Cup.

Creating a spec that says it all

Nearly as important as hiring the best developer is providing her with clear, thorough guidance, by drafting a *design specification* (*spec*); a blueprint of how you want your app to look and work. The spec includes what the finished app will do, how users will interact with it, and why they would use it.

A meticulously detailed spec makes development like walking on water; both are easy if they're frozen. That's because the developer working from a good spec has all the information he needs about the app and can simply start building it. Also, a detailed spec gives your developer confidence that you know your stuff. It shows that you put your design to the test, thought everything through, and won't be changing your mind halfway into the project. Developers like to go for the short wins and try to avoid a project that can change and drag on because that only burns everyone out.

Failing to write a spec is the largest unnecessary risk you could take, even if you're developing the app yourself.   **IMPORTANT**

Ideally, you want your spec completed *before* you start interviewing developers. The fine details help candidates establish a more accurate bid for your project, making it easier for you to select the best developer for your app. To have your spec ready in your hiring process, you should begin composing it while you're finalizing the designs of your app.

Although you want as much detail as possible in your app, the goal is to keep it simple, but not too simple. As a rule, images speak louder than words, so try to display your ideas graphically as much as possible. Also, images translate into any language, so they are far more effective if your developer doesn't share the same first language. Developers can *see* the idea, not *read* it. If your spec is *truly* good, you won't even need to pick up the phone or Skype with the developer. He'll just get it.

Pump your spec full of all that hard work you already did on your design. I usually use Google Docs for my specs, but you might feel more comfortable sharing a PDF file that can't be edited.

Your spec should include:

- Your product mission statement.
- A description of your target audience (tribe) and profiles of your tribe proxies.
- The story about someone using your app.
- A list of the app's main features and sub features.
- The screen flow diagram.
- An image of each screen in your app as it would look in final production.
- For each screen image, include a list of all the functionality of that screen, broken down by section (navigation bar, body, tab, or taskbar).
- For each screen image, include a list of all the screens that it connects to and how they transition.

- All variations of the same screen. For example, if a dialog box displays under some conditions, include a screen shot.

- A link or copy of the wireframe.

- Information about you or your company.

- A table listing when the spec was last modified.

- Milestones and important dates.

- Assumptions.

On the other hand, here are a couple of items to avoid:

- Long paragraphs explaining functionality. If the concept can't be explained quickly and graphically, it might be too complex.

- Slang or local lingo such as "end of the day" or "bottom line." If English isn't your developer's first language, this lingo will just add to the confusion.

Remember to include the kitchen sink

Having worked with developers all over the globe, I discovered there's one trait that most of them share: they follow directions down to the last detail. They do not add in their own logic or reasoning to interpret your intentions, but take your mockups and design specs at face value. If you are aware of this and make the effort to imagine how a developer will view your specs, it truly can work to your advantage, and your project will get done faster. If you aren't aware of this, you might be in for a few surprises. Figure 4-2 shows 3 of the 15 views I created for just one screen.

FIGURE 4-2: I created more than 15 different views of the same screen to include in my spec.

The design spec I created for my first app was awful. It included quick mockups of the screens that led to all sorts of confusion. For starters, the spec had an image of a journal entry screen with the text *"(entry goes here)"* in the center of it (see Figure 4-3). To me, this image made perfect sense; I was pointing out where the text would go when someone created a new entry. Sure enough, when I opened the first version of my app, the screen looked exactly as it did in the spec, complete with *"(entry goes here)"* hard-coded in the middle of the screen. Who's to blame? Me and only me.

Removing a few words from an app doesn't seem like much at first blush, but little changes add up quickly. For each detail excluded from the spec, expect more time to be added onto the overall project timeline. All of this creates a ripple effect, eventually resulting in a burned-out and frustrated team, or worse, the developer-who-suddenly-disappears syndrome.

FIGURE 4-3: It took me awhile to learn that details really matter. Mockups like this are just asking for the project to run over and the team to be burned out.

A six-year old can understand it

A wordy spec is as pleasurable to read as the instructions to your microwave and will be consumed in the same fashion—not at all. Chances are that the developers won't be reading in their native tongue either. Of course, spelling out each detail graphically is impossible, so anything you do write should be in very basic and simple English. Avoid any slang or idioms even if you're just punting your project around your local town.

If you can manage to build a wireframe of your app, you might almost eliminate words altogether. Ideally, the words in your spec will add to your document like extras in a movie. They aren't the main characters so barely get noticed, but without them the scene just isn't complete.

What your developer needs from you

After you've signed the contract and paid your deposit, make sure your developer has everything she needs to build your app. Here's a list of what you need to pass along to your developer for her to do her job most effectively.

- Access to the detailed design specification
- Access to wireframes
- An account in your project management tool (if you're using something like Basecamp)
- Copies of all the design elements in 1x and 2x sizes
- Copies of your icon in all sizes
- The name of your app as it appears on the device
- Any sound files included in your app
- Your account details for the developer's preferred source code control tools
- Access to bug-tracking tools

 NOTE Give your developer all your contact details and the best times to reach you. Note any holidays or other dates you plan to be unavailable, and make sure your developer shares the same details, especially the holidays. Some countries have quite a few national holidays; this can drastically affect your delivery time so be sure to ask upfront.

What you can expect from your developer

After your developer builds the initial framework of the app, she will send you a semi-working version of it. Request an update at least once a week so you can stay on top of progress. Bear in mind that the first builds probably won't get many "ooh's" and "aah's". In fact, they might not even look much like your app, but that's fine. And if you're new to building apps, you might find the files confusing. This section will help you understand exactly what to expect.

Your developer can send you your app in two ways: either as a full source code bundle or as an install file (see Figure 4-4). The first option is my preferred method because I can make small changes, such as swapping out image files. If she provides the source code, request that she use a version control tool such as GitHub and have her teach you how to use it.

The second method involves sending you an installable version of your app called an .IPA (iPhone Application) file. This file is all your code compressed into an application that will load on your device.

The process of installing your app on your device can be a little hairy, so make sure the developer holds your hand the first time. Apple has improved the process by leaps and bounds over the years, and there are plenty of helpful resources online, but having your developer walk you through it the first time is still the quickest way to learn. If it costs you a couple of extra hours of her time, it's worth every penny.

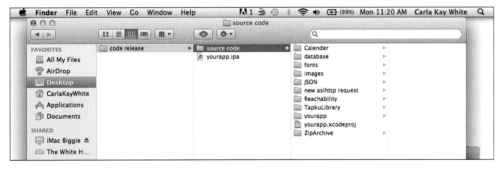

FIGURE 4-4: What the source code file will look like (top) and the installable file (bottom).

To get you started, the next section introduces you to Xcode and outlines some easy steps to install your app on your device. You'll also learn ways to test your app, track any bugs found, and get your tribe in on some of the action.

Issues, Bugs, and Tweaks: Testing Your App

Your developer has been staring at your app for hours and it needs a fresh set of eyes. It's up to you to test every one of your app's features and to make the final judgment call that your app is absolutely bug free. You cannot expect your developer to do this for you. It's *your* product, so you're ultimately responsible for its quality, not the developer.

To help you pinpoint exactly what to look for, the folks at TestPad (ontestpad.com) created a hefty list of every imaginable item to test before submitting your app to iTunes. The list is available at https://ontestpad.com/library/201/ios-app-store-submission-checklist. For convenience, select the items from the list that pertain to your app to create your own personal testing checklist, and then add any features in your app that aren't on the list. A checklist is the best way to be certain that you're successfully striking everything off it before your developer says "*Sayonara*!" and moves on to another project.

> We've developed a QA checklist that tests over 50 items including content accuracy, memory management, crash, connectivity, versioning, device/iOS compatibility, analytics tracking, App Store search optimization, orientation management, and more. We use a web-based tool to track and manage all issues, so the entire process is transparent and open to participation across our team.

> **—Christopher Taylor, founder of Playtend (Counting Ants app)**

To get you comfortable with Xcode, I first walk through a simple example, using a simulator. Next, you learn how to set up your device with the require certificate and IDs you need for testing. Finally, you learn how to use TestFlight to distribute your app to others for testing, and how to record and track any bugs they find.

Have you downloaded the SDK and Xcode?

Here's where the things start to get a just a little more complex. To test your app, you need the latest copy of the software development kit (SDK) and Xcode installed on your computer, as described in Chapter 1. You should have installed these tools earlier so you can use them to review code from prospective developers. This introduction will get you started.

The absolute beginner's guide to Xcode

Getting the hang of Xcode is pretty much like using any new software; it might be overwhelming at first, but after you find your way around the menus, it isn't nearly so intimidating. Most newbie tutorials kick things off with teaching you how to create the simplest program possible, typically called "Hello World." There are plenty of examples on the Internet if you care to learn, but in this section you walk through the steps of running a completed version of "Hello World" on the iPhone simulator, using the following instructions.

As you learned in Chapter 1, a *simulator* is a program that runs your app much like it would run on a device except that it displays on your computer instead. Using a simulator is a great way to quickly test your app, but all final testing must be done on a device.

---

1. A "Hello World" example is available for download from my website at ideatoiphone.com. Download this file, save it to your desktop, and unzip it.

2. Click the Xcode icon (Figure 4-5) to launch the Welcome screen.

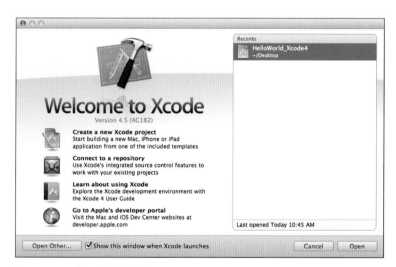

FIGURE 4-5: The Xcode Welcome screen.

3. From the Welcome screen, select File⇨Open. Navigate to the HelloWorld_Xcode4 folder you downloaded in Step 1, as shown in Figure 4-6, and click the file `HelloWorld_Xcode4.xcodeproj`.

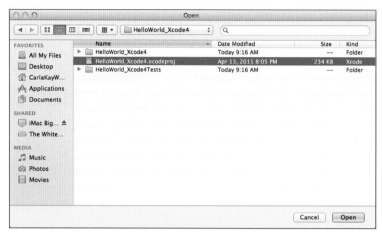

FIGURE 4-6: Open the file with extension `.xcodeproj`.

4. Selecting the file opens the Xcode interface (see Figure 4-7). To the left side of the screen are all the files that make up the code. In the middle and right panes, developers can edit files.

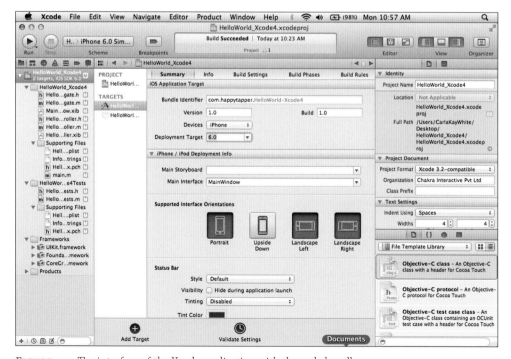

FIGURE 4-7: The interface of the Xcode application with the code bundle.

5. Before you run the code, it is good practice to clean the cache first. To do this, select
Product⇨Clean (see Figure 4-8).

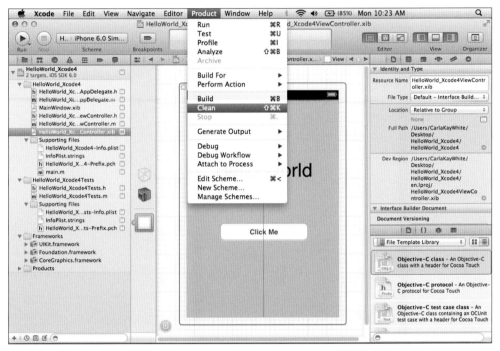

FIGURE 4-8: Clean the cache before running any code bundle.

6. Click the Scheme button at the top of the screen and select the iPhone 6.0 Simulator
from the menu that displays, as shown in Figure 4-9. Click Run (the button with the
triangle at the left end of the toolbar). This compiles the code and opens the simulator
on your computer to the Hello World app, as shown in Figure 4-10.

FIGURE 4-9: Select the iPhone 6.0 Simulator and click Run to start the code in the simulator.

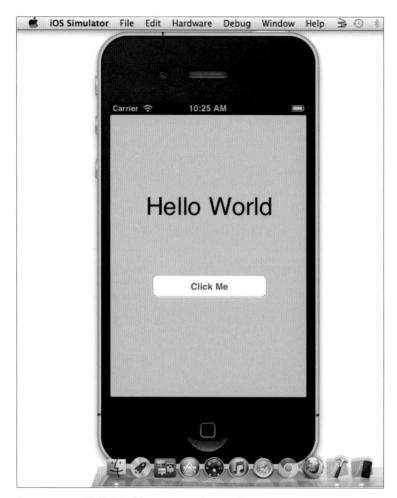

FIGURE 4-10: Hello World running in the simulator.

The Hello World app only has two screens that display when the button is clicked. If you go back to Xcode and look at the files in the source code, you will notice two files with the extension .xib. They are the screen layout files. Each .xib file has accompanying .h and .m files with the code. These are the *very* basics of what makes up an iOS app (see Figure 4-11).

Now that you know how to navigate around a bit in Xcode and how to use it with the simulator, I'll show you how to use it with your device. Before you can install testing software on your device, you need to set everything up first.

.xib files

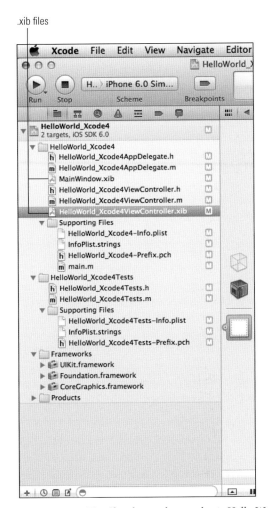

FIGURE 4-11: The files that make up a basic Hello World app.

Setting up your device for testing

The simulator is incredibly useful for quickly running an app, but don't rely on it for your testing. That's because apps might run like a charm on the simulator but crash on the device. Simply put, the simulator on your computer is a completely different machine than your device, so all code from your developer must be installed and tested on an iPhone and/or iPad, not the simulator. That's actually pretty simple to do. Here's the quick and easy way to get started.

Before installing anything from your developer, confirm that your developer tested the code on a device (not just on a simulator) and fixed any bugs she found *before* she sent it to you. This might sound fairly obvious, but some developers get lazy and only run the app in the simulator. You may have to ask her with every build she sends you, making you sound like a broken record, but hopefully after the first few builds she should get the message.

IMPORTANT   You must use the latest released version of Xcode and it will only work with a device that is compatible; for example, Xcode 4.5 requires iOS 5 and above, so any devices used for development and testing must have the latest iOS version installed. To meet this condition, you may have to upgrade your device before proceeding. The updates download to your device automatically but you have to install them yourself. To see if your device needs a software upgrade, open the Settings app on the device, select General, and then select Software Update.

There are two files that you must create and install before you can run an app on a device for development and testing. The first is a *provisioning profile* installed on the device, and the second is a *development certificate* installed on your Mac. These next steps guide you through a process that automatically creates these files for you.

1. Log in to the iPhone Provisioning Portal (always use the Safari browser). Log in to your Apple Developer account by going to http://developer.apple.com and clicking the link for the Member Center. Sign in using your Apple ID and password to access the Developer Program Resources (see Figure 4-12). From there, click the link to go to the iOS Provisioning Portal.

2. Install the WWDR Intermediate Certificate. From the iOS Provisioning Portal, click the Certificate tab in the left panel to display a link to download the WWDR Intermediate Certificate (see Figure 4-13). Click the link to download the certificate. After it is downloaded, double-click the file, and it is automatically added into the Keychain Access program on your Mac.

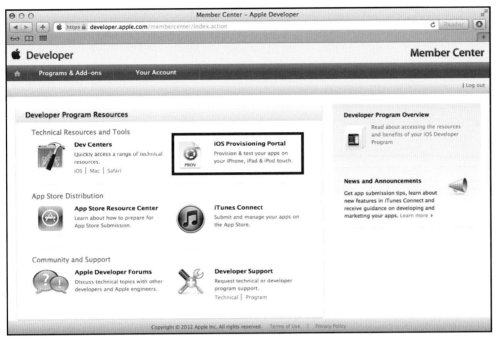

FIGURE 4-12: From the Developer Program Resources window, click to go to the iOS Provisioning Portal website, where you will manage all your certificates and IDs.

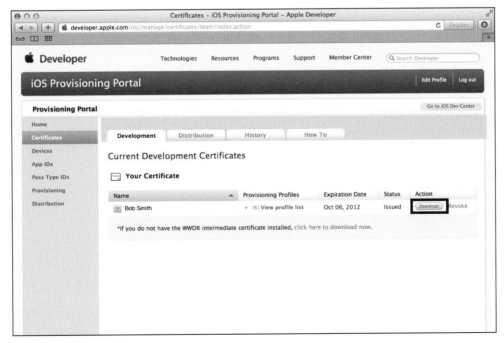

FIGURE 4-13: Download the WWDR Intermediate Certificate from the iOS Provisioning Portal.

3. Connect your device to the Mac and enable it for development. Next, connect the iPhone, iPod Touch, or iPad to your Mac. In Xcode, open the Organizer window by selecting Window⇨Organizer or by clicking the Organizer button on the far right of the toolbar (see Figure 4-14).

FIGURE 4-14: To open the Organizer window, select Window⇨Organizer.

On the Organizer screen, shown in Figure 4-15, your device should be listed in the left side of the screen. (You might have to click Enable for Development first.) Make sure your device is selected, and then click the Add to Portal button found at the bottom of the window. In the window that opens, you can enter your Apple Developer account email and password. This window also offers to request a certificate for you. Enter the requested information and select this option.

The icon beside the device will soon turn green. That means you can you can now select it from the device menu in Xcode and install apps on it by clicking Run. To do this, close the Organizer window to return to the Xcode interface. Follow the same steps as you did earlier to run the Hello World app in the simulator, but select your device from Scheme (Figure 4-9), instead of the simulator.

The automation of these steps is a serious improvement over earlier versions of Xcode, and I applaud Apple for simplifying the process and sparing us hours (maybe days) of headache and confusion. Here's a list of all Add to Portal accomplished behind the scenes:

- It creates a developer certificate for you. This includes a certificate that is added to your Mac keychain.

- It uploads a request to sign the certificate to the Apple iOS Provisioning Portal. Apple must sign your certificate before it will run on the device.

- It adds your device's Unique Device ID (UDID) to the iOS Provisioning Portal.

- It creates a Wildcard App ID in the iOS Provisioning Portal.

- It creates a provisioning profile in the iOS Provisioning Portal. This is the permission to run apps (with the matching App ID) signed with your key on only the devices with the specified UDIDs.

- It downloads the provisioning profile from the iOS Provisioning Portal and installs it to Xcode and on your device. You can check the profile on your device by tapping on the Settings icon. Scroll to Profiles and you will see the iOS Team Provisioning Profile installed.

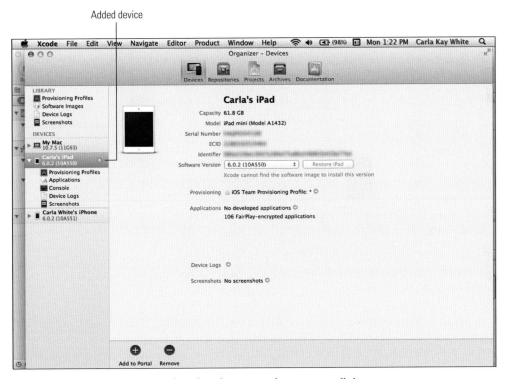

FIGURE 4-15: Your device is now listed, and you can select it to install the app.

Taking a look at Apple's iOS Provisioning Portal

Are you scratching your head, trying to understand what exactly you accomplished with all those steps? You can see what happened by going back to your Safari browser and have a look at the iOS Provisioning Portal site. This site is where you manage your certificate, App ID, devices, and profiles. You should now have a development certificate, your device should be registered, and both an App ID and a development profile should be created. Each link has a How-To's tab with step-by-step instructions to walk you through if you get stuck (see Figure 4-16).

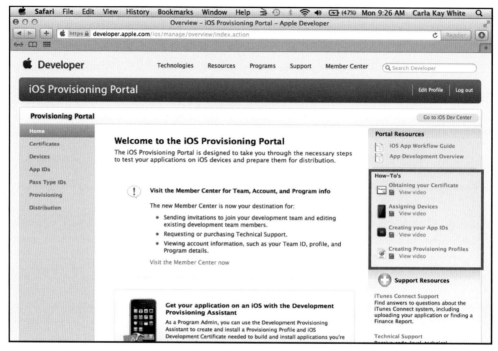

FIGURE 4-16: The iOS Provisioning Portal site.

If your app *doesn't* require Game Center, Push Notifications, or in-app purchases, you're all set to start development and can skip the next section. Otherwise, you have a few more tasks to take care of.

NOTE   Later you'll be using the iOS Provisioning Portal as part of the app submission process. To learn more read the section "Set up certificates, App IDs, and profiles" in Chapter 5.

Adding in Game Center, Push Notifications, or In-App Purchases

There are two types of App IDs that can be associated with a provisioning profile: *Wildcard App ID* and *Explicit App ID*. The ID created in the preceding steps is a Wildcard App ID and will work just fine for most situations. It allows you to enable iCloud, Passes, and Data Protection in your app. But if you plan to enable Game Center, Push Notifications, or in-app purchases in your app, you need to create a different type of App ID—the *Explicit App ID*.

To do so, you need to create a new App ID and provision profile. The easiest way to learn how to do this is to select App IDs from the left panel and open the How To tab link to see directions explaining the process. If you get stumped, ask Dr. Google. Dozens of blogs have done an amazing job explaining the process. And if you're not sure whether you need a Wildcard App ID or an Explicit App ID, ask your developer.

Find bugs and create buzz by enlisting your tribe

Testing your app is a lot like trying to get an eight-foot sofa out of your living room; at some point you'll have to ask for some help. No matter how many times you meticulously go through your app with a fine-tooth comb, you will always still miss bugs. That's because there are so many different devices and setups, it's almost impossible to account for all the various scenarios.

Feed two birds with one scone by inviting some of your fans to be your beta testers. Your invitation announcement stirs up excitement for your approaching app launch and the few lucky testers chosen to be members of your exclusive preview club will help you unearth some hidden bugs, saving you the disgrace of paying customers discovering them and posting about them on their iTunes review.

You really only need about five serious and good testers. Screen each applicant to filter the time-wasting tire kickers from people who will actually test the app and give you quality feedback. Ask what kind of device they have and why they feel they'd be a good beta tester. Ideally, you want people who do QA testing for a living because they will know how to break your app, not just look at it and tell you what they like. Select applicants from around the globe if you plan to distribute to other countries, and try to get a variety of devices. If you don't know the testers well, make sure they sign an NDA first and that you can trust that they won't run off with your idea.

Distributing your app using Test Flight

Passing testing versions of your app on to other devices used to be as hard as sneezing with your eyes open, until TestFlight (testflightapp.com) came along. This free service makes app distribution and testing a piece of cake.

To get the most out of the service, have your developer download the TestFlight SDK and integrate it into your app source code. This tool will automatically create all sorts of helpful reports that graphically display who installed your app, how long they used it, whether it crashed, and all sorts of other amazing details.

After signing up for the service, you can use the TestFlight Dashboard on the site to create a team, invite team members, add the team members' devices, and then upload code to be magically distributed to everyone. Anytime a new build is uploaded, testers are automatically notified and they can install your app just by clicking a button.

The Essential Secret Weapon

If you really want to brave the waters, hand your app over to a child to test it. Children don't worry about offending you or sounding ridiculous if they don't understand something. They will find design flaws faster than any adult because they're digitally savvy and accustomed to how interfaces should work. It doesn't matter if your app is a tax calculator or slingshot for shooting pigs; if your app isn't intuitive to use, a kid won't hesitate to tell you openly and honestly.

Find a clever and outspoken child between 9 and 12 years old and ask him to play with your app. He'll call it like it is and give you a straight answer as to whether it's any good or not. He'll reveal design and technical bugs that adults might not tell you about. He'll let you know if it will be a global success.

You can even keep tracking details *after* your app is live and distributing through iTunes. You can discover the time of day people used your app, for how long, on what screen they stopped using it, and how often they reopened it. This is some seriously powerful information that you can use to improve your app.

Working with our developers, we test our apps incessantly. Every iteration of the app sees multiple, intense sessions. Now, with the need to test on multiple devices, in a multitude of environments, we've created a core collective of friends and customers who help us with this process. Also, since we design for children, it's very important for us that we get our apps into the hands of children before we go live. While we can try to anticipate what the children might respond positively to, we never know until they take it for a test drive!

—Bobby George, Co-founder of Montessorium (Intro to Letters app)

Keeping track of bugs

Testing a new build may take only a few minutes, but creating the bug report to pass back to the developer can take hours. That's because the more details you can provide, the quicker your developer can fix it. I number each bug found, write down the exact steps taken, the results, and what I expected the app to do. I also include plenty of screen shots. I categorize each bug by screen name and record everything in a spreadsheet that we both have access to.

This level of communication might seem a little condescending to the developer, but trust me; it reduces confusion, keeps the project ticking along, and creates a fantastic working relationship. Programming is as much an art as a science, and everything is related. You might think you know the source of a bug, but in fact it may be a symptom of something seemingly unrelated that only the developer can correctly diagnose.

Keeping track of all the bugs you find can get pretty hairy, especially with a team of testers. You need a process for recording everything to ensure that all the details get passed along to your developer. There are plenty of free tools to use, or your developer might have one that he prefers. I like to use a Google spreadsheet and give my testers and developers access to it so we can all collaboratively edit it (see Figure 4-17). Everyone can see all the issues logged, whether they've been worked out or are still outstanding, and other details.

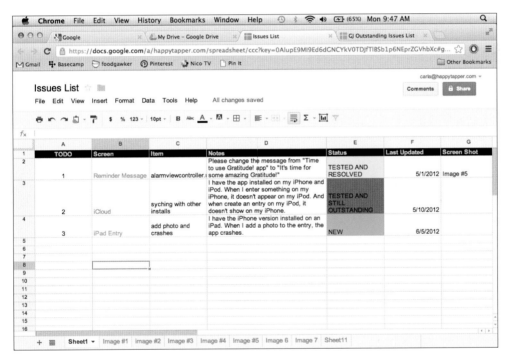

FIGURE 4-17: Google spreadsheet bug report.
Source: Google, Inc.

When you give your testing team access to this spreadsheet, also provide them with instructions on how to use it. It helps to include the instructions on a page in the spreadsheet as well so people can easily refer back to them. Here are the instructions I include with my builds:

1. You found a bug.

2. Search the spreadsheet to see if it's already been reported. If you find it already listed, add your name to the "Found by" column and you're done. If the bug isn't listed, go to step 3.

3. Provide the following information about the bug: your name, app screen where you found the bug, description, steps taken to reproduce the bug, app version, date, and screen shots if any. Please email screen shots to abc@abc.com.

4. My team will then check the spreadsheet and fix the bugs.

5. When a bug is fixed, we will change the Status column to "Fixed." If we cannot reproduce the bug, we will change the Status as "Cannot Reproduce."

6. When a new version is released, I will list the bug as fixed.

7. If you confirm the bug is fixed, move that bug to another tab of the spreadsheet labeled "Closed."

8. If the bug is not fixed, remove the "Fixed" status and make a note that it's been tested and still is not working.

Breaking the news to your developers

Developers despise bugs as much as you do, so when you find one, go easy on them. They take pride in their work, and hearing the bad stuff is like finding out their favorite team lost the playoffs. It hurts, so break it to them gently.

Start by complimenting them. Point out all the things you like about the build. If they fixed a bug, give them a high five. If they finished new development, thank them for that, too. Developers need to hear that they're doing a good job before you dish out the bad news about the bugs.

When you get to the part about the bugs, provide every detail you can imagine. Doing so will not only soften the blow, but also will make it far easier for them to fix if you relay every ounce of information about how you came across the issue, step by step. If it was raining and your Internet was spotty, let them know. If you have a different device, that information is important, too. You can't give your developers too much information.

Finish by praising them for all their efforts and let them know you enjoy working with them. Going to these lengths may sound a bit much, but who doesn't want to hear this? Doing so not only is respectful, but also builds a relationship that can last through the storm of bug fixes and scope changes.

Tweaking design after development: Don't do it

You'll have no shortage of new ideas for your app while it's being developed. But the truth is, after your designs are coded, changing anything can be extremely tedious and time consuming, so resist the urge to add in new features or change the layout. Your testers won't be shy about giving you ideas because, let's face it, you asked them for feedback. Every hot new app will inspire a new approach and style. Your developer friends might come across some cool whiz-bang-thingamajig and want a creator to dabble in it. As tempting as all this can be, don't do it.

Changing layouts and adding in new features or additional screens mean rewriting code, and that translates into more money, longer development time, and lost revenues. Save the new ideas for the next version release.

When It's All Gone Wrong

No matter how much work you put into hiring the right developer, the project can still always go wrong, for all sorts of reasons. Your developer may quit, and the shop secretly replaces her with a novice without your knowledge. Or a better offer may come along, and she would be a fool to pass it up. Or she may simply disappear. Prepare yourself for a Houdini act by requesting weekly updates of all your source code, so if the worst happens, you can move on without starting from scratch.

What to do if your developer disappears

If your developer is suddenly nowhere to be found, before slandering them on Twitter, your blog and Facebook, get your ducks in a row first. Stop any future payments right away. You might not be able to recoup any previous payments without hiring a lawyer, but you certainly can remove any future payments from escrow.

If you used a freelance site like Elance, you can file a dispute. The sites will want you and your freelancer to try and work out a solution first. If you can't come to an agreement, the site will step in (for a fee) with an arbitrator.

Freelance sites also give you a chance to leave feedback on your developer at each milestone. Do this as soon as you can. The window to leave feedback closes after a week or two so don't sit on your comments. If things aren't going well, try to work out the problem before leaving bad comments about your developer on the site. But if he still isn't responsive, by all means let other prospective clients know how poorly your project with him went.

Knowing when to fire your developer

You're the only one who gets burned if you choose to keep working with a bad developer, so as soon as you smell rotten work, take action. Don't wait for it to get worse. Give him three strikes and then he's out.

Builds that are so poor you can't even open them let alone test them, the app looks nothing like the design, or maybe no progress is being made at all—these are sure signs of sloppy work. Or maybe the bugs seem to be multiplying with each build. If your developer is delivering mud pies, stop everything and call a crisis meeting.

Strike 1—At the first sign of poor workmanship, call for a crisis meeting. Come to an agreement on a list of actions that can be accomplished in one week's time. This is a testing period and a chance for your developer to redeem himself.

Strike 2—If a week goes by and you don't see any improvement, give the developer a warning that you are planning to move on. Offer him one last chance to prove himself before you call it quits. Again, ask for a specific outcome that is reasonable with a few days' work.

Strike 3—Still no improvement? If your app is outsourced to a development shop, ask if there is a more qualified developer who can be put on your project. Sometimes shops swap around developers, so the one you initially thought was working on your project got replaced. As before, insist on seeing specific progress within a week. Note, however, that if you get to this point, it might be easier to cut your losses and move on. The replacement will need a few weeks to get up to speed on the code and may wind up being just as sloppy as the first guy. In the end, can you honestly trust a shop that does a bait-and-switch? It's your call.

Knowing When to Go Live

Development can go on longer than an Oscar acceptance speech if you let it, so at some point you'll have to decide that your app is good enough to submit to the App Store. If you're a small shop like me, waiting too long could be fatal. Instead, release early and incorporate feedback after you go live. Eighty percent complete was good enough for me.

The one thing you can't rush is the quality of your app. Fix every single bug. You may not find all the bugs, but fix the ones you do discover. If you don't, you will read about them later in your customer reviews and that will hurt. Aim to ship a bug-free product, not the best version you will ever have. Your app is probably ready before you think it is.

Marketing Ideas Checklist

Before making the big leap into product launch, be sure your app hits the ground running by keeping up with your marketing efforts. Here are a few suggestions on ways you keep your marketing ball rolling.

PROMOTE

- **Follow all relevant stories and share them.** Set up Google Reader to follow any stories that are relevant to your app project. Share the best stories with your tribe through your social media sites such as Twitter, Facebook, and Pinterest.

- **Write positive reviews about other apps you like.** Using your blog or Facebook page, mention apps you think are really well done. Send the link to the people who created the app and let them know you appreciate their good work and you hope the app you're about to release reflects the same high quality.

- **Create a new video of your app and share it.** At some point during development, create a new video of your app with shots of your screen. It doesn't have to be fully functional; you want to give only a glimpse of what's to come. Share this on your social media sites, your blog, email distribution list, and with other app developers you've gotten to know.

- **Update your email signature.** Be sure your email signature includes information about your app, the website, and other links. Update all your online profiles with the details, too. Make sure anyone who stumbles across your name can easily find out what you're up to.

- **Keep an eye out for competitors.** You don't want to be caught in the shadows of a similar app, so keep researching for apps like yours and see when they plan to go live. Likewise, you don't want releases from major players such as Sony and Apple to outshine yours, either.

Key Points

- Build up your network of iOS experts by hanging out at the places iPhone developers go, both online and offline. The developer community is packed with wonderful people all over the globe. Get to know a few so you can turn to them for technical advice.

- Download and start using the SDK and Xcode. These are the tools your developer will be using, and you will need to be familiar with them to test your app.

- A detailed spec with plenty of images to describe your app will make development go faster and save you money in development costs. Taking two minutes to add important information to a document could end up saving you thousands of dollars.

- Don't rush hiring your developer. Take the time to review all his apps; contact and interview his references. Cheap developers can end up costing you more in the long run. It's up to you to do plenty of due diligence to make sure the freelancer is qualified before hiring him to build your app.

- A happy developer is a productive one. While your freelancer is cutting code, do whatever you can to make his job easier so your project stays on schedule and you can continue to work together after your app launches.

- You're ultimately responsible for the quality of your app, not the developer. So it is up to you to test each feature and make sure the app is completely bug free. Recruit friends and fans to help. They'll feel invested in your app's success and find issues you'll miss, saving you from hearing about them on iTunes reviews later.

CHAPTER 5

Raising the Curtains and Going Live

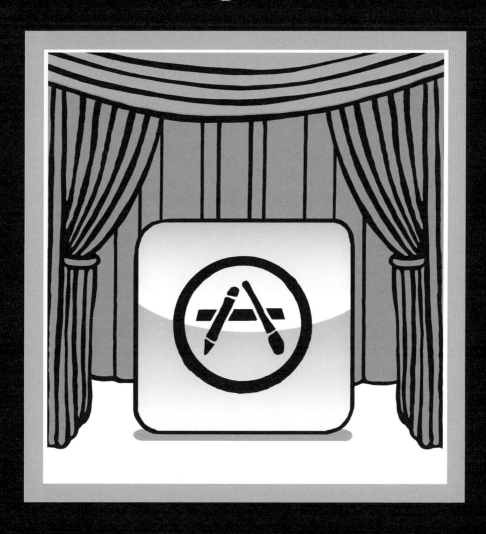

"Don't compare yourself with anyone in this world…if you do so, you are insulting yourself."

—Bill Gates

Your app is gorgeous. Your friends all love it. Your mom said she'd buy ten copies (bless her, if she only knew). Then come launch day, all you hear are crickets. Houston, we have a problem. That's because most developers follow the same cookie-cutter launch as the thousand developers before them, and it's predictable and dull. Or worse, they simply put their app out there and say, "Here you go." The competition on the app market is fierce and growing everyday, so you need a thunderous launch that gets heard. To do this you have to step up your game and step out of your comfort zone.

This chapter maps out a precise plan for everything you need to do in the weeks leading up to your launch. It unravels all the technical hurdles of submitting your app and reveals the secrets behind a launch that catches the media's (and Apple's) attention and gets your app off to a great start climbing the charts. You can't slow down now and put your feet up in the last stretch. Doing that could ruin everything. In fact, the real fun is just about to start.

The Ultimate App Submission Cheat Sheet

"Submitting your app" and "going live" may sound like the same thing, but they're as different as giraffes and goldfish. First you need to *submit* your app to Apple for its blessing and permission to add it to the iTunes Store. When you do that, you can also instruct Apple as to the exact date to release it; this is when you *go live* and everyone gets to download and enjoy your app. Both events require careful planning on your part.

Preparing your app before sending it to Apple involves a number of steps. No matter how often you do it, you may always wonder whether you remembered everything. The tutorials and checklists in this chapter should relieve you of that anxiety.

Careful planning also puts you in the driver's seat for when your app goes live. This is absolutely essential to gaining the maximum pomp and pageantry for your app release because you want to slowly let the launch unfold weeks in advance. Rather than thinking of it as one big take off, view it as a series of small conversations with key people leading up to the main event. The worst thing you can do is go live without letting anyone know.

 The biggest thing we overlooked was marketing. We spent all our energy in building the product, and when we launched we just then started to look into getting the word out. Make sure you start early with your marketing plan and try to build hype.

—Shelby Meinzer, founder of MindTapp (Photonest iPhone app)

Selecting a Powerful Launch Date

It might seem odd to delay the release of your app after working so hard to get it built, but you'll have far better results if you set a date and build up to your launch rather than going live as soon as your app is approved. Studies have shown that Sunday is the best day to go live due to the high volume of weekend downloads. However, I prefer to launch on a Wednesday, and I'll tell you why.

The App Store's prime real estate locations—Featured, New and Noteworthy, and Editorial Picks—are updated every Thursday at 4 p.m. Pacific time, just before the weekend rush. A well-staged launch on a Wednesday might create enough noise to get Apple to notice and select your app for a weeklong spotlight on iTunes' center stage.

You can also plan your launch to coincide with a holiday. Newspapers and blogs are always looking for an interesting angle on annual events such as the Super Bowl, Mother's Day, or even Groundhog's Day. If your app can fit that bill, plan to launch at that time and give them a story.

Christmas is incredibly powerful because the holidays are the slowest time of the year for news, especially between Christmas and New Year's Day. To a journalist, this slow time is dreadful, but to you, it's a golden opportunity. Build an app themed around Christmas, and the odds of the press picking up your story are a hundred times greater. Also, Christmas downloads are higher than those at any other time of year because of all the new devices that just got unwrapped.

At Least One Month Before Submitting Your App

After you select your launch date, go back 30 days and put a big circle around that date. That's the day you must complete your app and send it off to Apple for approval.

Plan to submit your app at least one month before you want to release it on iTunes. If you're planning a Christmas launch, this means Apple should have everything by mid-November. Approving the app might take only a week, but if Apple doesn't approve it, you'll need the extra time to turn around any issues.

To hit your targeted submission date, you can start taking care of the major pre-launch activities while your developers are still coding your app. Some things can take well over a month to complete and can be showstoppers, so it's smart to start early. Nothing is more expensive than missed opportunity.

SUBMIT

Get set up on Apple's iTunes Connect

We're all well aware that Apple doesn't work on a handshake, so the first thing you want to tackle is taking care of all the legalities, taxes, and financial details. You do this through iTunes Connect (itunesconnect.apple.com), which is the bigger brother to the iOS Provisioning Portal. You also use this web portal to submit apps to Apple for review (see Figure 5-1), and to manage all your app details such as price, description, and screen shots. It also has all your sales reports and iAd revenues, plus your contracts, banking, and tax details.

FIGURE 5-1: iTunes Connect web portal, where you manage your app and business details.

Before submitting your app to Apple, you have to set up everything on iTunes Connect. The easiest place to start is completing all the legalities, tax, and bank forms. In fact, some of these documents may not be effective immediately, so don't leave this step to the last minute.

1. Make sure you have an active agreement (free and paid apps). You must have an active contract with Apple first. You were asked to sign one when you stepped through the registration process for the Developer Membership Program, but make sure it's

current. Log in to iTunes Connect and click the Contracts, Tax, and Banking link to see whether updated versions need to be approved (see Figure 5-2).

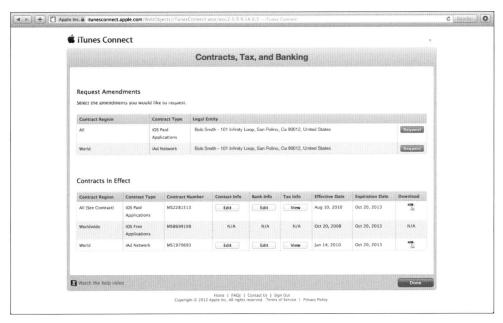

FIGURE 5-2: An active agreement with Apple allows you to upload free apps.

2. Accept a paid contract (skip if app is free). If you wish to sell your apps on the App Store for a price or have in-app purchases, you have to sign a Paid Application Contract first. If you don't already have one, a section titled Request Contracts will be displayed with the contract listed below. You also need to supply the following three pieces of information:

   a. **Contact Info**—Set up all your contact names. Apple wants to know the details for Senior Management, Financial, Technical, Legal, and Marketing contacts. All of these contacts could be just one or two people, but you need to specify each one.

   b. **Banking Info**—You also must supply bank information. All payments from Apple will be sent to the bank account you supply, and you can provide only a single bank account. You can't request payments to be split to multiple accounts. You can always go back and change bank account details later if you need to.

   c. **Tax Info**—You also must submit your tax details. Some tax forms must be downloaded and submitted, so allow time for this task. Tax info is cemented in place after Apple receives it and can't be changed on iTunes Connect.

Prepare for customer care

Imagine it's your big launch day, which means you're up by 5a.m., coffee in hand and ready to go. Everything goes smoothly; by noon hundreds of people have downloaded your app, and by the end of the day that number nearly triples. Then your buddy calls you and shares the bad news that he found a bug in your app. Sounds like a nightmare, I know. And unfortunately I lived it. The best advice I can give you is to have a customer support system in place before you go live.

A customer support system sends out a crucial message that you value your customers and *want* to hear from them. It's not just for damage control because customers will reach out to you with more than just suggestions and technical questions. They also want to tell you how much they love your app.

Select a support site

Because we all understand the importance of happy customers, customer service has come a long way in a short time and involves a lot more than answering support requests. Today there are a variety of online services all designed to let customers share ideas, praise, as well as questions. And customers can do this through any channel they like—your website, Twitter, Facebook, email, or chat. I use an excellent bulletin board–type service called Get Satisfaction (getsatisfaction.com). User Voice is a similar service (www.uservoice.com), and so is ZenDesk (www.zendesk.com).

These sites streamline support by trying to answer customers' questions as they are submitted into the site. If someone else has already posted a similar question, the site will attempt to find it and share it, so customers don't have to wait for your reply and you aren't repeating the same answer over and over. Most of the questions and comments that customers post tend to be some variation of the same few questions, so this feature is an incredible time saver for everyone. Also, the site helps build your community by providing a place for customers to have conversations and share questions and ideas, much like you see on forums. These sites also pull in outside information like customer profiles and the "buzz on Twitter" about the product.

You can set up the site so questions come directly into your feeder and email, so you can answer them as soon as they're posted. You don't want to miss a single one. Getting back to people quickly can turn an angry customer into one who's so impressed she's singing your praises on the social network scene.

Customers want to know they've been heard, and some can expect a lot out of a $0.99 app, but most are just dumping every idea they have because they want to help you to improve your product. Some excellent ideas are buried in there, and can be some of the best insight you can get. Later in this chapter we'll get into more customer care ideas.

Add a contact link in your app

Another way to let customers get in touch with you is to create a contact link in your app's settings screen that will send an email directly to you. I did this once hoping to improve customer service and my response times. My email inbox was flooded. Even if people didn't intend to send, they still accidentally tapped the button. Most emails repeated the same message, and I had to spell out the same answer again and again, so responding took nearly half my day.

The moral of the story is that it's a smart idea to offer support inside your app, but link to a website where customers can get their answer right away without having to wait for a response.

Using a series of screens explaining how to use the app is increasingly popular because these screens are extremely helpful to customers. Offer enough assistance inside your app so customers don't have to contact you with questions. But including a full user's manual suggests your app is far too complicated. | NOTE

Offer an FAQ page

If you don't want to answer requests, you can point people to a Frequently Asked Questions page on your website or in your app (see Figure 5-3). The downside is that you won't know what the most frequently asked questions are until after you go live and have given people an opportunity to get in touch and tell you. To be successful, FAQ pages have to actually give people the answers they're searching for; otherwise, they will find a way to hunt you down.

FIGURE 5-3: The Weightbot iPhone app created by Tapbot includes a support feature with answers to customers' most commonly asked questions. This saves customers the time of having to contact Tapbot for support as well Tapbot having to answer the same question over again.

Source: Weightbot iPhone app

Identify launch tricks you must start now

One secret to preventing a launch so quiet that you can hear a pin drop is to recruit some prominent people to help make some noise. This is where bloggers rule the universe. They'll improve your app's credibility, downloads, and visibility to heavy hitters like Apple employees.

Let's get one thing straight: The days of mass-mailing press releases are the thing of the past—although you'd be amazed at how many developers are still using this, shall we say, "traditional" method as their grand plan to get the media's attention. No matter how well-crafted your press release is, not one journalist will care. And why should they? It's a generic pitch and pretty much spam.

Instead of blasting out something monotone like most other app developers, get to know a few key bloggers and journalists and reach out to them. Take the time to learn what they care about, and share your app in a way that is meaningful so they pay attention. Post comments on their blogs and reply to their tweets. Then when you're ready to share the news about your app, craft a personal message. That's the way to stand out and get their attention.

In addition to finding key people to share your message, you also need to prepare all your promotional materials well in advance because you aren't just going to lift the curtains and go live. You're going to put on an incredible performance, using the tactics described in this section.

These tactics aren't exclusive to just introducing new apps. You also can use them to push existing apps ahead.   **NOTE**

Make the most of promotion codes

Rather than thinking of your launch as one quick blast-off, view it a story that *slowly* unfolds during the weeks leading up to the release date. Start taking baby steps and reaching out to bloggers and journalists who will impact your launch and show them some love. Once they know who you are, you can offer them an exclusive preview of your app by sending them a promo code.

Promo codes are coupons that let people download a particular app for free from iTunes. As soon as your app is approved, Apple gives you 50 codes to hand out (see Figure 5-4).

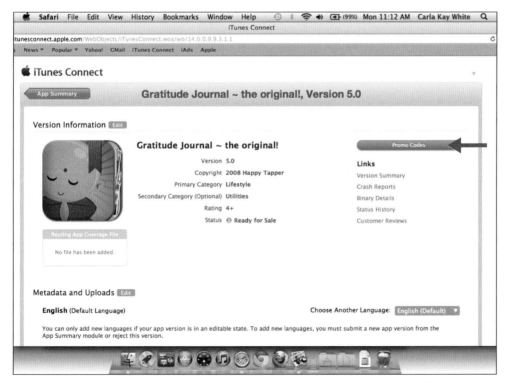

FIGURE 5-4: Apple provides 50 promo codes for your app that you can access through iTunes Connect.

Source: Apple iTunes Connect

Now, there's a secret to using promo codes that helps both paid and free apps boost exposure, but you have to start planning early. You can send these promo codes to the press and bloggers for review *before* your app hits iTunes. Your app won't appear in the iTunes Store, but people can still download it with a promo code, giving them an exclusive sneak preview before everyone else.

To make this strategy work, you have to first identify everyone you plan to invite to preview your app. Start with the most popular and influential bloggers your tribe reads. Follow all their posts for a few weeks to get to know their style. If a team of bloggers write for the site, select just one of them. Stalk all these bloggers as if you were their biggest fan, post considerate comments on their blogs and Facebook page, reply to their tweets, and slowly get to know them. You should also include your loudest fans with the biggest following on your exclusive list. Later in this chapter I discuss the art of composing a personal message these people will actually read, appreciate and most importantly, make them want to talk about your app.

> **NOTE** I created Twitter lists of journalists (twitter.com/carlawhite/press), Apple employees (twitter.com/carlawhite/apple-employees), and app developers (twitter.com/carlawhite/amazing-iphone-devs) to help me stay in touch with key people. Feel free to use them to get started.

Prepare your website for the red carpet

The "coming soon" site you created did a marvelous job of grabbing people's attention and gathering emails but soon will be retired, replaced with one for your launch. The new site will teach your audience about your app, give them a link to download it, and let them get in touch with you.

A quality website is an absolute necessity for every app creator. It's your app's "home" and the first place your customers, bloggers, and the media will look to learn more information about you and your app. So don't skimp. Your site should include images of your app, the app icon, a description, the price, and links to iTunes and support. Also include a way for people to contact you so the media can get in touch.

By this point, you probably are well aware that anything that involves a developer takes time and planning, and the last thing you want to do is to confuse people with your "Coming Soon" site still up on launch day. So it's wise to start preparing your launch site at least a month before you want it live.

> **NOTE** Check out the section "Creating a Compelling Website" in Chapter 6 for more details about getting your website ready for the launch.

Recognize the beauty of a great newsletter

Along with your website, you also want to prepare a newsletter to share the incredible news about your freshly launched app with everyone on your distribution list. Remember, these fans asked to be notified so have the newsletter ready to fire off on launch day.

It goes without saying that a newsletter that doesn't get read, let alone opened, is worthless. So aim to produce one that people actually look forward to reading and are happy to pass on to their friends and colleagues (see Figure 5-5). Your newsletter design should have one goal in mind: to get readers to download your app.

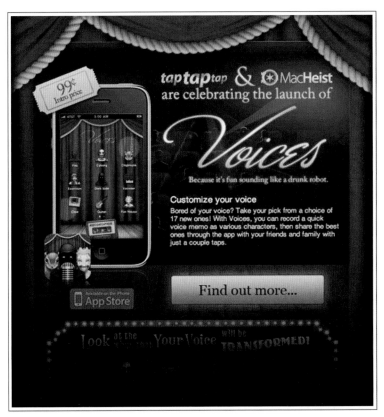

FIGURE 5-5: An announcement newsletter like this one for the Voices app is a must-read.

The newsletter is for your fans. The blogger celebrities will receive an individually crafted email with far more details. **NOTE**

If your distribution list is about as short as your grocery list, you can always beef it up with purchased emails. The people on these lists probably won't be the best prospects because they don't know you and never gave you permission to email them. But if 4 percent download your app, purchasing these lists might be a good gamble with a decent return on your investment.

NOTE   Check out the section "Tips for a Successful Email Campaign" in Chapter 6 for more details about creating an effective email campaign.

Build your press kit

Ask any successful developer, and they'll say that creating a good press kit is just as important as having a website or customer support system these days. That's because reporters have strict deadlines; they're working on way too many stories at once, spread across multiple projects, and slowly going nuts. Make it easy for the media to write about your app by creating a press kit they can download from your site. A well-put-together press kit gives them instant access to everything they need so they can download and use it immediately.

The first rule of creating a press kit is that modesty is overrated, so toot your own horn. Share your most triumphant work, greatest accomplishments, glowing reviews, and your own personal comments in a nice little kit that is as thoughtfully put together as your app.

First, create a folder on your computer with the name of your app, the words "press kit," and the release date (for example, AppName_PressKit_2013_12_20). Next, create three folders inside your press kit folder with the following names, and add the listed items in each one.

- **Artwork**—This folder includes your branding images. Create a high-resolution copy of your app icon and your logo in PNG format and add them to this folder.

- **Examples**—If your app allows users to create content such as a photo or a list, include at least six sample screen shots of the end result. Include before and after pictures if that helps.

- **Screen shots**—This folder includes screen shots of your app on targeted devices. Create a high-resolution screen shot of five screens and save them in PNG format using the Organizer window in Xcode. If your app is designed for both the iPhone and the iPad, create a folder for each with screen shots.

To really make reporters smile, create a document with your app description, link on iTunes, price, features list, and all your flattering achievements. When you're done, compress the press kit folder and put it on your web server with a link to download from your website.

The creators behind the Percolator app composed a remarkable press kit well worth checking out (percolatorapp.com/blog/press/).

Produce a viral video

As soon as you have a few functioning screens in your app, you're ready to produce a viral video. Keep it short: 15 to 30 seconds is enough. Try not to make it into an outright ad. You can mimic the style of Apple ads, go for the cute-as-kittens approach, parody something popular, or go for the shocking "Did that really just happen?" You don't need big equipment—just a clever idea.

You'll want to include some video of your app in action, which you can easily do with the Reflector app (reflectorapp.com). It lets you mirror your device's screen display on your computer, and then record it directly within the Reflector application. If you plan to do an over-the-shoulder shot, be sure to use a tripod and keep things in focus. If you can't afford to hire a professional to shoot the video, spend a couple of days learning about video making. Dig into the Internet and get some books from the library.

You'll also want to create a demo video showcasing your impressive design and interface, and telling a story of the app's hook, to pass along to the press and bloggers. Make sure the video highlights the core function through actually using the app, not screen shots. If your app's viral video is cleverly thought out, it could also work as the demo video for your bloggers.

For example, the team behind the Solar app created a noteworthy video (thisissolar.com) that can be both viral and great for showing bloggers their product. The app is pretty simple, but watching this video makes you wonder whether it will give you superpowers to control the weather.

At Least One Week Before Submitting Your App

When you're nearing the final couple weeks of development and the last bugs are being resolved, start preparing everything you'll need to send to Apple so it can approve and publish your app. This includes all the marketing materials that will be published along with your app on the iTunes Store such as screenshots and description. It's a good idea to hold off sending these details until your app is nearly ready just in case you have any last minute design changes to your app. Here is the full list of everything you need to prepare:

SUBMIT

Remember, the date you submit your app to Apple for approval should be at least one month before you want it to launch. That means you should be pursuing the following steps five to six weeks ahead of your intended launch date.   IMPORTANT

- The date when you want your app available on iTunes. (Set it to the latest date allowed and change it after your app is approved. If your app approval process takes longer than expected and the availability date is passed, your app will be released as soon as Apple approves it, meaning you miss your chance for a big launch.)

- A description of your app that iTunes will display to customers (I show you the art of a powerful yet short description in the next section).

- An app icon (1024 by 1024 pixels) ready for upload (PNG format).

- Five screen shots of your app ready for upload (you'll learn how to create screen shots that sell shortly).

This next section shares tips and suggestions on how to compose iTunes marketing materials that produce sales. First, you'll look at how people read the iTunes store because this influences how your marketing material should look.

> **NOTE**   You will use iTunes Connect to submit all the marketing materials for your new app. To do this, log in to iTunes Connect, select Manage Your Applications, and then Add New App. The next three screens walk you through preparing all the details to include about your app.

How people really scan the iTunes store

People read app product pages as quickly as they read a passing billboard on the highway. Our eyes instantly gravitate to the screen shots and then scan *some* of the text. Apple must have realized this when it redesigned the App Store app for the iPhone. The new layout moved the screen shots to the top with the product description below (see Figure 5-6). Only about 200 characters (five lines) of the description are shown (which is plenty for our fleeting eyes) unless customers tap More.

Apple also noticed that people pay more attention to the app reviews than the full app descriptions and moved the link to reviews right at the top. Based on Apple's new design, people see the icon, scroll through the screen shots, glance at the few lines of description, and then read reviews. If the majority of the first five reviews are positive, they'll go back to the description and scan it some more before deciding to download or move on.

Sifting through apps on your computer or iPad is a different experience only in the fact that there is more space for everything to reside on one screen. Our eyes still drift to the screen shots first and will skim over the descriptions. Most people breeze through the descriptions rather than read them line for line, so the key is making them easy to skim.

FIGURE 5-6: How people read the iTunes store on the iPhone and iPod touch. The screenshots (left) appear at the top; scroll down to see the description (right).

Source: Apple App Store iPhone app

The formula for an effective product description

The product description might be one of the most overlooked marketing opportunities available to developers. A well written product description can entice people to tap the Download button to get the full picture. More importantly, a good description is packed with just the right keywords so it's effective for search results, helping fuel discovery.

So why do so many app developers fail to use this marketing tool productively? Persuasive writing isn't easy, and many developers simply get app-store-writers'-block. To keep you from getting stuck, the following formula is designed to maximize searches and discoverability while also selling your app using the best words possible.

The perfect elevator pitch

To start, put yourself in the customers' shoes and pretend you don't know anything about your app. Then think really hard about the words that would make the app become irresistible to you. What adjectives truly describe the sterling qualities of your app? Pick two or three of its best benefits. Then work in a background or setting that will have an emotional meaning to your audience. Also, tie in the audience you're trying to appeal to. Keep your description to just two or three sentences and stop before you get into too much depth. For example, which of these two apps are you more compelled to download?

"The Bad Piggies are after the eggs again—but as usual, nothing is going according to plan!"

"The intuitive and responsive multi-touch user interface makes our game amazing and easy!"

To stir up some ideas, look at product descriptions of apps created by the larger companies for inspiration for your elevator pitch. These companies usually can hire professionals to write their descriptions so they should be fairly good.

Reaffirmations, reviews, ratings, and rewards

Before plying folks with your elevator pitch, dedicate your first 200 characters to really hook them. These are the precious few lines of text that show just below the screen shots (or above, depending on which device you're using; see Figure 5-7).

Grab their attention like this:

- Promote any price reductions and let folks know when the sale is ending.

- Brag about any awards your app received or blogs that recommend it.

- Boast whether it's been featured, highlighted, or promoted by Apple.

- Highlight any reviews by well-known publications, people, or your audience.

- Blow your horn about getting only five-star reviews.

- If yours is the number one selling app of its category, share the good news.

If you could think of only one thing you would want your audience to know about your app, this would be it. If your highlights are more than 200 characters, keep the list flowing but not so long that people never actually get to read what your app does. It's okay if people have to tap More to read a description about what your app does, but if they only discover endless lines of praise they'll get confused and hesitate downloading the app.

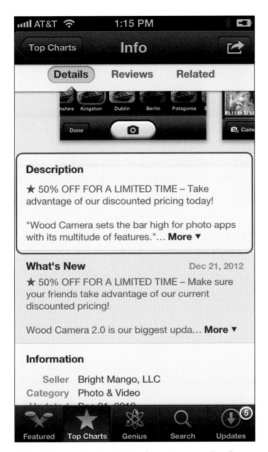

FIGURE 5-7: The first 200 characters are for the most important thing you want people to know about your app

Craft an awe-inspiring benefits list

Rather than listing the features of your app, list the benefits of using your app instead. For example, use "brings out your creative side" rather than "photo editor with filters". Also, people will read a short sentence over a paragraph of text, so try to keep your description to bulleted lists of four or five items.

Leave out the technical details, such as the supporting retina display. This list is intended to sell your app, not for someone to build it, so don't copy from your design spec. Think about all the ways your app benefits your customers and highlight those points.

Share upcoming enhancements

Create a "coming soon" section and share any future enhancements you're planning to add into the app. Customers might have been hoping to find certain features in the app, but they are willing to use your app as it is now knowing that those features are coming.

Add in a personal note

At the bottom of your description, include a personal note thanking people for helping make your app so popular. Include your social media links and mention how much you would appreciate it if they took the time to rate your app. At the very end, nudge them to tap the Buy button by saying something like, "Download [app name] today and experience the best [your app benefit] on the iPhone!"

How to design screen shots that sell

The value of a good screen shot skyrocketed after iOS 6 was released. After a potential customer taps an icon to learn more about an app on iTunes, the screen shot is the first thing he sees. Screen shots are a huge selling opportunity that is too often overlooked, especially with new apps. The following sections outline the essential elements of screen shots that sell.

An entire story with five images

Apple lets you provide five screen shots of your app to be displayed on the iTunes Store. They should be high-quality JPEG, TIFF, or PNG images. The required sizes for the screen shots are as follows:

iPhone 5 Screen Shots Full Screen
  640 pixels by 1,136 pixels (portrait)
  1,136 pixels by 640 pixels (landscape)

iPhone Screen Shots Full Screen
  640 pixels by 960 pixels (portrait)
  960 pixels by 640 pixels (landscape)

iPad Screen Shots Full Screen
  1,024 pixels by 768 pixels (landscape)
  768 pixels by 1,024 pixels (portrait)

To create a snapshot of your app, connect your device to your computer and open Xcode. Use the Organizer tool to capture images of your screen. Find your device to the left of the screen and then select Screenshots. Click New Screenshot at the bottom and then click Export to send it to a folder where you can later edit it. Do this with all the screens you want to highlight on your iTunes product page.

Screen shots that say it all

Screen shots have two purposes: to show potential buyers what the app looks like, and to act as mini ads of your app. Customers will give more attention to the screen shot than anything you write in the description, so take advantage of this opportunity to *show* and *tell* them what you want them to know. Just make sure any text you add is easy to read and can be understood in a glance. Also, the main screen shot has the important job of tempting people into exploring more, making it the most valuable of the five shots. Here are some clever ways to do just that.

- Show the app in action, with a blurred finger and a few descriptive words beneath (Figure 5-8). Be careful that the hand doesn't hide too much of the screen, especially in the main shot.

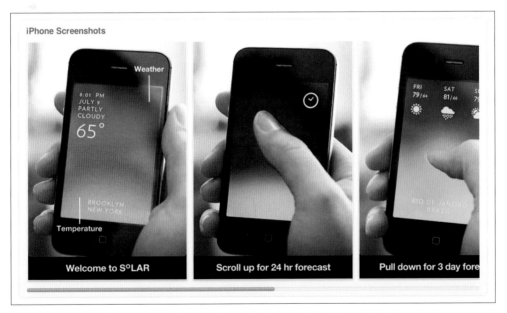

FIGURE 5-8: The Solar app screen shots on iTunes helps people envision using the app.

Source: Apple iTunes

- Create a sliced panorama of images to tell your story (Figure 5-9). People will be more tempted to view all of the screen shots to see how the story unfolds.

FIGURE 5-9: The Bump app screen shots on iTunes unfolds a story while showing the app in action.
Source: Apple iTunes

- Don't be afraid to cut off part of the interface or device to emphasize specific features or to share more of your app's design. (Figure 5-10).

FIGURE 5-10: The Momonga Pinball Adventures app has multiple screenshots together so people can see more of the app.
Source: Apple iTunes

■ Show the results of what your app can do (Figure 5-11). This sparks ideas in people's heads about clever ways they can use the app.

FIGURE 5-11: The Over HD app screen shots show examples of what the app can do (add text to your photos).
Source: Apple iTunes

Be careful not to turn your screen shots into an ugly infomercial. Also, it's a good idea to invest in a decent manicure before taking any hand shots. If you can, shy away from using any stock photos. Lastly, don't overload an image with too many screen shots or too much text so it won't look too busy.

Remember, the main screen shot must tell the story of your app in one quick look. The other four images support that story with at-a-glance details. You don't have to give away the whole plot, just enough to hook customers into tapping the Download button.

Improve discovery with the right keywords

Perhaps the second most overlooked marketing opportunity, just after the product description, are the app's *keywords*. These are the words or phrases prospective customers are most likely to enter in the App Store search box when looking for your app. You want to make sure that the app's keywords appear in either your app name, description, or iTunes Connect keywords. Selecting the right words for your app is absolutely essential for people to find it.

Because you have only 100 characters for your keywords, don't repeat the same words that are in your app name. Choose wisely because after you submit your app, you can't change the keywords until you submit an updated version of your app.

To discover the terms people are using to describe your product, ask the king of search, Google. To make it easy, Google's Keyword Tool (http://adwords.google.com/select/ KeywordToolExternal) tells you how many searches are occurring for specific words as well as other relevant words. Brainstorm all the words that would describe your app and type them into the tool. Google will help you discover new keywords you might not otherwise have thought of.

We do pay close attention to App Store search optimization. Build A Train is currently the top result in the store on a search for "train", which is a fairly high volume term that gets us some consistent exposure.

—Christopher Taylor, founder of Playtend (Counting Ants app)

Other keyword tactics involve searching competitor names or including their names in your own keyword search. You can also look at the keywords similar apps are using on their websites by following a few simple steps:

1. Go to a competitor's website.

2. Click View and then click Source. This opens the source code for the website.

3. Search for "keyword." It should be at the top portion of the code. Now you can see what might be your competitor's top keywords.

It's a good idea to test your keywords first by entering them in Google or Wikipedia, as well as running them past a couple of friends. Selecting the wrong words could actually hurt sales, so take some time to get them right.

Submitting Your App for Approval

The good news is that submitting your app is actually pretty easy to do, because essentially you're just sending Apple a file. You might have to request a little guidance from your developer, and if all else fails, have your developer submit the app for you.

There are three steps to submitting your app, outlined in Figure 5-12. First, you complete all the app details on iTunes Connect and let Apple know that your app is ready to be submitted. Next, you need to put your digital fingerprint on the app by creating a certificate, profile and App ID. Finally, you use Xcode to create a special build of your app that you'll submit to App. These next sections walk you through each step of the process.

Set up App Details on iTunes Connect

Complete all app details on iTunes Connect and let Apple know you are about to submit the app.

Create Certificates, App ID & Profile

This is your digital fingerprint on the app and lets you create a distribution build.

Submit App to Apple

Compile a distribution build of your app and submit it to Apple using Xcode.

FIGURE 5-12: The steps to submitting your app for approval.

Complete the app details on iTunes Connect

Before you can submit your app, you need to log in to iTunes Connect and complete one last task in the setup process:

1. In iTunes Connect, select Manage Your Applications.

2. Select your app.

3. Click View Details.

4. Click Ready to Upload Binary.

5. Answer the question and then click Save.

6. Click Continue, and the status of your app will change to "Waiting for Upload."

Now you're ready to submit your app. You must create a *distribution build* of your app, or in other words, a version that can be distributed on iTunes. The next sections walk you through the technical process of creating a distribution build and sending it to iTunes. The steps are fairly simple, so you certainly can do this yourself, but you may feel more comfortable with help from someone who has been through the process before.

Set up certificates, App IDs, and profiles

A distribution build of your app is just like the builds you created for development, except it has your digital fingerprint inside of the app—a special certificate, an App ID, and a Provisioning Profile. This fingerprint lets you compile a version of your app specifically intended for download from the App Store. The following steps walk you through the process of creating these three things.

> **NOTE** For a more detailed walkthrough including screen shots of the steps, check out the *App Store Submission Tutorial* on Apple's iOS Developer's site for step-by-step details of the entire process (http://tinyurl.com/b9fuk8e). You must be registered as a developer to access the tutorial.

1. Generate an iOS Distribution Certificate Signing Request. First, open your Keychain Access tool by going to your applications folder⟹Utilities⟹Keychain Access.

    a. Select Keychain Access⟹Preferences. When the window opens, select the tab labeled Certificates, and make sure both the Online Certificate Status Protocol (OCSP) and Certificate Revocation List (CRL) are set to "Off." Close the window.

    b. Select Keychain Access⟹Certificate Assistant⟹Request a Certificate from a Certificate Authority. When the window opens, enter the email address and organization name as they appear in your iOS Developer Program account. Leave CA Email Address blank and select the Saved to disk and Let me specify key pair information options before clicking Continue. You can keep the default name or change it, and then save it to your desktop.

    c. The Key Pair Information screen comes next. Make sure that the Key Size is set to 2,048 bits and that the algorithm is RSA before clicking Continue.

2. Send the certificate to Apple. The next step is to send the certificate you just created to Apple for approval using the iOS Provisioning Portal.

    a. Log in to the iOS Provisioning Portal link and click the Certificates link located in the left panel. Now select the Distribution tab in the center of the screen.

    b. Click the Request Certificate button. This opens the Create iOS Distribution Certificate window. Click Choose File and the certificate you just created; then click Submit.

    c. After submission, the certificate will be listed as Pending Issuance. Refresh your browser to reload the page, and the certificate should be ready to download.

3. Install your new distribution certificate. Download the certificate and save it to your computer. The file is saved as `distribution_identity.cer`. Double-click the file, and it automatically installs into your Keychain Access tool and is listed under Certificates.

4. Create and install a distribution provisioning profile. Apps destined for iTunes must be built with your distribution provisioning profile before they can be submitted. The steps are as follows:

    a. In the iOS Provisioning Portal, select the Provisioning link on the left panel and then choose the Distribution tab in middle of the screen.

    b. Click New Profile and select App Store as the Distribution Method. Enter a descriptive name for the profile.

    c. Select the corresponding App ID from the list and then click Submit. The profile is listed as "Pending" on the next screen. Refresh your browser and then click the Download button to save the profile to your desktop.

    d. Go to your desktop and drag and drop the profile onto either the Xcode or iTunes icon to install it on your system.

Create the distribution build yourself

After completing the preceding steps, you're all set up to create your distribution build. You'll be pleased to know that the most technically challenging steps are behind you. The app submission process went on a crash diet and has slimmed down considerably over the years, making it far simpler. Following is an overview of the steps involved.

If you aren't comfortable doing this task yourself, see the following section for details on having your developer handle this part.   `NOTE`

---

1. Open your app in Xcode and set the code signing identity to your distribution certificate.

2. Create an archive of your app using Xcode (Product➪Archive).

3. Validate the archive by selecting the app you want to upload. Enter your login details and then the name of your code signing certificate.

4. After it passes validation, select the archive again and click the Distribution button. This allows you to submit to the iTunes store.

After submitting your app, log in to iTunes Connect and notice that the status for the app has changed to "Waiting for Approval." Congratulations! You are nearly there. Although it might seem like a good time to kick back and put your feet up, you actually need to fill the waiting time by putting the final touches on your launch preparations. The "Countdown to App Approval" section coming up shortly shares exactly what you need to do.

Let your developer create the distribution build for you

If you feel completely out of your depth creating the build, you can request that your developer do the job for you. She needs to build the app with your development profile so you have to send two documents:

- A copy of your distribution certificate

- A copy of your distribution profile from the iOS Provisioning Portal (created in the previous steps)

To create a copy of your distribution certificate, open Keychain Access and select Certificates from the left side of the screen. Select your distribution profile and right-click Export to save it to your desktop. You need to create a password with the certificate and supply it to your developer, too. You can see if your developer successfully submitted the app by logging into iTunes Connect and checking the status for your app. It should now be changed to "Waiting for Approval."

Countdown to App Approval

If all goes well you will have only a week or two before your app is approved and you take the next colossal step of going live. While your app sits in a long line waiting for approval, it's a good time to craft your message to the bloggers who will get a backstage pass. You want to have it prepared because as soon as your app is approved, you can download your promo codes and start sending them to your bloggers, giving them an exclusive preview before you go live.

NOTE   When you set the release date in the future, Apple can approve your app but may not bother to inform you. So check on the status of your app on iTunes Connect every day and see whether it's changed to "Available for Sale."

Prepare your message

You've been post-stalking your favorite celebrity bloggers for weeks, so now it's time to finally share the news about your app. You should have already exchanged messages with them or posted comments to their blogs. Reaching out to them early is smart. Really successful developers will go so far as to take bloggers and journalists for a coffee or to lunch, but some of us aren't within a thousand miles to even consider such a treat.

Download only the exact number of promo codes that you plan to use because they expire. Save the rest to issue at later dates. **TIP**

I highly suggest reading the book *Pitch Perfect: Practical Advice From Professional Bloggers* by Steven Sande and Erica Sadun (Sand Dune Books, 2012) to grasp the best tactics to getting your app on important websites and in the press. Here I highlight some of the book's pointers, including how to craft your message.

To start, you need a strong opening in your email, and it helps to know the recipient's style and what he's been talking about. For example, you can reference a review the bloggers wrote and mention how your app relates to that post. Be honest and genuine because most bloggers can sniff out fakes pretty quickly. Here are some other important details for your letter, suggested by *Pitch Perfect*:

- **Motivational subject line**—Use 80 or fewer characters that say what the app is, the role it plays, and how it is different. Let them know they're getting an exclusive preview.

- **Name of the app**—Indicate exactly how the name should appear when they write about it. They'll also use that name to do a Google search.

- **Price of the app**—Provide a price in U.S. dollars unless it's specific to another region. If it's a freemium app, let them know this, too.

- **Links**—Include links to the iTunes product page and your product website. Your site might not be live yet, but you should still be able to give them a link.

- **Screen shots**—Add one or two shots or, better yet, a link to your press kit.

- **Demo video**—Include the link to your demo video. This is the bloggers' chance to quickly see the app in action without having to go through the hassle of downloading and installing it.

- **Description**—Add one paragraph that explains what the app does and why people should care. Who is the audience? How is it different? How does it work?

- **Features list**—Use simple phrases in a bulleted list.

- **Contact details**—Include details such as website, Facebook, Twitter, email, phone, and address.

- **Promo code**—Give them the code and expiration date.

- **Launch date**—Let them know the exact date and time that your app will go live. Be specific if you don't want them to publish anything until your launch date.

- **Specific blog category**—Let bloggers know if there is a specific place on the site you want to be mentioned—for example, iPhone App of the Day.

TIP Plan to send your personalized emails to bloggers and the press at least two weeks before your app launch date. These people are busy and you want to give them enough time to prepare their reviews so they're ready to publish on your launch day.

Close shop

Steal a page out of Apple's marketing book and close your shop the day before launch (see Figure 5-13). Closing your site just before you go live probably seems counterproductive, but it sends out a message that something important is happening and people need to pay attention.

FIGURE 5-13: Close your shop for a day to send out the message that something important is about to happen.
Source: Apple Inc.

Unlike Apple, you should let visitors know exactly when the site will be open and prominently share your app launch date. You can even continue to collect email addresses and share images or the video of your app. When you're ready to reopen, replace the "closed" site with the new website you designed to promote your app.

Backstage sneak peek event

While your shop is closed, give bloggers and journalists a backstage pass by letting them be the first to see your web design before you launch the new site. You can do this by sending them a link to your development site.

If you really want to make an event out of it, invite them to an exclusive webinar as well. Send them a paper invitation three weeks in advance to really grab their attention. A clever invite is hard to resist, so search Pinterest for inspiration on creating an enticing invite that reflects your app. The more the merrier, so invite your followers as well by creating a Facebook event page. Make the webinar short, punchy, and memorable. Be sure to record everything so you can share it later on your social networks.

Announce your launch date

Too often developers make the mistake of keeping their launch date a secret, hoping the element of surprise will generate incredible buzz. But the truth is a lot of people will decide to buy your app before they even see it, so as soon as you're confident about your launch date, share it with everyone and ask people to circle it on their calendar. Publish it on your website, send it out in a newsletter, and shout it out on social media (more than once).

3...2...1...Launch!

GO LIVE!

Your app's first day on iTunes is a birthday worthy of a grand celebration. Make sure all your marketing messages are ready so you're free to celebrate the day and share your excitement over Twitter, Facebook, and then later with friends at your favorite restaurant. The next chapter goes into more details on promoting your app, but the following sections cover a few things you don't want to miss.

Double-check the important stuff

Before anything, make sure Apple has your app listing flawless on iTunes. Double-check the spelling is correct, the icon and screen shots look great, and the category and price are accurate. Make sure the app is downloadable by installing it from iTunes. See how easily customers can find your app by testing some search terms.

You still have time to edit your screen shots, description, and details. Any changes you make at this point might take a couple of hours for Apple to roll out, and that might mean your app disappears from iTunes momentarily, so make edits before posting announcements.

Roll out your new site

Launching a website can be almost as tricky as developing your app, so plan it wisely. If you need to enlist the help of your developer, make sure she is available on your app launch day to go live with the site. Schedule the rollout early in the morning or the night before to allow plenty of time to fix any issues you might discover.

Also, if the web address you shared with bloggers and journalists is your development site, be sure to redirect that traffic to your new live site automatically.

Blog your big news

If all goes according to plan you'll be busy engaging new fans on launch day, so draft a blog post a few days in advance, but put the final touches on it the day you launch. You want to capture your enthusiasm plus include any other news such as being featured in a blog. Include screen shots of your app, your marketing newsletter, and any other materials you created, such as your video.

Get the word out on social media

Craft some newsworthy posts for Facebook, Twitter, and any other social networks. But don't just post and walk away. Start conversations and ask questions.

Share content that's meaningful and relates to your app such as videos, podcasts, photos, and news articles. Social networks are the perfect place to get your app in front of people that have already been "sold" on your product because they're used to getting their news and information from these sites—or rather, from their friends on these sites.

Ready, set, email!

In addition to sending out your carefully crafted launch newsletter, reach out to everyone in your contacts list and on your Christmas card list and share the big news. Reach out to your local community, too. Find your local news and radio stations' Facebook pages and get in touch. They're always looking for some newsworthy nuggets and might like to interview the newest local entrepreneur. Send a follow-up email to your blogger and press friends to thank them or remind them about your big news.

Get fans in on the fun

Your fans are your biggest asset, so create an experience that isn't about you or your app, but about your audience. Give your fans a once-in-a-lifetime moment by letting them showcase their talents.

Engaging your fans has to go beyond a contest or comments. You want the focus to be on them and their creation. Invite a customer to be interviewed on your blog. Showcase the wonderful works of art made possible with your app. Let your fans be creators as much as customers.

Keeping Track of Sales

Of course your biggest distraction on opening day won't be the frantic Tweets, Facebook posts, and emails. Instead, you'll be preoccupied with wondering how many people are actually downloading your app. Now, you can wait 24 hours for Apple's sales reports to find out how well it did, or you can install an analytic service and watch the numbers instantly. Sounds like a no-brainer if you ask me.

Add a free analytic service

Services such as Test Flight (testflightapp.com), Flurry (flurry.com), and Mix Panel (mix-panel.com) are all free analytic solutions. Install their SDKs into your app and you can log in to their sites and view sales, customer locations, how long customers use the app, and what time of day—all in real time.

This information is powerful. It's a lot more than what Apple tells you and a lot quicker. Details like this are critical for making business decisions. In Chapter 7, you learn more about using analytics to make business decisions.

What Apple tells you and doesn't tell you

Each morning your iTunes Connect account is updated with your sales estimates for the previous day. These estimates, as well as customer feedback, are broken down by region, which can be extremely helpful when you try to discover any regional issues with your app.

Other than sales and feedback, Apple doesn't share anything at all about your customers. You won't know their demographics or location, or even have a clue how they came across your app. And you won't have any contact details so you could ask them. There are ways around this lack of information, however. You can force customers to register or use an analytic solution to learn more, but some details might always remain a complete mystery.

Building Customer Love

After launch, you might be tempted to grab a margarita, sit in the sun, and finally relax. There's nothing wrong with a breather, but make it quick. More eyes are on you now than ever before, and what you do next is important.

Be a snoop and monitor social networks like a hawk. When you discover someone talking about your app, contact that person to say thanks and ask if he likes it. These folks are probably your biggest fans and would appreciate the personal high-five on your launch day. Keep sending personal notes as often as you can, even weeks after the launch. The following sections describe a couple of other ways to get customers to love you (and praise you).

Answer emails early, often, and sincerely

How many times have you contacted customer service and been told that you're important but then asked to listen to a 40-minute flute solo while you wait? It's no wonder most customer requests have such an ill-tempered tone. People would rather walk three miles backwards than contact customer service.

The unfortunate truth is that we've gotten terribly used to being put on hold or waiting a week for a reply and feeling as though businesses don't care. Most customer requests are rude and angry because people feel they have to be the squeaky wheel to get heard. It's nothing personal. Even the most successful app developers are called names and ridiculed.

The best thing you can do is to answer all customer queries the same day they arrive. An instant reply, even a short message, can turn a potentially bad situation into a good one, no matter how ugly it looked. Angry customers instantly relax because they've been heard. Give them a personal response, and they can even be swayed into becoming your biggest fan. Not having the perfect solution doesn't matter. Just let them know you're on the case and will get back to them.

Be real and they will reward you

If customers do manage to get through to a human, the next blockade is the canned and robotic responses. Businesses think these responses make them sound professional, but they just come off as boring and annoying.

Don't be afraid to show your true colors and be the real you. People can relate to flaws and will respect you, but they can't relate to a robot. Talk to them as you would a friend. Be open about your faults and dare to find humor in them. Leave the polished perfection for your products and let your flaws be in your favor.

The Pre-Launch Cheat Sheet

One Month Before Submitting App

- ❏ Take care of all legalities, tax details, and contracts on iTunes Connect.
- ❏ Prepare your customer support system.
- ❏ Identify your most influential bloggers and journalists, follow them, and introduce yourself.
- ❏ Build a new website promoting your app.
- ❏ Create a newsletter to send to your fans on launch day.
- ❏ Compose a press kit for the media to download from your website.
- ❏ Produce a viral video of your app as well as a demo one for the media and bloggers.

One Week Before Submitting App

- ❏ Research the best keywords for your app.
- ❏ Write the product description that will be displayed on the App Store.
- ❏ Prepare five screen shots of your app that will be displayed on the App Store.

Submitting Your App

- ❏ Complete the setup details for your app on iTunes Connect.
- ❏ Create and install your distribution certificate, App ID, and distribution profile.
- ❏ Create a distribution build of your app using Xcode and submit it to Apple.

While You're Waiting for Approval

- ❏ Prepare personal emails for each of your selected bloggers and journalists. Send them along with a promo code as soon as your app is approved.
- ❏ Draft your launch day marketing messages to share on social media sites.
- ❏ Announce your launch date on social media sites, your blog, and in any correspondences.
- ❏ Draft a blog post to be published on launch day.
- ❏ Close shop and invite fans and bloggers to a short preview webinar.
- ❏ Plan ways to engage your fans and customers on launch day, such as competition or sharing content they create with your app.

continued

continued

Launch Day

- ❏ Double check your app on iTunes to make sure everything is perfect and you can download the app. Make any required changes right away.
- ❏ Roll out your new website.
- ❏ Update the blog post you drafted and publish it.
- ❏ Send out your launch day newsletter to your fans.
- ❏ Email all family, friends, and acquaintances with the big news. Contact your local news and radio stations as well.
- ❏ Send out messages on the social networks throughout the day.
- ❏ Engage your customers, say thanks and have fun.

Key Points

- ■ Select a launch date coinciding with a calendar event that matches your app theme. Plan to submit your app for approval at least one month before your launch date.

- ■ Show your customers how much you appreciate them by creating a customer support site, answering emails early and sincerely, and including them in on the launch fun.

- ■ Start following bloggers and journalists who are your tribal leaders and can make an impact on your launch. Reach out to them and form a relationship with them.

- ■ Give journalists and bloggers a sneak peek at your app before it goes live by sending them promo codes. Craft each email individually and include everything they will need to write a glowing review for your app.

- ■ Plan your marketing materials early. Create a stunning website, prepare a marketing kit, craft a viral video, and put together a newsletter that people will read and forward to their friends.

- ■ Make your app stand out on iTunes with a well-thought-out description and screen shots of your app. Keep the content simple and easy to read, and show everything at a glance.

CHAPTER 6

Promoting Your App and Making a Profit

"Try not to become a man of success. Rather become a man of value."

—Albert Einstein

With the number of apps available on iTunes rapidly approaching the gazillion mark, a common misconception is that you need massive PR and a huge marketing budget to have a hit. So let's get one thing clear, especially if you're just joining us now; the secret to getting noticed is kicking off your marketing campaign as soon as you decide to create an app, not once it's live on iTunes. Also, marketing isn't hustling, exaggerating, or tricking people into buying your app. It's sharing stories and engaging your audience.

This chapter reveals the ingredients of a compelling story and teaches you how to leverage the power of the social networks. It shares tried-and-true marketing tactics, laying the groundwork so you can pioneer your own marketing trail without breaking the bank. Rather than throwing away money on advertising and PR, you'll learn how to make your audience come to you because they *want* to hear what you have to say. It shares a formula for creating hype and shows you how to listen to your fans. Lastly, it walks through creating websites, handling email campaigns, and successfully pricing your app to sell.

PROMOTE

The Art of Attracting Attention and Creating Hype

Every second, millions of people hear about new products and ideas thanks to the social networks—a phenomenon powered solely by people sharing things that moved them. Word-of-mouth marketing is like rocket fuel, and is the single most important and powerful tool you have. Ad clutter is everywhere, and we just ignore it. We don't trust ads, and they cost too much anyway. But humans have used stories to illustrate, entertain and persuade since we used rocks as tools. We're naturally built for them; whether it's gossip, news or the muttering in our heads.

So how do you harness the powers of YouTube, Facebook, Instagram and Twitter to make your app famous in a week? The simple answer is you need to either have a famous trendsetter spot your story (like Oprah), create something that lets the world participate (think of all the parodies of *Gangnam Style*), or create something unexpected (like the cannonball leap into a freezing pool). But the basis of any good story is that it's simple and touches the audience's imagination. For example:

- It reveals something personal or unknown about you or your brand.
- It taps into a specific emotion such as fear, joy, anger, playfulness, or shock.
- It makes people feel empowered and casts them as the hero.

- It lets people believe in a solution.

- It surprises, amuses, and takes people on a journey.

We'll dive deeper into these tactics in a minute. First, understand that half of your time should be spent connecting with people and sharing, and the other half creating. Start with the people you already know and build from there. Remember, word-of-mouth marketing is about interacting with people and enticing them to participate. This is how you do it.

Our Instagram reach of 275,000 wasn't a bad place to start, but we knew to reach the top of the charts we'd need something more. We communicated with Mobile Media Lab (Instagram-centric marketing services) and decided that they would be a good fit for us and our marketing plan for Wood Camera.

The plan was to do a number of posts over several days on Instagram. All we asked was that people use the #WoodCamera hashtag and point to the @WoodCamera Instagram account in each image caption. Other than that, we trusted each photographer's creativity to shape the style, feel, and timing of their posts—as well as their viral impact.

—John Barnett, Founder of Bright Mango on how Wood Camera became the #1 paid iPhone app

Give people a story to tell

Give people something to talk about—that's the entire crux of word-of-mouth advertising. People naturally *want* to tell each other stories, so give them one. What gives a good story life? Yes, it's interesting. But more so, a good story makes the person sharing it interesting. You want to give people something to talk about because it makes *them* compelling and gives them an edge. Here are a few ways to do that.

Although most of the following examples are about videos, these tactics can be used in any medium. | NOTE

Pull on the heart strings

Content that touches people's emotional sides is by far the most effective. Reveal the heart-break of loss, the tremendous power of loyalty, and the triumph of the human spirit. These are stories that move us and stick with us. They motivate us, shake our awareness, and stir up emotions that connect us all.

The mobile journaling app *Path* relaunched its app with a touching video titled "Share Life," shown in Figure 6-1. In the two months after *Path 2* launched, it attracted a million new users, according to Path CEO Dave Morin (allthingsd.com, February, 2012). That's roughly the same amount Path got in its entire first year.

FIGURE 6-1: Path 2 launch video that helped it double the number of users in just two months.
Source: YouTube

Build identity

People want to share content that reflects who they are and where they stand on issues and ideas, whether it's social, political or emotional. For example, when President Obama won reelection in 2012, he tweeted three words, and his message broke the record for most retweets. The tweet simply says "Four more years," and shows a photo of the President and the First Lady embracing (see Figure 6-2).

FIGURE 6-2: The tweet sent by President Obama surpassed 500,000 retweets, making it a record breaker.
Source: Twitter

Another example is the 30-minute documentary film *Koney 2012* about Ugandan rebel leader Joseph Kony. With more than 100 million jaw-dropping views in six days, it became the most viral video in history, according to Mashable (http://mashable.com/2012/03/12/kony-most-viral/). Throughout the video, the filmmaker Jason Russell makes the story about the viewers by repeatedly referencing Facebook. He uses the Facebook's Timeline feature to help viewers visualize his story, all the more powerful because of the fact many people watched his video after discovering it on their Facebook news feeds.

Make it cute as kittens

Whether or not you're a feline lover, a kitten playing the piano is going to make you smile at least a little. It's not just dolled-up cats that are suddenly in need of a good talent agent; children and adorable grandparents are also easy pickings.

Esther Huffman was trying to show her husband how to take a photo using the camera on their laptop. She couldn't get it to work because it was taking a video, unbeknownst to them. She unknowingly recorded their struggle, and the video, titled "Webcam 101 for Seniors," has been viewed more than 10 million times (see Figure 6-3).

FIGURE 6-3: An adorable couple attempt to use their web camera.
Source: YouTube

Make us laugh

Perhaps the most common of all viral content are the things that make us laugh. As comedian Yakov Smirnoff says, laughter is the shortest distance between two people. It not only brings people closer, but also can also sell a lot of product.

The Dollar Shave Club (dollarshaveclub.com) launched in March 2012 with a hilarious video of the CEO, Mike Dubin, walking through the warehouse (see Figure 6-4). The ad went viral and was viewed 2 million times its first four days on YouTube. Within the first week, Dollar Shave Club had 25,000 new members. None of which would have been possible if the video wasn't funny.

FIGURE 6-4: The Dollar Shave Club video cost less than $5,000 to make and gained the company millions in sales.

Image reproduced with permission of the Dollar Shave Club. ©2012 Dollar Shave Club All Rights Reserved.

Create nostalgia

We all love to reminisce about the good old days. Big hair and horrible fashion, celebrity teen crushes, music, old toys—the list is endless. The familiarity with comfortable classics and our beloved heroes from yesteryear connects us to a more hopeful time. Rather than creating new plots with new characters, take your fans back to their fond memories.

The creators of Hipstamatic (hipstamatic.com) have earned more than $10 million from their app, which transforms photos into really cool retro images. They're sticking with the '70s pop culture feel in their latest app, SwankoLab (hipstamatic.com/swankolab), shown in Figure 6-5.

FIGURE 6-5: The SwankoLab app promo video uses retro images and throwback tunes.
© 2009 - 2012 Hipstamatic, LLC.

Try taboo, unusual, or outrageous

When all else fails, there's nothing like sex, lies, or bathroom humor to spice up some content. It suddenly becomes far more interesting. Stupid pet tricks, the wild, eccentric, and unpredictable are all mainstream viral content. The video *Tootin' Bathtub Baby Cousins* is a simple little song about the bubbles these kids make in the bath after eating too many beans, and it has over 250 million views.

Apps that make you bald or fat, change faces, wiggle body parts, or produce farts are obviously in no shortage on the App Store. There is unquestionably a huge market for anything that is shocking and appeals to teenage male humor.

Monitoring buzz to create more interest

Perhaps one of the easiest ways to be interesting is to be interested in what people are saying. In other words, it's better to listen to what your audience is talking about than to show off your brilliance and then turn a deaf ear. Listen and let your audience lead the conversation.

There are dozens of free and low-cost tools designed to monitor activity on the social networks. They let you measure your social media reach and gauge how fast your online community is growing. You can set up alerts to notify you whenever someone mentions your app. If you have a tweet or post that went viral, you can track it as it spreads. Here are some of my favorite tools:

■ **TweetDeck**—Even if you decide not to use Twitter, you still want to keep track of what is being said about you and your product on Twitter. TweetDeck (tweetdeck.com) is the Swiss Army Knife of a Twitter account. If you have more than one Twitter account, you can arrange all of them in one place. You can schedule tweets and set up searches and customized feeds. You can also set up groups you want to follow.

Using this tool can be a great way to find out who purchased and is using your app and what they're saying about it. You can reply to people who mention your app with a thank you, and you can retweet glowing comments. Best of all, TweetDeck is free.

■ **Google Alerts and Reader**—Google Alerts (google.com/alerts) notifies you whenever certain keywords appear in blogs and news posts. You specify the keywords you would like to be notified about, and anytime they appear on the Internet, the article is sent directly to your inbox or news feeder.

Google Reader (google.com/reader) enables you to follow selected news in real time. You can track posts created by both your audience and influential bloggers. It's easy to set up, and you can read all the articles from one website. Plus, plenty of really good apps are designed to bring all your content to your iPhone and iPad, so you can read everything there too.

■ **Social Mention**—A bit like Google Alerts, Social Mention (socialmention.com) enables you to track who is talking about you, your app, or any other topic you're curious to learn more about. It pulls conversations from hundreds of social media sites and can send the results directly to your email or reader.

■ **Facebook Insights**—You can see what impact your Facebook posts have and track your audience growth using Facebook Insights (facebook.com/insights). The dashboard of analytics data related to your Facebook page enables you to better understand your audience and know what content reaches the right people.

The $5 Marketing Plan

The tips I share with you in this section are fairly straightforward, but best of all, they're free. They don't cost you anything more than your time. The five bucks is to treat yourself to a cup of coffee to keep you going while you're busy promoting your app.

The following pages offer the basic, time-proven marketing tactics that you need to master. But don't stop there. These ideas are only the beginning. It is up to you to break the rules and formulate a marketing campaign that no one has ever seen before.

Have a sale

Celebrate a big event or milestone with your tribe by dropping the price of your app for a short period, or better yet, make it free. You earn nothing when you give your app away, but this tactic certainly can boost the popularity of your app and increase your audience. Lower the price or offer it free for a couple of days and watch your download numbers soar.

Discounting your app can gain you extra press too. Sites such as AppShopper (appshopper. com) and Free App a Day (freeappaday.com) feature apps that are on sale to help developers get a boost.

> **TIP**   Consider offering your first app for free as a strategy to gain millions of fans so you have a strong fan base for the launch of your *second* app.

To make sure everyone is aware of your sale, plan for it as you would a launch. Let influential bloggers know about it in advance and market it around another campaign, like a contest. Be sure to update your iTunes product description with your price drop details, too, so potential customers know they're a saving a couple of bucks.

Give out promo codes

Everybody loves a freebie, so give some lucky people a promo code and score some positive reviews in return. Apple grants app developers 50 free download codes for each app on the iTunes Store. The company recently changed the rules promo codes so people using them can't post a review of the app on the iTunes Store. But that doesn't prevent someone from posting a review about your app on his blog, Facebook page, or Twitter feed.

When you give someone a promo code, ask if he would write a review on his blog, Facebook, Twitter, or all of the above if he has them. Another option is to request that he send you a couple of glowing comments about the app. You can post his statement to your own website and on the App Store product description.

Promo codes expire after 28 days, so don't download them all at once. Instead, download only the number of codes you need. You get 50 more codes each time your app is updated and the revision is approved, but your old codes won't work after that point.

Unfortunately, this tactic works only for paid apps at present. Apple doesn't provide promo codes for in-app purchases, but that could change.

Promote your app inside your app

There's nothing like getting a recommendation from a happy customer. When you have her full attention on your app, make it easy for her to share it with others. Offer incentives and rewards for doing some marketing on your behalf. This approach is all about asking the right people at the right time in the right way.

Build in social and sharing features

People *want* to share what they find in your app, so give them a quick and easy way to send it around the social circles with a tap of a button. It could be a screenshot of a map, a product, or the weather. Whatever it is that your app creates, let your customers share it on Twitter, Facebook, and email at the very least.

To help others discover your app, automatically tag the content they create with your app name. For example, if your app name is *Wonderboy*, place the tag #wonderboyapp in the Facebook or Twitter post, but let people edit it. You can also place a small overlay of the app icon and name on images, but be sure it doesn't ruin the content of the image. The stamp should be so subtle that people barely notice it's there.

Request a review

Having only a handful of really great reviews on iTunes is better than having hundreds of reviews littered with a handful of bad ones in their midst. The key is to get *happy* customers to leave feedback on iTunes while trying to have the negative comments to come directly to you.

A recent trend is to ask customers by throwing out a pop-up message requesting a review as soon as the app opens. It's important to ask for a review only *after* people have a chance to use your app a few times. If they opened your app just one or two times, you probably won't get a good review, so don't even ask them.

People will also leave a poor review if you interrupt their flow, so be careful about when your pop-up appears. If it appears right when they open the app, they might be put off because they want to use the app, not review it. Always give people three options: to rate the app, to do it later, or to never be bothered about it again.

A better option than hijacking users to ask for a review is to put a Review button in the Settings screen. It will link to your app in iTunes so that so users can review the app when it's convenient for them. If a user is perusing the settings screen, he isn't in the middle of creating content, so the timing is much better.

If your app sends messages or notifications, you can create one to send to your customers after they have used your app for a while asking if they will review it. Include your iTunes link in the message to make it easy for them. You can also ask them to send you a reply with any ideas to improve the app. This approach helps filter negative feedback directly to you while the good stuff hopefully ends up on iTunes.

Most people would rather have an answer to their issues than slam your app on iTunes, so give them that option. Put a link in your app with a statement like "Found a bug?" This statement can automatically create an email or link to your support page. If you're able to help these people, you could wind up with a glowing review out of them rather than an unpleasant review about a bug.

Also, anytime customers contact you with kind words about your app, thank them and ask they leave a review on iTunes. Always include your iTunes link. You can even suggest they just copy and paste their comments from the email.

Tell a friend

Asking for referrals is a marketing tactic that is as old as the trees. An easy way to elicit a referral is to place a button in your settings screen that automatically creates an email with a link to your app on the iTunes Store, making it incredibly easy for customers to share your app with their network.

Now that Twitter and Facebook are both integrated in the SDK, you can easily add buttons that let customers create a tweet and Facebook post with a link to your app. Even if only a fraction of your audience shares your app, you're still expanding your reach.

Reward handsomely

Reward your customers for marketing your app and getting the word out by giving them a freebie. It can be extra storage, a theme, a character, or a free upgrade. It can cost you nothing and be just the right push your customers need to convince their friends to download your app.

You can do this by adding buttons that automatically let customers follow you on Twitter or be a fan on Facebook. When customers tap on them they receive a pop-up message with the great news of the freebie you just unlocked for them. Another option is to let customers know that you'll be sharing promotional codes every week to your fans through Twitter and Facebook. Or you can offer them a prize if they invite at least ten friends to try the app. Be creative with ways to reward people for sharing your app.

We did our best to make sure fans of our first app, Koi Pond, were aware of our new app Distant Shore's release by adding a newsfeed tab to the Koi Pond interface. That's what really drove Distant Shore's initial sales.

—Andy Skirvin, co-founder and engineer at The Blimp Pilots (Koi Pond app)

Teach to reach

You're now an expert on creating apps and your app's domain, so you have valuable information that your audience would gobble up if you disclose it. Be generous with your knowledge and teach others. Write articles offering tips related to your app or your market. Create a series of educational videos. People will trust and respect you more when you openly and generously share your knowledge and experience.

Write, write, write

Send out newsletters, write posts on your or someone else's website, publish an e-book, and post comments on blogs. The more your company name is seen and read by your audience, the greater the awareness of your apps and the more credible you and your brand will be.

Concoct a series of blog posts that will reveal secrets, educate your audience, or share a story. Plan to release a post from your series on the same day each week so readers know when to expect the next installment of your series.

Contact bigger blogs and offer to write an article for them. You are now an expert on app development, your product's domain, and launching a business. The opportunities are endless.

Collect everything you write and formulate a book. E-books are incredibly easy to publish and distribute on Amazon and other sites. Publishing yourself will open opportunities to public speaking and teaching. It's a big, bright feather in your cap.

Reveal your secrets

Disclosing everything you know is actually a competitive advantage, so don't be obsessed with secrecy and filter everything you disclose. Share all your secrets openly. Don't worry if your competitors learn everything you're doing. There is no way they'll be able to copy your business exactly. Tell the world about how you do things, what works and doesn't, and your "secret recipe."

Whereas most developers hold their sales numbers closely to their chest, app developer company Tap Tap Tap publishes its numbers on a regular basis (www.taptaptap.com/blog). It has done this from the start, and doing so has only attracted more fans. The company is now a household name in the app developer world.

Praise other apps

Review your favorite apps on your blog and let the app owners know about it—they might return the favor. If you don't have time to draft a full review, mention great apps on Twitter and Facebook. Share design elements you like and new features you noticed.

Create videos and presentations

Take a page out of marketing great Gary Vaynerchuk's book and create a video series. His network is worth more than $10 million, and it started with video blogging about good wines. If the thought of getting in front of the camera stirs up stage fright, create a series of PowerPoint presentations and upload them to SlideShare (slideshare.net).

Share everything

In addition to sharing your secrets and expertise, share your customers and your brand. Doing so costs you nothing and shows how generous you are with your fans and friends. It also builds really good karma, and that goes a long, long way in word-of-mouth marketing.

Share customers

Join forces with other entrepreneurs who run businesses that share the same customer base. Create a cross-promotion. Enthusiastically endorse each other's business to your customers and reward them with special two-for-one deals.

Share your brand

Create banner ads and wallpapers with your logo, app mascot, or other unique graphics and share these freebies with your fans to download from your website. Facebook and Twitter covers are also hot freebies. Figure 6-6 shows you how to do it.

Banner ads—To create a banner ad, you can either search for banner ad templates online or use a free banner ad service. The service stamps its web address on your ad, so another option is to post a design contest on 99Designs (99designs.com). Thousands of talented designers "compete to create a banner ad design you love, or your money back!"

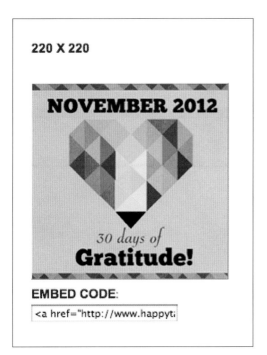

FIGURE 6-6: Display the banner ad on your site with the ad image at top and the HTML code beneath.

After your banner ads have been created, add them to the "freebie" section on your website. The banner ad will appear at the top with HTML code below the image. Fans can copy and paste the code to automatically add your banner to their site. The HTML code looks like this:

```
<a href="http://www.yourlink.com"><img
  src="http://www.yourwebsite.com/images/220x220_banner.jpg"
  width="220" height="220" border="1" style="border-color:
  #CCC"/></a>
```

You have to edit the code with your link and image details. If you aren't familiar with HTML, it's pretty basic code, so any web developer should be able to give you a hand. Figure 6-7 shows an example.

FIGURE 6-7: I stumbled upon this free wallpaper created by Scott Jackson (iamscotty.com) and later hired him to create the mascots for my apps. He now is his own boss.

Used with permission of Scott Jackson, iamscotty.com

Wallpaper—If you think creating free wallpaper is a waste of time, just hear me out. The artist who created all my icons created a wallpaper that I fell in love with and downloaded while I was in the process of designing my app. His web address was subtly stamped in the corner. I got in touch, and he sold me some designs to use in my apps. His wallpaper was picked up by a major blog, Smashing Magazine (smashingmagazine.com), and plenty of other people got in touch with him too. He went on to quit his job and now is a full time artist.

Creating free wallpaper for iPhones and iPads doesn't require any templates, but you need some design skills. Create a layout the same dimensions as the iPhone and iPad screens and keep the design very simple, with your app name and website subtly placed in the corner. You can add elements from your app, such as a character, or design something that reflects what your app stands for. Use purchased stock images or a simple quote. Add the wallpaper to your site with a link to the image for people to download (see Figure 6-8).

FIGURE 6-8: Facebook cover image created for my November Gratitude project.

Cover photos—Facebook's not-so-new Timeline design introduced the use of the cover photo—the large picture at the top of the page designed to let people personalize their wall. The market for unique cover photos and designs is hot.

Facebook cover photos are 851 pixels wide and 315 pixels tall. You can create your own design using an image editor like Photoshop. You can also use an online service that puts together an image for you. Here are three:

- timelinecoverbanner.com
- pagecovers.com/facebook-cover-generator
- thesitecanvas.com

Twitter also rolled out cover photos, giving you another large space for fans to personalize and identify themselves with your tribe. Twitter cover photos are 1,252 pixels wide and 626 pixels tall. Twitcovers (http://twitter.com/TwitCovers) is a great place for inspiration and for sharing your designs. Figure 6-9 shows my Twitter cover image.

The key to good wallpaper and cover image designs is to keep the personal identity to your fans and subtly place your branding in the corners, or not at all. These aren't advertisements like banner ads, but a way for your audience to add to their own identity.

FIGURE 6-9: My personal Twitter cover image.
Source: Twitter.com

Put your name on everything

Update your email signature with your app name and iTunes link. Mention it in your voice-mail greeting. Use your app icon as your image on all your social media sites. Update your stationery, business cards, and Christmas cards.

Hit the streets

It might not occur to you to go offline and promote your apps, but you will be amazed how many people want to learn about everything you now know. Wherever you go, always come prepared with freebies in hand—buttons, cards, anything that they can walk away with that has your name and app icon on it.

Speak Out

You can find opportunities to present and participate on panels at conferences, seminars, and other events. This is your chance to say something interesting and build awareness of your brand and app. Tell stories that illustrate a point, share personal stories about your kids, and make fun of yourself.

In addition to public events, visit local colleges and schools. Share your experience creating and promoting apps, building a brand, and marketing apps. Some of my most engaged audiences have been students because they're hungry for this information. Get in touch with college business and advertising departments and let them know you're available to give a talk.

Pull a stunt

To really catch the media's attention, get outside and try some guerilla marketing. Start a pillow fight in the park. Too violent? Give away cookies with a smile. Bring your app to life outside for everyone to see. Create a scene that will make people smile, wonder, and even jump with excitement and then catch it all on video. Share your stunt live over Twitter, Facebook, and Instagram. Even if you live in a remote mountain-top village, the Internet makes it possible to spread stunts quickly.

Promotion Tactics That Don't Work

In more than five years of creating apps I spent less than $600 on advertising, yet always managed to have an app in the iTunes top charts. Sudden bursts in sales can be a mystery. The numbers magically go up for a few days, and I have no idea why. A post about my app in *MacRumors* might have caused the jump, or it could have been the storm of tweets, or maybe both.

What I do know is that there are a few tactics I've tried with zero results. Perhaps they work for other developers, but for me they seemed like a waste of time.

Press releases are spam

Before I stand on my soapbox about press releases again, let me confess that I also tried to push my state-of-the-art app with this traditional marketing tactic. I invested $350 in a press release, and although it was extremely well written, it got me nothing in return. Not one blogger or journalist even read it.

It's no secret that newspapers are underfunded and desperately trying to adapt to the digital era. Some developers try to exploit busy and competitive reports by putting the right "spin" on their press release, trying to disguise it as news. I personally feel that manipulating the press isn't necessary if you genuinely have a killer app. If you followed the steps in this book, your audience will plaster your app across the world stage.

Think before leaping into banner ads

A banner ad was one of my big marketing splurges. I spent $200 for a 125 pixels by 125 pixels ad on a well-known website. It went up the day my first app was live on the iTunes Store and stayed on the site for a couple of months. When I decided to discontinue it, my sales weren't affected one bit.

I put the same banner ad on my website so my tribe could copy and paste the code to easily add it onto their websites. I was amazed at all the places that ad showed up, and it didn't cost me a penny. Remember, your customers want to brand themselves as part of your tribe, so give them a way to do it.

To be fair, banner ads have come a long way. Because they still exist is proof that they actually are effective if done correctly. Before you jump into creating banner ads, here are a few tips:

- Headings should be short and captivating.

- The call to action should be clear and visually engaging.

- Animation should be very subtle and not annoying.

- Colors and graphics should blend in and compliment the site it's being displayed on.

- Run more than one banner ad in a campaign so you know what is working.

- Measure your success and make adjustments to your campaigns.

Never slam competitors' apps

Leaving bad reviews on iTunes for competitors' apps might sound fairly innocent, but it can cost you your whole business. If Apple gets wind of it, the company takes away your developer membership and pulls your apps. Going this route is completely pointless anyway. Who cares what your competitors are doing? Focus on *your* app and customers instead of pouring your energy into your competitors' businesses.

With the preceding tactics in mind, you may be dreaming up a campaign that uniquely reflects you and your app. But to truly be ahead of the game, you can't stop there. You need a website to get some online presence for your app, and an email strategy to reach out to potential customers.

Creating a Compelling Website

With all this talk about Facebook and Twitter you might be wondering if you truly need a website. The answer is YES. In fact, it's even more important because these social media sites make it easier for people to find your site, generating more traffic to it.

Not only does a site make it easier for people to find you, it's easier for you to control what they see. Your site only shows content that you want people to see, in a way that makes it easiest for them to find what they're looking for. Most importantly, you control the branding and own all of the information and content. So yes, you need a website. In fact, you need at least two: a teaser site and your app live site.

This section outlines some basic steps for creating a website. It also breaks down the anatomy of a good teaser site and an app product site. The next section steps you through the basics of email campaigns. If you're considering hiring someone to create your site for you, it's wise to see if they can create all three elements (teaser site, product site, and marketing email).

Registering a domain name

Even if you have an existing site or blog, having a stand-alone site for your app is helpful. Tagging a web page onto an existing site can turn the web address into an ugly long mess. It's far easier to share the address "pingpongapp.com" than it is "myblog.com/iphoneapp/ping-pong/." Not only is this name simplier to read, but you can also have an email address with the unique domain name, making it easier for people to remember.

When you find a domain you like that is available, you can go to a number of websites to purchase it, such as GoDaddy.com and Register.com. The process of purchasing the domain is as easy as entering your address and credit card number. Some sites try to upsell you with all sorts of additional products, but you really don't need them.

Purchasing web hosting

After you buy a domain, you have to find a server to "host" your website. A Google search for *web hosting* will turn up all sorts of great bargains. The site that sold you the domain may offer hosting as well. Make sure the service has a guaranteed up time, meaning the service (and your site) doesn't suddenly go away for any period of time. You also want some decent customer support in case you run into any snags setting up your site.

Tips for creating a memorable teaser site

An effective teaser site pushes people to react by signing up, sharing it, bookmarking it to come back to later, or possibly all three. The site should reveal just enough to intrigue viewers.

The way to get people to remember your site, hand over an email address, and share it with friends is to use a gimmick. You can tell a story about what your app does, share your teaser video, or try some subtle animation. Another way to entice visitors into sharing their email address is by offering beta testing invites or giving them a freebie in return.

After visitors sign up, make it easy for them to instantly share your site on Twitter or Facebook with a click of a button. Trust goes a long way, so assure them that you won't share their email with anyone or spam them with unnecessary newsletters. And include all your social networking links so they can get in touch and start following you.

A good teaser site

- Has content that is memorable and informative, and builds your brand.

- Includes all your social networking links.

- Includes a teaser video.

- Allows email signup and rewards people with beta offers or freebies.

- Makes it easy to share the website link.

- Includes a press kit (not necessary, but if you have one, why not put it out there?).

Should you use a landing page service?

You can use a website service to quickly generate a teaser page of your own, saving you from having to devote precious time and resources building a sign-up and invitation system that will be used only once. Here are a few options:

- Launch Rock (launchrock.com)

- Unbounce (unbounce.com)

- Prefinery (prefinery.com)

With the exception of Prefinery, most teaser page services require that you redirect your domain name to their site. Doing so gets your site up quickly and cheaply; plus, it saves you from hosting a site, but there's also a downside to it: it will be harder for people to discover your site in Google searches.

I won't get into the entire science of search engine mechanics, but I will share two ways around this dilemma. You can purchase a template to quickly get a teaser site up and running. Theme Forest (themeforest.net) has templates for as little as $8. Another option is create a custom site. Either option will require that you hire a developer; you can do that through Odesk or Elance. You can also post a competition on 99designs.com, or hire a professional shop that will really give you a polished site.

Collecting names and addresses

One of the main goals of creating a teaser site is to collect email addresses. But what do you do with those addresses after people hand them over? Some website services, like Launch Rocket, collect email addresses for you and the list can then be exported to a CVS file. But you still need a place to store everyone's details, yet keep them separate from your work contacts and personal contacts.

This is where a marketing email service such as MailChimp (mailchimp.com) or Campaign Monitor (campaignmonitor.com) is important. These services are designed to manage your subscribers, send newsletters, and track the results. They make it easy to send out beautiful newsletters, and provide reports on who opened the letter, the links clicked, and how long it was viewed.

Both services provide a snippet of code that is easy to embed and style on your website, so email addresses collected on your site go directly to your MailChimp or Campaign Monitor account, saving you the time of having to add each one. You just put a little code on your page, and they handle the rest. Both of these services are affordable, easy to use, and well worth looking into.

Tips for an effective app website

If an app's website is stunning and informative, the app will be just as smokin', right? That's what your customers, bloggers, and media think, and it's the first place they'll look to learn more about your app. So as soon as your app goes live, launch a striking website along with it. The majority of visitors to your site will decide whether to buy your app within a few seconds, and you only have one chance to get it right.

The first thing your app site must do is *tell* people what the app does. Right below the app name, create a tag line that explains the purpose of your app. Make sure it's just one short sentence that can be read and understood in a glance.

The second thing your site must do is *show* what the app looks like. Include at least one screen shot above the page fold. If you have a video, put it next to an image of the app. Don't ever make people click to view an image of your app.

The third thing is to briefly *summarize* the benefits of using your app. Include an attention-grabbing description of your app's functionality, and a feature list that can be quickly scanned. Include your big pat-on-the-back stuff and rewards, but leave out the nitty-gritty technical details.

The download button should be huge and obvious. Don't throw up any obstacles to getting to the iTunes Store by making visitors register or subscribe to a newsletter first. These obstructions will just kick off an angry relationship and leave you back paddling.

Make the price obvious. If it's a freemium, let customers know that they'll have to pay to unlock the best features. Now is the time to be completely transparent and honest about your prices.

Figure 6-10 shows all these elements on the Gratitude Journal webpage.

FIGURE 6-10: The webpage for my Gratitude Journal app is an example of how to lay out the elements of a good app site.

Customers, bloggers, and the press will want to get in touch with you, so offer an email address or a contact form. Communication is exactly what you want, so don't try to hide from people. They'll just wind up not trusting you in the end.

As people scroll down the page, unfold the story of your app. Show additional images and highlights of your app. Include the long list of testimonials. Add your newsletter signup form and links to your freebies.

Your header and footer should also have links to your social media sites and blog. If your site enjoys a healthy stream of traffic, show it off with visible counters from Twitter and Facebook. You can tuck away your link to your press kit in the footer where reporters are used to finding them.

The process of building and maintaining websites is trickier than you might think. It also costs more than you might expect. But if you spread the cost of the site over four or five years and consider your potential return, that amount starts to seem a lot more palatable.

One way to lower the investment cost is to build a one-page site. The development time will be shorter. It also forces you to cut through the clutter and include only the most important content. The downside is that it's really only good for showcasing one app, which might be a problem in the future as your app portfolio and business grows.

Tips for a Successful Email Campaign

Sending an email campaign is like stepping into the living room of each person on your distribution list and paying him a visit. Like any good guest, you don't want to intrude too often or overstay your welcome. Respect the fact that they even let you in the door, and consider your visit on borrowed time. Make it quick, punchy, and to the point. The following tips will help you.

Repeat after me: no spam!

Make your emails a rare and special occasion. If you contact people too much, they'll mark your address as spam, and your next message won't even reach them. Worse, services like Google will also tag your address as spam, so all future distributions end up in the junk folder whether or not the reader wanted it. Send email only when you have reached a really big milestone or go live with your app. Other than that, keep your messages on your blog and social media sites.

And you are?

Introduce yourself immediately. Put your name and business in the "from" field so people know who is contacting them without having to open the email. Clearly place your website and social media links at the top of the email where people can find them.

Boring subject lines actually work better

You may think a clever, catchy title is the way to grab interest, but actually you should use a straightforward, non-salesy subject line. The email service MailChimp recently reviewed the subject lines of over 40 million emails sent from customers through its service, and analyzed the ones with the highest open rates and the ones with the lowest (see http://kb.mailchimp.com/article/how-do-i-know-if-im-writing-a-good-subject-line). MailChimp discovered that the subject lines that were honest, direct, and perhaps even boring did the best and emails that even *hint* of spam just get deleted. At the top of the list was this subject line:

[COMPANYNAME] Sales & Marketing Newsletter

At the bottom of the list were emails that sounded like advertisements, such as this one:

Last Minute Gift – We Have the Answer

Don't write your subject line like something found in a Sunday flyer. Worse, don't use one that is completely different from the content of the email such as "Thanks for coffee" or "You won the lottery." We've all had our fair share of those, thank you. Be direct and honest, and use as few words as possible.

Use space wisely

The top part of the email is the most precious real estate, so don't make readers scroll to get to the most important information, like the download link. Also, expect most of your readers to view the email on their mobile device, so optimize it for mobile users.

You want the name of your app, the tag line, a screen shot, and a link to download all above the page fold. Anything below won't be viewed unless your newsletter is really good.

Make it quick and reward them

You have only a few seconds to grab the readers' attention, so make your email easy on the eyes and a quick read. The content must be meaningful and interesting, and the next step as plain as the nose on their face. If it's to download your app, the button should be big and obvious. Also, give them a reason to take that next step right now. For example, if you're announcing the launch, give them an incentive to download the app now rather than waiting.

Use images sparingly

Most mailboxes are configured to automatically block images in emails, so don't use too many. Test that your message can be clearly read with images turned off. If it can't be understood, your campaign will fail, and your message might just end up in spam boxes. Emails with attachments will almost always end up in spam, so avoid those as well. Figure 6-11 shows an example of an image that works well in an email.

FIGURE 6-11: The Readability app launch email was easy to scan, used very few images, and had the "next action" buttons clearly above the page fold.
Source: Readability

Make it easy to share

Include icons so readers can easily share your email with a single tap. They should be able to forward to a friend as well as share on all the social networks. You want to extend the reach of your audience as much as possible. If even a fraction of your readers share your email, you'll be that much better off.

Answer replies

If readers invested their time to reply to your email with warm wishes, you should return the gesture and thank them. A simple hello back builds trust and respect. The next time you ping them, they will be sure to open your message and possibly share it with their network.

Making Money from Your App

It used to be that selling apps was the best way to strike gold in the app market. But some developers hit the jackpot by giving away their app, whereas others are finding profit outside the App Store. The truth is that not all roads lead to profits, and picking the best revenue model for your app can be tricky.

Remember, if one revenue model isn't working, try a new tactic. Changing tack halfway through the journey is okay and may actually help sales. Here are a few suggestions to get you started.

Pricing your app in the paid model

Apple lets you price your app as low as 99¢, on up to $999.99 per download. The sweet spot for the impulse-buying app crowd tends to be the bargain price 99¢. Plenty of developers are just following the herd, selling apps for peanuts and hoping for a huge volume of downloads.

Because competition has pushed app prices to the floor, customers now expect most iPhone apps to be either free or 99¢. But an informal market study done by *Business Insider* found that around 75 percent of people willing to pay 99¢ would also pay $1.99 or $2.99 (read more at http://www.businessinsider.com/how-to-figure-out-if-your-iphone-app-will-get-you-rich-2009-8#ixzz28GQ8PRk0). If your app is clearly a Maserati in a sea of beat-up Dodges, don't be afraid to charge more. You can always drop the price later.

The interface and features of any iPhone apps higher than that golden 99¢ price tag must stand head and shoulders above the other apps; otherwise, people will feel ripped off and won't hesitate to leave negative feedback. Sure, your app cost less than their skinny latte and was a darned sight harder to make, but they will still feel fleeced.

Universal apps and apps targeted solely for the iPad are a different story. At the time of writing, only *8* of the top 50 iPhone apps are priced above 99¢ compared to *30* iPad apps that are higher. With fewer of these devices on the market, there are simply fewer app sales.

Pricing your app can be agonizing. You might simply decide to follow the 99¢ trend because it seems safe. How many times have you contemplated purchasing an app, thinking that it's only a buck? It's a gamble, but for that price, any buyer's remorse is short-lived.

You can see what your top competitors are charging and try to undercut them or match their price. You may also try to do some research to calculate how many people will actually download your app and do the math. I found the latter to be more like asking a crystal ball.

Make sure to price it low enough that people would buy it on impulse even though they have no need for the app.

—Mark Jardine, co-founder and designer at TapBots (Tweetbot app)

When to give it away for free

You could actually make a lot more money giving your app away for free. Just look at Instagram's $1 billion success story. Other apps like Snapseed and Glancee were also snatched up in Google's and Facebook's shopping spree. Because these apps became so wildly popular, they were acquired by software giants for millions. There's no limit to what a good app could turn into.

Because social networking apps depend on a large customer base for their content, it might be smart to offer them for free, at least for the first month. Customers are doing these apps a favor by installing and using them, adding to their value. Also apps that are advertising for companies are blessed when customers choose to have the apps' message on their phone. Let them have it for free.

Being acquired by a billion-dollar tech firm, building a huge social network, or promoting a business might not be what your app is all about. There are still profitable reasons to give it away. Launching a free app can get you noticed. You can make money through ads or in-app purchases. Or you might be creating a taster of a bigger app. Let's look more closely at these models to see whether one fits your app.

How the free-to-paid model might be the ticket

It goes without saying that free apps typically get more downloads than those for sale. Giving away your app for free for a limited time can give it the spotlight exposure it might need to be pushed into the top of the charts. When an app goes from paid to free or launches for free for a limited time, the blogosphere pays attention. We all love free things and will brag to everyone about an incredible steal when we discover one. Some sites even specialize in tracking price drops, like AppShopper.com.

Free can be a great way to launch your app because it attracts reviews that are critical for future sales. It also lets bloggers and fans try out your app without having to pay for it first. You won't make any money from the app, but futures sales drawn in by word-of-mouth hopefully will more than make up the difference.

The difference between free and lite

Who doesn't like a free sample? A stripped-down version of your app lets people sample it before paying for a fully loaded version. This marketing tactic has boosted sales for a lot of developers. A try-it-to-see-if-you-like-it version is more than a demo, and Apple has some pretty strict rules about "lite" apps.

Every app needs to be fully functional and stand on its own. If it's a game app, for example, you can leave out some levels of your game, but you can't remove the app's core features. This is where you get into that gray area of what exactly is considered a core feature, and unfortunately Apple hasn't fleshed it out in detail. Lite versions might not be stripped down at all, but in fact fattened up with ads that will go away only when users fork out for the paid version.

The drawbacks are that a lite app doesn't make any money unless you fill it with advertising or it entices people to buy the full version. It will also cost extra money to design and develop. In the end, lite apps could actually hurt your sales because people will just get the free version and never bother with paying for a full version. Because of these drawbacks, many developers are using the in-app purchase model instead.

The latest fad: In-app purchases

The in-app purchase model is spreading like wildfire, and proving it can be a lot more lucrative than charging people 99¢ up front. Almost all the top 25 grossing apps are "freemium"— free with in-app purchases. The company NaturalMotion reported earning $12 million through in-app purchases in just a single month with its game *CSR Racing* (www.tuaw. com/2012/08/15/natural-motion-on-track-to-make-12-million-a-month-with-csr-rac/). When your in-app purchase is done right, the micro-moola adds up pretty quickly.

The trick is to give people an app robust enough to get them to download it in the first place, and then find a way to convince a majority of the customers to part with a couple of dollars. A free app is the more popular method because of the higher volume of downloads, but well-designed paid apps can also profit from in-app purchases.

The app must be simple, engaging, and addictive. Give users plenty to play around with so they get hooked. When they're in the zone, confident about using it, and enjoying it, drop in the in-app purchase.

You can also offer an in-app purchase when users get to a critical stage in the app, such as buying a player to win a game. Or customers can buy more tools, themes, or options. Or purchase the full subscription for a radio, magazine, or dating service. Customers can purchase coins, new characters, and food for those characters. Just to give you an idea of the potential, the company TinyCo made $50,000 selling the character The Cash Cow, according to Chief Executive Suli Ali.

Infomercials are great for inspiration for in-app purchase strategies. Make an offer available for a limited time only, or the next purchase is reduced or half price but only if the customer buys before the offer runs out. Most people are already familiar with the buy-now-or-lose-it-forever sales tactic. Limited quantities or time on a discount creates a feeling of urgency, and it works.

Making money with iAd and other advertising options

Bombarding customers with ads in hopes that they will click to make a penny may work for some developers, but I shy away from the advertising model for a couple of reasons:

- If you do the math, whatever you make from selling your app for just 99¢ well outperforms giving it away and hoping your customers click on the ad.

- Your app would have to flood customers with adverts to make up the difference.

The advertising model is best for apps that are sticky. *Sticky apps* get used on a daily basis, over and over. Facebook, Twitter, and Instagram are all good examples of sticky apps. I use them at least a half dozen times a day. The more people open the app, the more they'll see the advertisement, and the higher the chance they will click and you'll make a few cents.

Various services automatically rotate different advertisements in your app, including Apple's iAds program. Only the ads that are relevant to your app are supposed to appear, but when I toyed with iAd in an app designed to improve health, ads for potato chips were displayed.

Only free apps should have advertisements. Charging customers for an app filled with ads will only create an uproar of protests. You can give customers the option to turn off the ads through an in-app purchase. After the customer buys this from you, the annoying ads no longer appear.

Think outside the app

Now we can all go to sleep snuggling our Talking Tom plush toy, resting on an Angry Birds pillow in our Where's My Perry pajamas. Spinoff products of your app's character or customers' creations are becoming increasingly popular.

Your app doesn't have to be a top seller to push your other products. An accompanying mobile app is now the must-have accessory to books, artists, services, or businesses. The app itself might not make any money, but it's driving sales elsewhere.

Sincerely Inc created a line of apps all designed to sell printed cards. Customers enter credit card details directly in the app to have a printed card sent through snail mail. The secret is to offer products you can sell at the same prices as apps so you can capitalize on spontaneous purchases. Larger ticket items might sell too, but perhaps not in volume.

The Generosity Principle

Although I create apps, my real-life business icon is the owner of a simple little coffee shop. He's incredibly nice; sneaks me a free cookie or coffee every now and again; remembers everyone's name; and is just downright respectful, cheerful, and awesome. He takes his time with each customer, shares a laugh, and sends people on their way with the most delicious coffee and scone. His little shop survived the recession just fine because his business model is to be ethical, decent, and giving.

If you want to build a truly great app business, reflect these same high ethical standards. Give back to society, be helpful and honest, and do what is right.

Donate to a charity

Supporting a charity was the easiest and best decision I ever made in my career. It's something I chose to do to pay back to society. You don't have to show a profit to give back. There are other ways to help out either with your time, expertise, or simply encouragement.

I selected a charity that reflected the goals of my apps and committed to donate a certain percentage of my app profits. The more my app sells, the more I can give back and that's a huge motivator. Charitable donations are the ultimate pick-me-up when everything around you is going crazy. They make the madness entirely worthwhile. Not only that, giving speaks volumes about your personal character because it shows you have integrity and concern for others.

Find a launch sponsor

Everyone wants to be in the app business, but most people don't want to have to create an app. Look for a business or an individual with a background that gels with your app and ask if they would like to co-sponsor your launch. Your chosen charity might already have a sponsor. A familiar brand or face teamed up with a new app may attract new audiences for you while helping the other business, charity, or personalities get ahead as well.

Create a promotion

Plan a contest, sweepstakes, or quiz to gain both exposure and new fans. Invite your app sponsor in on the deal and let its product or service be the prize. Start with a small promotion to test the waters, and then create a bigger one for your launch. Google's Wildfire (wildfireapp.com) service lets you rapidly create and launch promotions across multiple social networks, including Facebook, Twitter, LinkedIn, and YouTube with its "Pay-by-Day" campaign.

Order some business cards and freebies

Order about 200 cards and be prepared to hand them out to everyone you meet. As soon as people hear that you create apps, their eyes will light up and they will want to know more. Have a card handy to pass along that says everything. The site moo.com offers inexpensive cards that you can customize.

Hand over a small gift, and the recipient will probably download your app then and there. You can create buttons or stickers, or put your brand on some candies, pencils, USB sticks, and all sorts of other products. Keep a stash on you at all times and hand them out. It's not just new fans that will get a kick out of the freebies. Bloggers, media, and even multi-millionaires will remember you for the take-aways, too. Have a stash handy when you go to meet-ups, conferences, and drinks with friends.

App Marketing Checklist

Every app marketing plan is different because every tribe is unique. Use these steps as a blueprint to help you build your own marketing strategy. You can begin any of these activities during whichever phase of your project that works best, as well as add other activities to the mix.

Before designing your app

- ❏ Identify your tribe. Does your audience share a passion, idea, stage of life, or desire for change? How will your app impact their lives?
- ❏ Get started on social media. Try to post something each day to at least one social media site. Start sharing your story and build your fan base.
- ❏ Make friends with bloggers and journalists. Pick the most influential writers your tribe follows and follow everything they write. Post comments on their blogs, respond to their tweets. Start to reach out and build a relationship.
- ❏ Start writing. You don't need to be a prolific writer; just share information and make yourself an expert. Post comments on blogs your tribe follows. Create content for other sites.
- ❏ Create a teaser video. A short, cryptic message to entice people about what's to come builds up the anticipation and your audience.

continued

continued

❏ Register your domain name. If you're not sure of your app name yet, that's fine. Get a domain name that reflects what the app does.

❏ Set up your email address and add your social networks and website to your signature tag.

❏ Create a teaser website to build your brand and start collecting email addresses.

❏ Sign up for a marketing email services such as Mailchimp or Campaign Monitor.

After design

❏ Update your teaser website with screen shots, logos, and your app icon.

❏ Start sharing your design on social networks. You don't have to reveal the entire screen. Just a section will ignite curiosity.

❏ Tell people the time frame of the launch and give them a reason to mark it on their calendar.

❏ Send an email to your subscribers sharing your designs. Offer them a freebie download or an exclusive look that is available only to subscribers.

❏ Update all your social media sites with your logo and icon. Use your app icon or your logo as your image and get it in front of people so they start to recognize your brand.

After development

❏ Create a viral video. Show your app in action in the video. If it's good, it can also be your demo video for the press.

❏ Publish your launch date. Put it on your website and social media sites, and email your distribution list. Let people know the date to expect your app.

❏ Write all your promotion copy. Compose your product description for iTunes, the content for your website, and other marketing materials. Proofread it multiple times and get someone else to read it, too.

❏ Create screen shot "mini-ads" of your app. Capture five screens of your app and put together mini-ads of each one to be posted on iTunes.

❏ Put together your press kit. Create a zip file that has high-resolution copies of your icon, app screens, and logo. Also include a reviewers' guide to really make the press happy.

- ❏ Create a new website with your products. A one-page site is all you need. Continue to collect email addresses. Share your social media links, your press kit, and let people contact you. If you created a uniquely designed website, submit it to design galleries to be featured.

- ❏ Put together a support site. You can use a bulletin board–type service such as Get Satisfaction, User Voice or Zendesk, or you can create an FAQ page. You must have a support link to provide to Apple when you submit your app.

- ❏ Create a launch marketing email. Produce a newsletter people not only will read, but are happy to pass on to their friends. Templates are available online, or you can hire someone to create one for you.

- ❏ Prepare blog posts and other social media content. Draft your blog post before launch so you have time to proof it.

- ❏ Craft emails to journalists and bloggers. Prepare a personalized message to each of your blogger and journalist celebrities with your app details.

Launch

- ❏ Send out promo codes giving bloggers and journalists a sneak peek. As soon as Apple approves your app, get some promo codes and send them off to your journalist friends for a special preview of the app.

- ❏ Close shop for exclusive first lookers. Take a note out of Apple's book and close shop for 24 hours before launching. This gives you a chance to update your live site and use it to replace your "coming soon" site.

- ❏ Double-check everything on iTunes. Make sure Apple listed your app correctly, you can download it, and it works fine.

- ❏ Roll out your new site. Do this the night before you launch to make sure it all goes smoothly. Make sure all the links are working and spelling is correct. Redirect any old links to the new site.

- ❏ Send out your launch newsletter. Double-check it for spelling one last time and then send it off to your fans.

- ❏ Post your blog and get on the social networks. Update your blog post with any new details the day of launch and post it as soon as your app goes live. Send out the message on the social networks. Start conversations with anyone who mentions your app.

- ❏ Send personal messages to your best fans. Recognize those who have supported you through your journey. Send them a tweet, or post on their Facebook wall. Express your gratitude.

Key Points

- Give people a story to tell. Pull at the heart strings, stir up some emotions, or just be adorable and funny. Half of your time should be spent connecting with others and the other half creating.

- Don't pay for advertising. Instead, have people come to you because they want to hear what you have to say. Share your knowledge, secrets, and brand openly. Give away your app regularly and reward people for helping you spread the word.

- Keep writing. Write on your blog and for other blogs, post comments on sites, and put together a book of everything you learned.

- Your app website must tell people what the app does, show them how it looks, and let them download it. Don't make people click a button to see the interface, and make the download button the biggest one on the page.

- Keep email campaigns short, punchy, and to the point. Use a mail marketing service to help you manage your contact lists and email campaigns.

- Play around with the various pricing models. If one isn't working, lower your price or give your app away for a few days.

- Be generous with your customers. Give back, be helpful and honest, and do what is right. Your generosity goes a long way in both respect and karma.

CHAPTER 7

Maintaining Your App and Going the Distance

"Success is not final, failure is not fatal: it is the courage to continue that counts."

—Winston Churchill

While most developers would agree that the first sales are the hardest, staying in the game is actually the bigger challenge. The truth is that most apps lose 76 percent of their customers after the first three months of use (*Entrepreneur Magazine*, August 2012). That's over three-quarters of your hard work deleted from devices. Poof! No matter what your pricing model is for your app, revenue streams dry up pretty quickly. To go the distance you need to not only keep improving your app but also focus on the larger picture. The longer you're around, the more your customers and onlookers can say good things about you, spreading word-of-mouth and increasing profits. So rather than thinking of achieving your goal as the finish line, see it as the launching pad for achieving more.

This chapter helps you prioritize your workload so you can keep growing your app and your audience slowly over time. It shares ways to research new features before investing in them. You learn how to expand your app to new markets as well as other smart devices. The chapter steps you through the process of updating your app and explains when it might be best to create an entirely new one. Lastly, it reveals the one biggest secret to long-term success.

Working on Your Business as Well as Your App

Every day is an opportunity to expand your audience, increase your knowledge, and improve your app. At least half of your time will be spent on the bigger picture of *growing your business* and the other half on *maintaining your app*. Too often app developers get lost in the finer details of their apps and lose focus on the bigger picture. Set aside time to connect with others: answering support emails, replying to messages on the social networks, reaching out to influential people. Keep learning about the technology and advancing your talents, and look into ways to grow your business with new apps, byproducts or partnerships.

The other half of your time will be devoted to improving your app. Continue to study other apps and the market. Download at least one app each day and try to learn as much as you can about the newest design ideas. Devote time to improving your app's usability, working with your developers on bugs and testing, and exploring new features or designs to enhance your app. Most importantly, just keep taking action.

UPDATE

Tweaking Your Way to the Top

Perhaps the most obvious way to cultivate happy customers is to continually tweak your app over time. You want to periodically release updated versions of your app with small changes, starting with bug fixes. Even if your app happens to be the first piece of software ever created in the history of mankind to be completely bug-free, you can always improve the interface and features.

Start by focusing on small changes rather than large reworks, so you can turn around new builds a whole lot faster. Incremental changes are quicker to do and can have just as big an impact. Also, releasing a series of small tweaks will help you set up a reliable process so you master the art of updates. Each time you work on an update, it will be easier because you have a series of steps and a proven process already in place.

Regular updates send the message to both your customers and onlookers that your app business has a pulse and is alive and thriving. These updates give them confidence in you and your products, and that translates into more downloads and sales. Let me explain how this process works.

The boomerang theory

When an update appears on your customers' devices, it's a subtle reminder to them that your app is on their device, so they tend to use it more. It also shows your commitment to them by improving and supporting your app.

After updating the app, customers tend to open it and use it to see what has changed. People who may have stopped using your app for whatever reason could return, increasing your app's overall usage. Usage is especially critical if you're depending on advertisements in your app or in-app purchases for your revenues. Regular updates nudge customers to use your app again and give them more opportunities to tell others about it.

In addition, their loyalty in your brand increases, and that will make any future sales a whole lot easier. Customers will *want* to come back and purchase from you again, including new apps you release as well as in-app purchases, because people are more likely to buy products from brands they already trust.

The addicts model

We're all addicted to something. Some are good habits, some bad. One of my biggest vices is my beloved coffee shop's rich triple chocolate brownie. And how did this addiction start? Not with just one free sample—I think my willpower could have countered that—but with a little freebie every time I stepped foot in the door. After a while I was hooked. Real bad.

Let me show you how you can use the addicts model as your marketing tactic. You launch your app for free so everyone can try it without paying a cent. This free release quickly grows a large customer base and exposure. You then update your app with bite-sized improvements to keep your customers coming back for more.

After a few updates, you introduce an amazing, can't-live-without-it feature that your customers can devour, all for a small in-app purchase fee. It can be a theme, characters, extra points, or backup services. Your addicted customers will come back for more—this time with money. People are more likely to buy the in-app purchase now because you already gained their trust and loyalty.

The children's book app Nighty Night (see Figure 7-1) initially launched for a fixed price and was enjoying wonderful success. After the app gained a strong following of satisfied customers, the developers capitalized on their good reputation by introducing an in-app purchase of new characters for the story. It became a gravy train for them because customers were already familiar with the quality of their products and features. After they had earned their customers' loyalty, sales were much higher.

FIGURE 7-1: The Nighty Night iPad app was originally launched for a fixed price. It wasn't until after the app had a following that the developers offered new characters available for in-app purchase.
Source: Nighty Night iPad app

It's an easy sale booster

Here's something you might not have thought about. When potential customers are considering purchasing an app, they notice when the app was last updated before they decide to download it (see Figure 7-2). If they see that an app hasn't been updated in months, they wonder whether it's neglected and may doubt if it even works, and you end up losing a potential customer.

Continuous updates show that you care about your products as well as customers, and that you value user input and are listening. Putting your business on autopilot is simply throwing away all the hard work you put into your app to begin with. Apps take tender loving care, just like any other living thing.

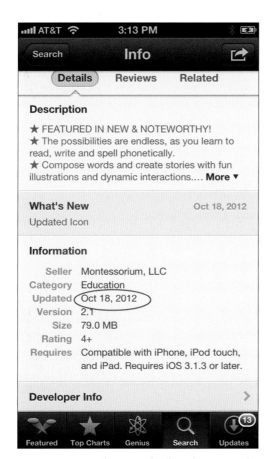

FIGURE 7-2: People notice the date the app was last updated when deciding whether to download an app, as shown here on the iTunes store.

Source: Apple iTunes

What to Tackle First

Although it might be tempting to get all those great features that didn't make it into the first release developed, tested, and in your customers hands, don't jump the gun. You need to think twice about what you do next because adding in new features is quite different after the app is already on iTunes and your customers are using it.

First, you have a lot more information to work with to help you make educated decisions about managing your app. You also have a lot more at stake. Tweaking your app takes some business literacy. If your first updates aren't in the best interest of your existing customers, you could risk losing future sales because of poor reviews. Not only that, you need the biggest bang for your buck. Investing all your hard-earned revenues into more coding might not result in a decent return on your investment. This next section steps you through all the things you need to consider when deciding how to improve your app.

Feedback and reviews

One of the best things about going live is that you finally get genuine feedback on your app. Some feedback might catch you completely off guard and surprise you. Some requests are flat-out crazy and impossible. And some comments might be exactly what you intended with your app.

Whatever your customers tell you, pay attention to it. *Write down the comments and track them* in a spreadsheet. You'll soon see the most popular requests add up while the odd ones sit abandoned at the bottom of the list.

TIP   If you use a tool like Get Satisfaction (http://getsatisfaction.com) for your customer support, all questions, ideas, comments, or praise is recorded and organized for you.

Your knee-jerk reaction might be to charge ahead with the top-requested features to keep your audience happy. But before beefing up your app, you must make sure all your existing designs and code are tiptop and running smoothly. Otherwise, you could be throwing good money after bad. So before we get into enhancing your app, let's talk about making it bug free.

Keep it simple. It takes discipline and restraint to keep an application focused on the task it was designed to do. Don't add features just because customers demand it.

Customer feedback is very important, but in the end it's your application and your job to make sure features directly support the purpose of your application. Less is more, especially on a portable device.

—Mark Jardine, co-founder and designer at TapBots (Tweetbot app)

Fix the bugs first

Take any bug reports as seriously as you would a tax audit because they're not just annoying, they can wind up costing you everything. You should plan to fix all bugs before adding any new features. As soon as customers start writing about bugs in their iTunes feedback, your app just hit a big iceberg and is going to slowly sink.

The first rule is to make it easy for customers to contact you with bugs, so the bad news comes to you directly rather than through an iTunes review. Also, take the time to reply and let them know you're on the case. Test each issue immediately and track all the details in the same spreadsheet you used for development. If you can't re-create the issue, see whether the customers will give you more details such as the type of device they're using, the iOS version installed, as well as the version of your app they're using.

Each update of your app has to go through the same approval process by Apple as the initial release. Because the approval can take weeks, try to lump as many updates as you can into a single release. Completing all the fixes might take longer this way, but using this approach saves you from waiting through dozens of approval processes; plus, it's easier on your customers to download only a single update.

Nothing is more annoying to both you and your customers than a buggy app. Of course, some bugs are clearly more important than others, so you should obviously concentrate on the high-priority ones. Really unimportant issues can wait, or perhaps even be addressed with a redesign. Some might not be technical bugs at all, rather confusing user interface design.

Ladybug, Ladybug

True story. I once released an update of my journal app that caused some people to lose their entries. To make matters worse, it only happened to the folks with more than 150 entries in their journal—my power users. The fallout was unbearable.

My gut reaction was to just delete all the angry emails I received and focus on a fix. Instead, I decided to sit down and reply to each one, explaining exactly what happened. Those customers did a complete one-eighty on me and offered to help me any way they could. Without them, I never would have discovered a fix to the app. Owning up to my mistake and taking the time to personally apologize to each complaining customer saved my business.

Improve usability

Equally as annoying as software bugs are any flaws in your design, so look at improving usability first, before tackling your new features wish list. Customers will wonder why you're investing time in new features when the current designs are less than optimal. Often tweaks to your app's usability are easy to change or enhance; plus they add just as much value to your app as a new feature.

Examine the analytics

We discussed integrating an analytic solution in Chapter 5, but how do you make heads or tails of the data? What does all that information tell you, and how do you use it to make decisions about your app?

One thing all analytic services offer is crash reports. These reports make it easier for your developer to discover what is causing a bug so it can be fixed sooner. Plus, crash reports flag any issues immediately, so you don't have to wait to read about a problem with your app in a precious review on iTunes. This gives you a timely advantage to addressing the problem.

If it's a big bug, the best thing to do is to fess up to the problem right away on your customer support site as well as in your blog and social network tools. Let everyone know you found a bug and are on the case, even if no one reported it or noticed it. People will respect you more if you go public and are honest about it.

Analytics also tell you how, when, and how long people are using your app and what screen they are on when they close it. For example, if people tend to stop using your app on the same screen, it might have a design flaw and be confusing users. Or perhaps they're missing the last step in a process. The data is most often real-time so it can be almost as valuable as if you're sitting right next to your customers and watching them use your app in person.

These services also report your user demographics and locations, which can help you determine where your strongest audience is located. You may discover that your greatest sales are from another country and you should consider localizing your app to make the most of the sales opportunity. Some app translation can definitely pay off, especially in Asia because apps in China, Japan, and Korea have proven to do better in the local language. Let's look into what is required to tap into new markets through localization.

Localize the description on iTunes

Perhaps the biggest sales opportunity that most developers let fall between the cracks is localizing their app on the App Store. Non-English-speaking countries account for more than half of the global revenue shares of iOS apps, so targeting these markets can be an easy boost in sales. Translating your app description is easier than localizing the app itself, so it's a good place to start to make huge strides into new markets. In fact, an even better place to begin is to simply translate your app name.

If people can't understand your description or name because they don't speak English, you are relying on your app icon, screen shots, and price to convert them into a sale. That's not the strongest approach to scoring more downloads from potential customers.

You can use one of the many online translation services to do a quick and cheap localization of your app name and description text. Also, localizing the name could have a big impact in countries such as Japan and China where localized character text will make your app stand out from the rest.

Be aware that a mistranslation can do more harm than good so it's wise to have everything double-checked by a native speaker to verify that the translations are not only accurate but don't cross any cultural boundaries. You don't want your app to be another legendary embarrassment such as the famous T-shirts sold to commemorate the Pope's visit that were supposed to say "I saw the Pope" (el Papa) , but actually translated as "I saw the potato" (la papa).

Unfortunately you cannot add translated descriptions and app names to submitted apps, so you need to submit a new release of your app to update the localization on iTunes. The best approach is to translate your app name and description before you submit the first release of your app so you can go live with a strong international foothold. That could really influence your launch.

Localize your app to expand your market

You may have heard the advice that if your app isn't successful in English, you shouldn't bother to localize it for other countries, but I beg to differ and your analytics data might also. Certain apps simply do better in other countries for a variety of reasons, and localization might just be the push your app needs. And it goes without saying that if your app is already a hit, it seems the next logical step to target international markets.

Start with one or two languages to keep your costs down while you learn the process, and use your data to select the strongest markets. The iOS SDK is designed so a single app can offer various languages, saving you the hassle of creating and maintaining different versions of the same app. It also has all the fonts needed.

The best time to start localizing your app is while you're designing it. Try to keep any use of language in your app to a minimum. If you can replace text with an icon and users can still easily understand it's purpose, do it. Doing so will automatically make your app simple to understand in other languages.

It's smart to let your developer know upfront that you plan to localize your app down the road so your project can be setup to accommodate it later. Make it a point to discuss how she would plan to handle localization.

Other factors to consider in localization include word length. Something short in English like "Tram Stop" translates into "Strassenbahnhaltstelle" in German. Yup, that word takes up nearly the entire width of the iPhone screen. If you have an input field next to that text, your design falls apart. Also, localization can affect the whole navigation of the app. For example, Arabic text is written right to left, and that can influence the entire design of an app.

Adding New Features to an App

At some point, adding new features to your app is inevitable, but before breaking out the checkbook to invest them, think hard about whether those features will pay for themselves in sales. In the traditional software world, people have a say in what version they want to own. For example, I'm perfectly happy with my Photoshop CS5, but I could upgrade to CS6 for a price if I felt like it. However, iOS apps don't work that way. For iOS apps, everyone who purchased your app gets all updated versions for free, so the development costs for your new features must be covered by new sales.

The way iOS code is structured doesn't make apps very flexible. You can change things, but if you take it too far, the app may stop working. Adding an email button on the About screen might not take that long, but you cannot integrate Facebook or iCloud in just a few hours, and doing so will drive up your costs and your workload. Depending on the feature, you might be better off creating a second app instead (see the upcoming section, "Should you create a whole new app instead?" for more on this approach).

The process of designing and adding new features is just like creating a new app. Start with low-fidelity mockups and work your way up from there. Always ask your app developer for input on your enhancement ideas before going forward with them. The new feature might actually do more harm than good if it's too difficult to integrate.

The first enhancements should always be the easiest to give you an opportunity to learn the update process. Pick the lowest hanging fruit first so you can set up a system of designing, development, testing, and submission. The last thing you want is to introduce new features riddled with bugs, so start with baby steps before you try a sprint.

Rocking the boat

It might surprise you, but nothing will create a tempest in a teacup faster than introducing a new feature or removing something. Don't panic. It's normal for people to resist change and react unfavorably.

People get used to doing something a certain way, and they can get upset when things become different. They'll write angry emails and ask you to change it back to how it was before. That behavior is perfectly normal.

Your immediate reaction might be to just give in and revert your app to its earlier incarnation. But sometimes it's better to stick to your guns and give people a chance to get used to the change. Even minor changes can cause an outraged response.

Unfortunately, the negative feedback you receive feels as if it outweighs the positive because it includes stronger language and more exclamation points. You may actually have more happy customers than dissatisfied ones, but you're unaware because the complaints sound louder, and satisfied customers are less likely to post comments. I know because I've been there.

Another True Story

After having my first app on the market for nearly four years with the same design, I decided to give it a complete overhaul with a modern look and beefed-up features. I basically created the app all over from scratch. Figure 7-3 shows images of the original and redesigned versions.

The outrage I received from customers after I launched the new design caught me completely off guard. I was so devastated that I was up for days trying to sort out the best way forward and even considered throwing away the new app and putting the old version back on iTunes.

Instead, I let things simmer down and replied to each message, telling people I understood their concerns. I explained that I was considering various solutions but needed to let it go for a while and see how it all panned out. What a wise choice that turned out to be.

continued

continued

FIGURE 7-3: The app before the redesign (top) and after (bottom). Changes this big should be rolled out with careful planning.

A few weeks later Apple selected the redesigned version of my app to be featured in the "New and Noteworthy" section on iTunes (see Figure 7-4). That would have never happened if I hadn't redesigned the app and stuck to my guns about keeping it on the store.

FIGURE 7-4: The redesign made the "New and Noteworthy" section. Sometimes change is good.

Taking your time to release

When you have real customers, you *really* have to sweat the small stuff. Test even the most minor features, because as the app goes through iterations, new problems can surface where none previously existed. No matter how much testing you do before releasing your updated app, you will almost always have issues, bugs, and problems that show up only after the app is out in the wild, so you need to do what you can to minimize them.

Your customers are using all sorts of devices and iOS platforms, so you'll also have to test your app on as many different devices as you can. An analytics solution in your app can help you determine which devices are being used the most so you know where to focus your testing efforts.

NOTE

Your testing plan needs to be as rigorous as before you first launched. Even if the new feature is on the Settings screen, you still need to test all the other screens and features to make sure they all are working perfectly. Remember, the app architecture isn't flexible, so even tiny changes can flame into disaster.

Should you create a whole new app instead?

The idea of building your app all over from scratch might sound ludicrous, but hear me out. If you're planning an extensive new design and features, starting over from scratch and releasing an entire new version of your app might actually be far more economical. Your current customers can continue with the old version as long as they like and won't be forced to update and change their habits. Your development costs could be significantly lower than if you tried to remodel an existing app. Plus, you can bank on all new sales.

Existing customers might not be happy to have to pay for the app again. You can offer it free for a period of time to smooth over the change with your current users and then start charging the regular price. Another hurdle to consider is that you will have to work on an entirely new promotion campaign, but you can use your existing app to give you a boost. A common approach is to update the existing app with a message that appears when users open it, letting them know about the new app with a link to the store.

It's not very typical for developers to release a new version of their app instead of an update to the existing version. That's not to say that such releases haven't been done with great success. Some customers may complain, but they will probably do that anyway if you change the existing app.

Managing Your App on iTunes Connect

Sometimes app developers get so engrossed in promoting their app on the social networks and through the Internet that they lose sight of the absolutely most important marketing tool: the App Store. Regardless of how people discover your app—through the media, friends, or by trolling iTunes—their final decision to download it is based on what they see in the App Store.

To avoid falling into that trap, make it a point to view your app on iTunes at least once a week to see how everything looks. After promoting your app for a while, you will have a better idea of what helps sales. You will also have new content such as glowing comments, reviews, and your audience's creations. Make the most of every bit of ammunition and put it on the front lines to help drive sales.

Keeping your app fresh and current

You can update some of the details about your app without submitting an updated version like the app description, screen shots and web addresses. If your app has been featured on iTunes, a major blog, or news publication, make sure you update your app description with the great news. Keep the screen shots fresh and include your new marketing messages on the images, too.

Your screen shots and description are working hard to sell your app, but it's easy to simply upload them and forget them, and that can give the impression that you're sloppy or neglectful. Studious shoppers scrutinize even free apps. If they return to your App Store page to find fresh screen shots and an updated description, the new material gives the impression that you're careful about the details and investing in the app.

Submitting new updates

Submitting updates for approval is pretty much the same process as sending the initial build. You use the iTunes Connect portal to inform Apple about the details of new updates for your app, and then submit your update using Xcode.

Just like going live, you have to wait for approval. You can also select when you want Apple to release the update. If you created a major release, it might be wise to plan the release date so you can have all your support crew on deck and ready to rally. When you submit your app, you need to provide a version number along with it. The following section explains the difference between major and minor releases.

Understanding software versioning

You're probably familiar with software versions (like iOS6) but might not be aware that there's actually a purpose to each number. Let me explain.

Each release of your app has a corresponding software number starting with version 1.0, the initial release. The most common number scheme is to assign a version number starting with 1, followed by a number for minor updates (like a small feature) and then a second number for revisions or bug fixes. The pattern is major.minor.revision, as shown in Figure 7-5. Together, these three numbers indicate what has been changed in the app.

2.3.4

major minor bug
updates updates fixes

FIGURE 7-5: Version number format explained.

In this example, the current version is 2.3.4. The "2" signifies it is a second major release. The "3" suggests that it is the third minor update of that release, and the "4" indicates that it is the fourth revision or bug fix. To further help you understand, the next section explains the difference between a major and minor release as well as a bug fix.

Major updates

Increasing the first number of your version from 1.0 to 2.0, for example, suggests that the app has some significant changes to its features, interface, or both. This is the big release for an app.

For example, Evernote recently released version 5.0 of its app with new features and layouts, including note creation, browsing, and advanced organizational options accessible with just one or two taps. The app's UI was also entirely redesigned to emphasize notes, notebooks, tags, and places. This was a major update.

Minor updates

Adding or removing features from an app isn't quite a major release, but is more than a bug fix. For example, when Facebook released version 5.1, it included multiple new features such as gift giving and photo filters.

Equally important to adding new features is removing existing functionality. Sometimes it's better to pull a feature because it isn't working correctly and is causing your audience stress. Dropping that feature might be better than fixing it and is considered a minor update.

Revisions and bug fixes

Most updates are small revisions to fix bugs. They don't change the features or the app structure like major or minor updates do, but rather make sure everything is working as intended.

Keeping Up with Apple and iOS Releases

As Apple customers, we know this story perhaps all too well. Just as soon as we finally break down and buy the latest Apple device, the company releases a newer version a few weeks later. It was less than six months after the iPad 3 hit the market that the iPad 4 was released; the new products ship that fast. Each new device and software update will potentially impact your app with code changes, designs enhancements, or both.

What new iOS updates mean for your app

Apple is pretty good about keeping developers in the loop about major iOS updates that will hugely impact your app by emailing you well in advance. The press and blogs like macrumors. com and appleinsider.com are also good at spreading the news.

But sometimes when Apple releases a major update or is about to introduce a new device like the iPhone 5, it lets only a few top developers in on the news before the release, while the rest of us play catch-up later. However, not being among the "chosen ones" can actually work in your favor.

Apple is known for not providing a lot of guidance in these exclusive releases, so the chosen developers often have to figure out how to make their app work on the new device or software under a very tight deadline if they want it to be available as soon as the device is publicly released. In the case of the iPad Mini or iPhone 5, the developers didn't have the devices to test on either. But let's face it; if Apple picks your app to be featured in a new release, you do whatever you can to make that happen. By the time the rest of the developers get in on the new product or update, the difficult hurdles have already been worked out by the pathfinders, and they generously share their insights.

> If you can see a major update or new product release on the horizon, hold off on adding any new features until after the release is out. Doing so might save you weeks of rework. **TIP**

Most iOS updates aren't too dramatic. But each time Apple releases a new update, you will have to download the SDK and update the version on your computer. Downloading is really easy to do now that the SDK is part of the Mac App Store. Just open the App Store program on your computer and click Updates. You will see Xcode listed; click on the Update button. It will automatically overwrite the current version on your computer.

After you update your iOS SDK and your devices, test all your app features on the new release. You should plan to do this with small updates as well as the big ones. You never know what might cause a feature to stop working.

> You should never use beta versions of Xcode or iOS to code an app because Apple won't accept apps developed on a beta version. **IMPORTANT**

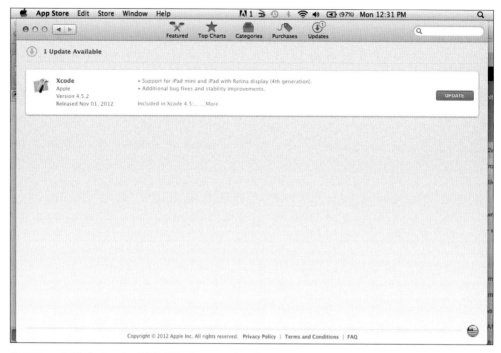

FIGURE 7-6: Updating the iOS SDK using your App Store app on your computer.

Porting your app to a new iDevice

If your app design is focused solely on one device, porting it to other devices might be a truly wise investment. Porting can give a fading app a new breath of life. But if your app is doing extremely well, it's pretty much a requirement.

Chapter 2 walked you through the decision of choosing which device(s) you want to design for: iPhone, iPad, or both. If you are considering porting your device, you face a similar decision as to whether to continue with separate apps for each device type or turn to a universal app.

> **NOTE** You might want to refer back to the section "Which Device Is Right for My App? iPhone, iPad, or Both" in Chapter 2 now for a quick refresher on the factors that go into making that decision, as they are relevant to porting your app as well.

Apps designed for the iPad are normally more complex than iPhone apps. Because they have more screen real estate to work with, most apps require entirely different interfaces and designs. Although the two devices are similar at what they do, the code can be drastically different under the hood.

Porting your app requires creating new images and rewriting a lot of existing code, so you may find it simpler to create a new app for the second device type. A lot of the existing code can be reused, thereby reducing costs, but it may still require a significant investment of time and money depending on your app design.

Here are some pros and cons to consider when deciding what is the best strategy for porting your app.

Universal Apps

Pros:

- Existing users will be delighted when they update and suddenly see support for all devices.
- You benefit from the existing ranking, reviews, and traffic to the app, rather than starting from scratch.
- You have only one app to manage.
- Apple likes universal apps, so it is more likely to promote your app.

Cons:

- You suffer a loss in sales in contrast to selling for two device types.
- Ratings and reviews may be misleading because they don't specify the device type.
- The app will take longer to download because it has assets and code for both platforms.

Two Separate Apps

Pros:

- You can set different pricing for iPhone and iPad.
- You can market the new app differently, in a way that suits the device best.

Cons:

- Existing customers may not know a new version is available for their other device.
- Having to migrate their data across devices can annoy current customers.
- Paying for the same app twice won't make customers happy.
- It's more work to manage two apps.

If your app appears identical on both devices, there is no question that you should release a universal app. Some app developers might tell you otherwise. Personally, I think it's worth more to keep customers happy than it is to make them pay twice for the same app.

Expanding to Android

If Android is the number-one-selling smartphone, why aren't developers clamoring to build apps for it? More to the point, why aren't all apps developed for Android first?

My career started with Android apps, but I never spend much time building for Android, so I don't have firsthand knowledge to comment on the revenue disparity between the two markets. A report in January 2012 by Investopedia.com states that Apple's App Store has earned about $4.9 billion in gross revenue for paid apps, whereas the Android Marketplace is estimated to have earned just $330 million in that market. That's a huge difference. Why? Because far more free apps are available for Android.

Even though there are more devices, Android is a Google product and people are used to getting Google products for free in exchange for putting up with the advertisements, whereas people are used to paying a premium for Apple products.

So why do app developers bother with Android if revenues aren't so hot? The Android market is growing rapidly, and expanding their customer base only benefits these developers. Also, the tools needed and costs for development are far lower for Android. And the operating system is completely open source, so you can do pretty much anything you want to do on the system.

Before launching into the land of Android, remember that it is *not* iOS. The platform is extremely different. The style and user interface guidelines aren't the same as the iPhone. Android owners have learned to use their devices in certain ways, so apps should be consistent with that design to make them easy to use and adopt. Apps that follow iOS guidelines are easy to use on iOS, but not so much with Android.

Before hiring a development team to re-create the exact same app on Android, invest in an Android device and study the interface. You might feel as though you're saving time and money creating an exact replica on Android, but it could actually damage your brand. One design doesn't fit all platforms.

The Law of the Vital Few

Before you close this book, I want to recap why we spent this time together in the first place. Some say the App Store gold rush is over, yet I'm still witnessing indie developers making a killing in app sales with one hit app after another. They're breaking all the rules and smashing some of the biggest plays out of the park. Why? Because small shops have less to work with, so they *have* to be creative and resourceful. They have less, so they have to use it wisely. It all boils down to the 80–20 rule.

An Italian economist named Vilfredo Pareto came up with the *80–20 rule*, or the *law of the vital few*. It states that 80 percent of the effects in a given sphere come from 20 percent of the causes (http://en.wikipedia.org/wiki/Pareto_principle). For example, the richest 20 percent of the world's population control 80 percent of the world's income. In business, 80 percent of the complaints come from 20 percent of the customers. Microsoft discovered that by fixing 20 percent of the bugs, 80 percent of the issues would be eliminated.

What does this have to do with app success? Let me tell you.

Ever since the App Store first launched, I have met some truly talented app developers who threw in the towel because their incredible apps earned them peanuts while really mediocre apps were climbing the charts. In their frustration, they gave up. As an outsider, I noticed that they all made the same big mistake.

They focused 80 percent of their time and energy into the development, when it accounts for only 20 percent of the app's success. They got too engrossed in the coding part of the project, pouring their efforts into the features and functionality, believing that if they build a truly stable and feature-loaded app, people will come. The app will simply sell itself. When the App Store first opened, organic growth was possible, but in today's market it takes more than that to get your app noticed among the millions of others.

The 80 percent of your app's success comes from putting your elbow grease into a meticulous design and a well-thought-out marketing strategy. That is why the longest chapter in this book is about design. It is also why I stress the importance of marketing right from the beginning and through every stage of the process. A halfhearted approach to either one of these efforts means you'll be begging your family at the next reunion to download your app.

You don't need big budgets to apply the 80–20 rule. There are countless things you can do yourself that will directly contribute to 80 percent of your app's success. You can do the initial designs, build relationships with the media and bloggers, and grow your audience. These tasks don't take any special skills or talents. They just take time and dedication. Pour your heart into your app project, and the rewards are beyond what you can ever imagine. Remember, if you can draw a circle, you can design an app. And if you can tell a story, you can build an audience.

Let Your Inspiration Guide You

As Garrison Keiller says, "Be well, do good work, and keep in touch." I hope you stop by my website, happytapper.com, and hook up to the social sites from time to time.

Most of all, I hope you enjoy the ride. Building a successful app is a huge challenge. Anyone who even takes a good shot at it has my deepest respect.

This book should take some of the bumps out of the road and make your journey a lot smoother. Of course, these ideas and methods aren't the only path to creating great apps. If you have a better way of doing something, go for it. Pursue your app dream in whatever path it leads you.

Index

A

accounting, 17
action sheet, 98
activity indicator, 97, 99
actors, for teaser video, 72
ad campaign, to micro-test, 65–66
ad clutter, 224
Add to Portal, 178
addicts model, as marketing tactic, 261
advertising, 253
agencies, as choice for developer, 154
alerts, 99, 126–127
Ali, Suli (TinyCo chief executive), 252
AlphaWriter, 7
Amazon, 62, 147, 235
Amazon Web Services, 62
ambassadors, 38
amusing (app strategy), 41–42
analytics
    to determine customers' devices, 271
    to determine who's downloading, 53, 271
    examining of, 266
    Facebook Insights, 231
    free services, 219
    Google Analytics, 66, 231
Android, expanding to, 278
Android Marketplace, 278
Angry Birds app, 15
animation, 97
API (application programming interface), 62
app approval
    countdown to, 214–219
    time for, 24
    while you're waiting for, 221
app creator, as CEO, 16
app IDs, 180, 212
App Lingua, 268
App Store
    Editorial Picks, 191
    Featured, 191
    as game of chance, 16
    history of, 14
    iPhone app, 82
    as labyrinth, 25
    layout for iPhone, 202
    as marketing tool, 272
    New and Noteworthy, 191
    for scouting out developer talent, 146
App Store Submission Tutorial, 212
app strategies, 40–42
app submission cheat sheet, 190
Apple
    active agreement with, 193
    advertisements as model, 72
    App Store earnings from paid apps, 278
    automatic icon adjustment by, 129
    Calculator app, 120
    Compass app, 120
    Developer Membership Program, 192, 232–233
    Development Program Membership, 32–33
    Find Friends app, 120
    getting paid by, 26–27
    grabbing Apple's attention, 24
    Human Interface Guidelines (HIG), 78, 80
    iAd program, 253
    icon collection, 95
    iOS updates, 275
    on length of app name, 130
    Member Center website, 32
    newer version releases of devices, 274
    pricing guidelines, 250
    promo codes, 197, 232
    sales reports from, 53
    what it does and doesn't tell you, 219
    working with, 23–27
Apple Design Award, 7
Apple Developer Portal, 145
Apple Inspires Me (design gallery), 101
Apple of My Eye (film), 70
Application Definition Statement, 57
application programming interface (API), 62
appreciation, for people who help you out, 147
apps. *See also* specific apps
    adding new features to, 268–272
    articulating benefits of, 40, 205, 245
    attracting attention to, 224–231
    average price for, 250
    benefits of targeting both iPhone and iPad, 51

apps *(continued)*
   cautions about including features that require
      moderating, 62–63
   corresponding software number of, 273
   creating second app compared to adding new
      features on first, 268–269, 272
   developing separate apps for different
      platforms, 54
   doing research for, 56–57
   first 200 characters of as most important, 205
   going live, 186, 190
   importance of being intuitive, 20–21
   importance of being obvious, 20–21
   indication of universal apps, 51–52
   installing on your device, 169
   keeping fresh and current, 273
   keeping your idea confidential, 64
   maintaining, 260–264
   never slam competitors' apps, 242
   as not very flexible, 268
   as offering something valuable, 46
   praise for other apps, 236
   protection of your idea, 64
   response to touch, 44
   as taking tender loving care, 263
   tucking away unnecessary elements, 126
   tweaking, 260–264
   types of, 51
   upcoming enhancements, 206
   updates, 60, 261–265, 273–274
AppShopper (website), 232, 251
Art Institutes, 72
artistic ability, needed to create app, 14
ASIHttpRequest, 156
AsyncSockets, 156
atebits (app company), 7, 40
audio, 42
autism, apps designed for people with, 25

B

backstage pass, 217
bad alerts, 127
bad notifications, 127
banking info, on app submission, 193
banner ads, 236–237, 241–242
Barnett, John (founder of Bright Mango), 225
bars, types of, 92–95
Basecamp (website), 31
BBC News app, 88
Beautiful Pixels (blog), 101
Behance (design gallery), 101, 137

bento box navigation, 85–87
beta testing, 64, 181
beta versions of Xcode or iOS, cautions with, 275
bid proposals, developers, 158–159
Big Nerd Ranch (code camp), 146
binary size, 53
Blimp Pilots (app company), 7, 235
blogs
   author's, 8
   Tumblr, 70
   using in launch, 195–196, 198, 214, 218
   using post-launch, 235
   WordPress, 69–70
blueprinting, 14
Bonjour (software), 156
book apps, 52, 89
bookstrapping, 16
boomerang theory, 261
Brichter, Loren (founder atebits 2.0), 7, 40
Bright Mango (app company), 225
broken flow, 101
budgeting
   advantages to of withholding key feature, 60
   to finance with own money, 15
Buffet, Warren (business magnate), 18
bug report, 182
bug-free, importance of being, 19
bugs
   apologizing for, 265, 266
   defined, 183
   fixing of, 186, 265, 274
   keeping track of, 182–184
   telling developers about, 184
   testing for, 176, 181
Bump app, 208
Burst app, 136
business cards, 255
Business Insider, 250
button and tab combo navigation, 91
buttons
   detailed disclosure button, 98
   five-button limit on iPhone, 82
   guidelines for, 22
   purpose, 99
   seven-button limit on iPad, 91
buzz, 181, 230

C

C++, 152
Cacoo (wireframing tool), 109
Calcbot app, 88

Calculator app, 120
camera (sensor), 42
Camera + app, 7, 18
Campaign Monitor (website), 245
captivating (app strategy), 41–42
carousel, 136
Casasanta, John (co-founder tap tap tap), 7, 18
celebrity bloggers, 195–196, 199, 215, 217
celebrity mobile designers, 137
charisma, 44
charitable donations, 254
charming (app strategy), 41–42
Churchill, Winston (UK prime minister), 260
class, 154
Classics app, 7, 127
Clear app, 14, 44, 45, 89, 100
Clever Coding (app company), 8
clever idea, as biggest factor in successful app, 36
click-through, 108
Clock app, 22
close shop day before launch, 216–217
cloud (flow diagram shape), 103
Cocoa (framework), 152
Cocoa Touch (framework), 27
code, not needing to know how to, 12
code camps, 146
code sample, from prospective developer, 156
coding, not core to successful apps, 19
color combinations, 44
colors, guidelines for, 22
Compass app, 120
competition, keeping eye out for, 187
compiler, 28
computer mockups, cautions with, 106
computer-generated prototypes, 112
conferences, 240
connecting with people/places (app strategy), 42
contact info, on app submission, 193
Contacts app, 96, 97
contest, as promotional tool, 254
contracts, 139–140, 161
contrast (design principle), 122
Convert app, 18
Convertbot app, 7, 45
copy (content), 44, 63, 97
CoreAnimation (framework), 156
CoreData (framework), 156
Counting Ants app, 8, 38, 67, 89, 123, 170, 210
cover photos/images, 239
Craigslist, 30, 146
crash reports, 266

critical tasks, 18
critical thinking, 17
cross-promotion, 236
CSR Racing app, 252
customer care
    adding contact link in app, 195
    apologizing about bugs, 265, 266
    within app, 195
    offering FAQ page, 195
    responding to negative reactions to new
        features, 269–271
    selecting support site, 194–195
customer love, building, 220
customers
    attrition of, 260
    expectation of for price of apps, 250
    reactions to new features, 269
CVS file, 244

D

Dandelion app, 45, 46
Data Protection (application), 180
decision (flow diagram shape), 103
decision making, 17
`Default@2x.png`, 139
`Default.png`, 132, 139
demographics, traditional, consideration of, 36
design
    ABC's of, 121–127
    as crux of successful app, 19
    skill, 17
design collection, building, 101
design inspiration, 100–101
design principles, 121–127
design problems, 79
design process
    avoiding letting ego dictate design, 104
    creating natural flow, 101–104
    dumping mental baggage, 104
    editing, 113
    feel-good factors, 125–127
    getting the ballpoint rolling, 78–80
    as iterative, 105
    making first impression count, 127–136
    navigation models, 80–92
    outsourcing, 137–141
    Pareto Principle, 279
    pixel perfect design, 119–120
    scaling up/down, 116
    shifting ideas into killer design, 104–110
    skeuomorphic design, 120–121

design process (continued)
   standard controls/elements, 92–99
   stealing good stuff, 100–101
   tests/testing, 110–113
   transforming mockups to masterpieces, 114–119
   tweaking after development, don't, 184–185
design specification (spec), 164–168
design tools, 30
designers, 137–141
designers block, 106
detailed disclosure button, 98
developer certificate, 178
Developer Membership Program, 192
Developer Program Resources, 176, 177
developer review checklist, 152–154
developer tools, 30
developers
   bid proposals from, 158–159
   breaking news of bugs to, 184
   connecting with online, 14
   creating distribution build, 214
   dealing with issues, bugs, tweaks, 170–185
   determining start of work, 159
   filtering out posers/rookies, 152
   finding dependable and talented ones, 144–151
   hiring, 13, 145
   hiring second developer to advise, 145
   interviewing prospective, 154–155
   job descriptions, 150–151
   keeping them happy, 162–163
   kicking off development, 164–170
   knowing when to fire, 185–186
   learning to trust your gut, 160
   list of, 6–8
   not enough experienced ones to meet
      demand, 144
   posting project and letting developer find
      you, 150
   rates for, 147
   reviewing prior work of prospective, 156–157
   scouting out talent, 146–151
   screening candidates, 149
   selecting best for your project, 152–161
   setting expectations upfront, 164
   signing contract with, 161
   spreadsheet of prospective, 157
   test-drive with mini project, 160
   time estimate for delivery, 160
   what they need from you, 168
   what to do if developer disappears, 185
   what you can expect from them, 168–169
   working with, 162–164

development certificate, 176
Development Program Membership, 32–33
DevRocket plug-in, 118
dialog box, 134
Diamond Dash app, 49, 50
discomfort, as sign on right track, 43
discount sale price, 232
Distant Shores app, 7
distribution build, 212–214
distribution certificate, 213
distribution provisioning profile, 213
Dollar Shave Club (website), 228–229
Domain Hole (website), 33
domain names, 33, 73, 243
donations to charity, 254
Donnelly, Paddy (co-founder Wee Taps), 8, 80,
   110, 111
download button, 245
download time, considerations in, 53
Dribbble (design gallery), 101, 129, 137
Drinkspiration app, 96
drop shadows, 129
Dropbox (website), 31–32, 62, 138

E
eBay, 30, 105
e-book, 235
editing, 113
Editorial Picks (App Store), 191
80-20 rule, 279
Einstein, Albert (physicist), 1, 224
Elance (website), 12, 146–148, 161, 185, 244
elevator pitch, 204
email addresses, collecting, 244
email campaign, 247–249
email signature, 187, 240
emails, 47, 215–216, 218, 220
emphasizing (design principle), 121
Engagement Letters, 161
entertainment apps, 89
Entrepreneur Magazine, 260
Etsy app, 83
Evernote app, 274
exclusive webinar, as promotional tool, 217
Explicit App ID, 180, 181

F
Facebook
   adding button to, 47
   author's page, 8
   as best way to stay in touch, 69

blue and white color combination, 44
harnessing the power of, 224
integrating with, 49–50, 57
iPhone app, 61
one-click sign-on via, 48
posting stories relevant to app project, 186
posting teaser video to, 72
for scouting out developer talent, 146
slide-out navigation, 84
as sticky app, 253
Timeline feature, 227, 239
Facebook 5.1, 274
Facebook ads, 66
Facebook Fan Page, 69
Facebook Insights, 231
Facebook SDK, 49, 50
Faces app, 7, 47, 48
FaceTime, 32
factory, 144
failure, 15
fan experiences, 219
FAQ (Frequently Asked Questions), 195
fat thumbs, 22–23
FBI, 63
Featured (App Store), 191
features
    adding new, 268–272
    customer reactions to new, 269
    identifying key, 58
    to leave out, 61–64
    prioritizing, 59–60
    starting with bare minimum, 16
feedback
    capturing of in design testing, 111
    from customers, 264
    on developer, post-project, 185
    on developer's skills, 157–158
    filtering negative feedback, 234
    providing to user, 97
    tracking of, 264
feel-good factors, 125–127
15-second rule, 20, 40, 59, 104, 112
file (flow diagram shape), 103
filename conventions, 119
filtered freelance sites, 146
financing, 15–16
Find Friends app, 120
Fireworks (software), 139
first impressions, 127–136
five-second test, 113
fixing a problem (app strategy), 41

Flickr (website), 62, 70
Flight+ app, 58
Flipboard app, 85, 91, 135
flow, 101, 102–103, 104
flow diagram, 102–103, 138, 165
Flurry (mobile analytics firm), 14, 219
font size, guidelines for, 21
Ford, Henry (industrialist), 144
formula, to creating successful apps, 10
framework, 144
Free App a Day (website), 232
free model pricing, 251, 252, 253
freebies, as promotional tools, 232, 234, 236, 237,
    240, 243, 244, 247, 255, 259
freelance job-posting sites, 146
Freelancer (website), 146, 147
freemium, 245, 252
Frequently Asked Questions (FAQ), 195
full app descriptions, 202

G

gallery apps, 85
game apps, 52, 89
Game Center app, 180
GameKit (framework), 156
Gangnam Style, 72, 224
Gates, Bill (business magnate), 190
generosity principle, 254
George, Bobby (founder Montessorium), 7, 25, 182
George, June (Montessorium team), 7
gestures, 44, 126
"Get it" testing, 111
Get Satisfaction (website), 194, 264
Giant Ant Design (website), 20
gift ideas
    for developers, 164
    for promotion, 255
GIMP, 31, 114, 118
Git Version Control (system), 32
GitHub (website), 169
Glancee app, 251
gloss effect, 129
Go Silk (website), 73
godaddy.com (website), 243
Godard, Jean-Luc (film director), 100
golden 15-second rule, 20, 40, 59, 104, 112
good alerts, 127
Good Morning America (TV show), 1
good notifications, 127
good stuff, stealing of, 100–101
Google, testing keywords in, 210

Google AdMob, 66
Google Alerts, 231
Google Analytics, 66, 231
Google Docs, 31, 138, 165
Google Drive, 31
Google Presentation, 103
Google Reader, 186, 231
Google spreadsheet bug report, 183
Google's Android, 278
Google's Keyword Tool, 210
Google's Wildfire, 254
Goop app, 85, 86
GPS, 42
graphicriver (website), 129
Gratitude app, name on phone screen, 132
Gratitude Journal app
    before and after redesign, 270
    App Store listing, 132
    banner ad, 237
    email to author from developer, 160
    Facebook cover image, 239
    mascots, 128
    origin of, 41
    redesign on New and Noteworthy, 271
Gratitude Journal webpage, 246
grid screen navigation, 85, 86
grouped style of table view, 97
grouping (design principle), 121, 122–123
GroupTalent (website), 146
growing your business, 260
guides, formats for, 134–136
Guru (website), 146, 147

H

.h files, 156, 174
Hack-a-Thon (website), 146
Hackatopia (website), 146
Haddad, Paul (co-founder Tapbots), 7
headaches, avoiding, 61
"Hello World" program, 171, 174, 175
"help" section, 134
hidden elements, 126
HIG (Human Interface Guidelines), 78, 80
Hinman, Rachel (designer), 80, 85
Hipstamatic (website), 228
holding position, 23, 54
Holmes, Oliver Wendell, Sr. (physician), 36
hottest apps, studying of as toxic, 43
HTML code, 237
Huffman, Esther (designer), 227
Hufkens, Alain (co-founder Wee Taps), 8, 59

Human Interface Guidelines (HIG), 78, 80
humor, in teaser video, 71–72
hype, creating, 224–231

I

iAd, 253
iBeer app, 120
iChat, 32
iCloud, 62, 180
icons
    Apple's standard collection of, 95
    design of, 127–129
    guidelines for, 21
    shortcuts to creating, 129–130
    sizing and naming of, 131
    templates for, 129
ideapreneurs, 2
ideas
    fresh and new ones as unnerving, 43
    ingredients for magnificent ones, 42–49
    transformations of compared to outright copies
        of, 100
identity, building, 226–227
iDevices
    deciding which to go for, 51–56
    porting to new one, 276–278
    purchasing the right one, 29–30
    screen size/image name by type, 116
Illustrator, 114, 139
image name, by device type, 116
image resolutions, 115–116
images, guidelines for, 21, 22
immersive apps, 88
iMovie app, 70
in-app purchase model, 252
in-app purchases, 180, 252–253, 262
inappropriate content, 63
incentives, to customers, 233
Indiegogo, 16, 56
infomercials, as inspiration, 252
input elements, 98–99
input/output (flow diagram shape), 103
Instagram
    described, 69
    as example of app development, 10
    harnessing the power of, 224
    improving on proven idea, 57
    screen shot, 11, 63
    as sticky app, 253
    as success story, 251
install file/installable file, 169

Intellectual Property (IP) attorney, 64
interface, 78
Interface Builder, 116, 156
intermediaries, 38
interruptions, 126
interview questions, for developers, 155
Intro to Geography app, 7
Intro to Letters app, 7, 182
Intro to Math app, 7, 25
Investopedia (website), 278
iOS
    cautions with beta versions of, 275
    defined, 28
    development of, 17
    keeping up with releases, 274
iOS App Designs (blog), 101
iOS developers
    bad rap of, 144
    as consultants on app features, 60
    as helpful, friendly, supportive, 145
    websites for hiring of, 13
iOS Distribution Certificate Signing Request, 212–213
iOS Provisioning Portal, 176–180, 192, 212
iOS SDK
    on Apple's Member Center website, 32
    defined, 28
    developers as needing to have experience with, 152
    Facebook SDK as more robust than, 49
    as one of two main development tools, 30
    standard controls/elements from, 92
    updating, 275–276
iOS Simulator, 28
iOS Team Provisioning Profile, 179
iOSpirations (design gallery), 101
IP (Intellectual Property) attorney, 64
iPad
    advantages of designing for, 54–56
    design galleries, 100–101
    navigation opportunities, 90–92
    price of apps for, 250
    purchasing, 29–30
    references to, 5
    required sizes for screen shots, 206
    resolution specs, 114
    screen size/required name, 134
    sideways (horizontal mode), 55
    sizing and naming of icons, 131
    status bar, 93
    vertical mode, 56
iPad 1 ... iPad 4, screen size/image name, 116

iPad Mini
    references to, 5
    resolution specs, 114
    screen size/image name, 116
    screen size/required name, 134
    sizing and naming of icons, 131
.IPA (iPhone Application) file, 169
iPhone. *See also specific topics*
    advantages of designing for, 54
    design galleries, 100–101
    price of apps for, 250
    purchasing, 29–30
    references to, 5
    required sizes for screen shots, 206
    resolution specs, 114
    screen size/required name, 134
    sizing and naming of icons, 131
    status bar, 93
iPhone 3G, 116
iPhone 4, 116
iPhone 5, 116
iPhone Application (.IPA) file, 169
iPhone Provisioning Portal, 176
iPhone simulator, 171
iPod touch
    purchasing, 29–30
    references to, 5
    screen size/required name, 134
    sizing and naming of icons, 131
iterative design process, 105
iTunes
    helping/hurting sales, 25–26
    how people scan, 202–203
    iPhone app, 83
    length of name displayed on, 130
    localizing app description on, 266–267
    reviews on, 53
iTunes Connect
    checking status of app on, 214
    completing app details on, 211–212
    getting set up on, 192–193
    managing app on, 272–274
    sales estimates posted on, 219
    screen shot, 197
    using to submit marketing materials, 202
iTunes Hall of Fame, 7

J
Jackson, Scott (creator), 238
Jardine, Mark (co-founder/designer at Tapbots), 7, 106, 113, 251, 264

job descriptions, for developers, 150–151
job interviews, with prospective developers, 154–155
Jobs, Steve (entrepreneur/inventor), 7, 25
Johnson, Victor (co-founder Playtend), 8
Jotly app, 70–71
Jotly—Rate Everything (video), 70, 71
JPEG images, 206

K

Keillor, Garrison (author), 279
key informants, 38
key task testing, 112
Keychain Access program, 176, 212
keywords, 210
Kickstarter (website), 16, 56
Koi Pond app, 7, 12, 235
Koney 2012 (documentary), 227
Kony, Joseph (head of LRA), 227

L

labels, guidelines for, 22
Landing Pad (app gallery), 100
landing page, 65, 73, 244
languages other than English, 267–268
launch day/launch date, 191, 217, 222. *See also* release date
launch email, example of, 249
launch image/launch screen, 132–136
launch sponsor, 254
launch tricks, 195–201
launchrock (website), 244
law of the vital few, 278–279
layered navigation, 90
layout, creating, 117–119
Lennon, John (musician), 41
Letterpress, 2, 7, 40, 121, 124
LinkedIn, 44, 146
lite apps, 251–252
Little Big Details (website), 45
LiveView (website), 110
LLVM (Low Level Virtual Machine), 28
LLVM Compiler, 28
localization, 266–268
location-based apps, 42
Lose It! app, 2, 7, 40, 51, 129
lovely ui (design gallery), 101
Low Level Virtual Machine (LLVM), 28
lynda.com (website), 140

M

.m files, 156, 174
Mac App Store, 275
Mac computer, 30
Mac Mini, 30
Mac OS X, 30
MacHeist (website), 7
MacRumors, 241
magic, planted in app, 45
Mail app, 56, 96
MailChimp (website), 245, 248
major updates, 274
marketing. *See also* promotion
　　checklists, 141, 186–187, 255–257
　　as crux of successful app, 19
　　email service for, 245
　　materials, submission of to Apple, 201–202
　　skill, 17
　　word-of-mouth, 224, 225
marketing plan, meaning of, 67
marketing plan, the $5
　　giving out promo codes, 232
　　having a sale, 232
　　promoting your app inside your app, 233–235
　　sharing everything, 236–241
　　teaching, 235–236
Martin, Dan (co-founder MindTapp), 8
mascot, 128, 236, 238
Mashable (website), 227
Matching with Friends app, 58
MBA (Master in Beautiful Apps), 100
Meetup (website), 13, 146
Meinzer, Shelby (co-founder MindTapp), 8, 103, 147, 190
memory management, 156
metaphors, 89, 129
micro-testing, 65–67, 73
MindTapp (app company), 8, 190
Minecraft, 101
minor updates, 274
mission statement, 57–58, 102, 138, 165
Mix Panel (website), 219
mobile devices
　　layers of distractions when using, 19–20
　　newer version releases, 274
Mobile Patterns, 100
The Mobile Frontier, 80, 85
mockups, 105, 114–119, 138, 167
MOMA's iPad app, 91, 92
Momonga Pinball Adventures app, 208

money
    making money from your app, 250–253
    as motivator to developer, 163
    needed to create app, 12, 15–16
Montessorium (app company), 2, 7, 25, 182
Morin, Dave (Path CEO), 226
motherhood tribe, author as member of, 37
The Murtaugh List (website), 73, 74
myths, debunking, 10–15

N
Name in Lights app, 7
Name Station (website), 33
name/naming
    of apps, guidelines for, 130–132
    of icons, 131
NaturalMotion (game development company), 252
navigation bar, 81, 93–94
navigation models
    bento box navigation, 85–87
    grid screen navigation, 85, 86
    immersive apps, 88
    as metaphors of real-life objects, 89
    nested doll model, 80–81
    slide-out navigation, 83, 84
    sliding cards navigation, 87–88
    swiping tabs navigation, 83
    tab bar navigation, 81–82
NDA (non-disclosure agreement), 64, 138, 154, 181
nested doll model, 80–81
New and Noteworthy (App Store), 191
newsletters, 141, 199–200, 235
.nib file, 116
Nigela Quick app, 88
Nighty Night app, 262
99Designs (website), 236, 244
The Non-Designer's Design Book (Williams), 122
non-disclosure agreement (NDA), 64, 138, 154, 181
non-English-speaking countries, revenue shares of iOS apps, 266
normal display (1x), 116, 117, 139
notifications, 126–127

O
Obama, Barack (US president), 226–227
Objective-C, 27, 144, 152, 156
oDesk (website), 12, 13, 146, 147, 149, 150, 244
office location, 27
Om Nom Stories (video), 70
OmniGraffle (software), 103

One Page Love (website), 73
online design galleries, 100–101
online translation services, 267–268
online tutorials, 140
Organizer screen, 178
originality, most amazing apps are not purely original, 100
OS X Lion, 30
OS X Mountain Lion, 30
output elements, 99
outsourcing
    for bootstrapping your project, 16
    for design process, 137–141
    Elance for advice on, 148
    experience, 17
Over HD app, 209

P
page (flow diagram shape), 103
page covers (website), 239
Paid Application Contract, 193
paid model pricing, 250
Panabee (website), 33
Pandora app, 52
Paper app, 128
paper prototyping, 106, 107, 111, 113
Paper Town Friends app, 45
Pareto, Vilfredo (engineer), 279
Parse (website), 62
Passes (application), 180
passion, importance of, 43
Pastebot app, 7, 94
Path 2 launch video, 226
Path app, 96, 226
Patterns of Design (website), 101
PDF file, for spec, 165
pencils and paper, as first design tools, 79, 106
Percolator app, 201
personal note, in product description, 206
personality, role of adding in app development, 44
PhotoNest app, 8, 103, 147, 190
Photoshop
    alternatives to, 118
    building designs that scale, 116–117
    described, 31
    learning, 140–141
    steps for making images, 118
    template generators, 129
    transforming mockups into layouts, 114
Photoshop PSD files, 118, 139
picker (input element), 98

Pinterest
    described, 69
    gift ideas on, 164
    for inspiration on creating invite, 217
    posting stories relevant to app project, 186
    screen shot, 90
    storing design ideas on, 101, 118
Pitch Perfect: Practical Advice from Professional Bloggers (Sande and Sadun), 215
pixel perfect design, 119–120
Pixelmator, 118
plagiarizing, 100
Playtend (app company), 8, 89, 170, 210
PNG file type, 114, 118, 139, 206
PopBooth app, 125
popovers, 54–55
porting app to new iDevice, 276–278
PostSecret app, 63
PowerPoint, 103, 236
Prefinery (website), 244
pre-launch cheat sheet, 221–222
presentations, as promotional tool, 236, 240
press kits, 200, 201
press releases, 196, 241
pricing your app, 250
primary task designation, 59
prizes, 45, 234
product description, formula for, 203–206
project management, 17, 31–32
promo codes, 197–198, 215, 232
promo videos, examples of, 227–230
promotion. *See also* marketing
    addicts model, as marketing tactic, 261
    advantages of withholding key feature, 60
    building identity, 226–227
    creating a website, 242–247. *See also* website for your app
    creating hype and attracting attention, 224–231
    email campaign, 247–249
    as first phase of project, 3, 16, 18, 67
    $5 marketing plan. *See* marketing plan, the $5
    giving back, 254
    inside your app, 233
    marketing ideas checklist, 141, 186–187
    monitoring buzz, 230–231
    offline, 240–241
    Pareto Principle, 279
    as part of every phase of project, 3, 18
    spinoff products, 253
    tactics that don't work, 241–242
    telling a good story, 224–230

pronunciation, of app name, 130
Proto.io (wireframing tool), 109
prototype/prototyping, 104–110, 112, 113
provision profile, 180
provisioning profile, 176, 179, 180, 213
proxies, tribe, 38, 79
pttns (design gallery), 100
publishing book, 235
pull power, testing, 65–67
Pulse app, 85, 86, 87
Push Notifications (application), 180

Q

Quip iPad app, 45
quiz, as promotional tool, 254

R

ratings, 204
Readability app, 249
reaffirmations, 204
real-world objects, designing app to resemble, 120–121
Recorder app, 130
reference, 121
referrals, 234
Reflector app, 201
register.com (website), 243
registering, as Apple developer, 32
rejection, handling, 24
release date, 197, 200, 214, 273. *See also* launch day/launch date
repetition (design principle), 122–124
Request Contracts (section of app application), 193
researching
    to find any app remotely similar, 56–57
    name of app, 130
    other designs, 100
resolution requirements, 114
retina display (2x), 116, 117, 139
Retina Display (application), 114–115
revenue models, 250
revenues, breakdown of, 26
Review button, 233
reviews
    from customers, 264
    how to request, 233–234
    how to use, 204
    never slam competitors' apps, 242
    people paying attention to, 202
revisions, 274

rewards, 204, 233, 234
Rohde, Mike (designer), 4
Rosenfeld Media, 80
Rovio (app company), 15
row height standard, 97
Russell, Jason (filmmaker), 227

S

Sadun, Erica (author)
    *Pitch Perfect: Practical Advice from Professional
        Bloggers*, 215
Safari app, 55, 95
St. Francis of Assisi (friar/preacher), 78
sale boosters, 263
sale price
    Apple keeps 30 percent of, 26
    discounting of as marketing tool, 232
    higher for iPad apps, 56
sales/sales numbers
    keeping track of, 219
    publishing of, 236
Sande, Steven (author)
    *Pitch Perfect: Practical Advice from Professional
        Bloggers*, 215
Savio, Nadav (designer), 20
scaling up/down, 116
Scheme (device testing), 178
scope creep, avoiding, 58–59
Scoutzie (website), 137
screen header, 82
screen resolution, 114
screen shots, 206–210
screen size, by device type, 116
screen transitions, 44
Screenshot Journal app, 101
SDK (software development kit), 28, 170, 275
search engine mechanics, 244
secondary purpose, of app, 103
secondary task designation, 59
secrets, revealing, as promotional tool, 235–236
seminars, as promotional tool, 240
server, cautions about owning your own, 62
server alternatives, 62
Settings app, 80, 97
shapes, for flow diagram, 103
"share" button, 82
sharing everything, as promotional tool, 236–241
short message service (SMS), 47
sidebar navigation, 91
Simon, Carly (singer-songwriter), 132
simplicity, in teaser video, 72

simulator, 28, 171, 175–176, 178
site canvas (website), 239
Sketch 2 (software), 118
sketching, as first design step, 80, 106
skeuomorphic design, 120–121
skills needed, 16–17, 18
Skirvin, Andy (founder Blimp Pilots), 7, 12, 235
Skype, 32, 152, 154
slide-out navigation, 83, 84
slider, 99
SlideShare (website), 236
sliding cards navigation, 87–88
Smashing Magazine, 238
Smirnoff, Yakov (comedian), 228
SMS (short message service), 47
Snapguide app, 85, 91
Snapseed app, 251
snapshot of app, 206
sneak peek, 217
social interaction, 46–48
social media/networks
    jumping on social media bus, 69–70
    monitoring of for talk about your app, 220
    navigation model on, 84
    for scouting out developer talent, 146–151
    sharing your ups and downs on, 141
    using in launch, 218
Social Mention (search engine), 231
social networking, 37
software, downloading/installing, 30
software development kit (SDK), 28, 170, 275
software testing, 17
software versioning, 273
Solar app, 86, 87, 126, 127, 128, 136, 207
sound, 44
SoundCloud app, 122
source code, 169
space (design principle), 123
spam, do not, 247
speaking engagements, 240
specifications/spec documents, 138, 164–168
spinoff products, 253
split views, 54, 55, 56
sponsor, for launch, 254
standard controls/elements, 92–99
Statements of Work, 161
statistics
    app downloads per week, 14
    App Store customers, 14
    Apple's App Store earnings from paid apps, 278
    apps received daily by Apple approval team, 24

Statnut app, 86
status bar, 93
stencil kits, 107, 108
sticky apps, 253
storytelling
    basis of good story, 224–230
    on flow diagram, 104
    as part of promotion, 68
"stretching" layouts, 116
students, as option to use as designers, 137
stunts, as promotional tool, 241
subclass, 154, 156, 162
submission date, 191
submitting your app
    app submission cheat sheet, 190
    steps to, 211, 221
    what to do one month before, 191, 221
    what to do one week before, 201–202, 221
subscribers, 245
surprises, planted in app, 45
SwankoLab app, 228–229
sweepstakes, as promotional tool, 254
swiping tabs navigation, 83
switch, 99

T

tab bar navigation, 81–82
table view, 95–97
tables, 95–97
tag line, 245, 248
tagging, 233
take-aways, as promotional tools, 255
talent, committing your own, 15, 17
tap size, 110
tap tap tap (app company), 2, 7, 236
Tapbots (app company), 2, 44–45, 100, 113, 196,
    251, 264
TapFancy (website), 100
TappGala (website), 100
target audience, 36–40, 58
tax info, on app submission, 193
Taxi Magic app, 10, 11
Taylor, Christopher (co-founder Playtend), 8, 38,
    67, 170, 210
teaching, as promotional tool, 235–236
teaser page services, 244
teaser site, 73–74
teaser video, 70–73, 187, 201
tech or startup center, for scouting out developer
    talent, 146
Teehan & Lax, 118

template generators, 129
Terms of Service (TOS) agreements, cautions about
    including features that require, 64
test checklist, 170
TestFlight (website), 181, 219
TestPad (website), 170
tests/testing
    asking children to test your app, 182
    beta testing, 64, 181
    of designs, 110–113
    enlisting tribe in, 181–182
    of even most minor features, 271–272
    "Get it" testing, 111–112
    informing designer about findings from, 138
    key task testing, 112
    micro-testing, 65
    as part of iterative design process, 105
    setting up your device for, 175–179
    software, 17
    user testing of paper prototype, 107
    your responsibility for, 170
text field, 98
text view, 98
ThemeForest (website), 65, 244
They Make Apps (website), 146
thumbs, 22–23
TIFF images, 206
time
    committing your own, 15
    15-second rule, 20–21
    needed to create app, 14
time management, 17, 225
Timeline Cover Banner (website), 239
TinyCo (website), 252
tips, 135
toolbar, 93, 94–95
tools, to get started, 29–30. *See also* design tools;
    developer tools
Tootin' Bathtub Baby Cousins (video), 230
TOS (Terms of Service) agreements, cautions about
    including features that require, 64
Toybox app, 128
trademark, 130
traditional demographics, consideration of, 36
translation into other languages, 267–268
transparency, 136
tree view, 80
tribe
    enlisting to find bugs/create buzz, 181–182
    identifying key characteristics of, 38
    your audience as, 36–38, 58, 68–69

tribe proxies, 38–40
tribe proxy template example, 38
Tumblr blog, 70, 72
Tweetbot app, 7, 106, 113, 251, 264
TweetDeck (browser), 231
Tweetie app, 7
Twitcovers (website), 239
Twitter
    author at, 8
    author's list of people to market to, 198
    author's Twitter cover image, 240
    buttons for sharing on, 47
    cover photos/images, 239
    described, 69
    harnessing the power of, 224
    launch screen, 132, 133
    nested dolls navigation, 81
    one-click sign-on via, 48
    "pop" sound when done refreshing, 44
    posting stories relevant to app project, 186
    pull-down-for-new-content feature, 100
    Quip iPad app, 45
    for scouting out developer talent, 146
    screens, 81
    sharing link to promo video on, 72
    as sticky app, 253
    TweetDeck, 231
@2x (Retina version display), 114, 115

U

UITableView, 156
Unbounce (website), 65, 66, 244
Unique Device ID (UDID), 178
universal apps
    benefits of, 52–53
    defined, 51
    pricing of, 250
    strategy for porting, 276–277
universal lite, 51
USA Today (newspaper), 1
usability, 266
user (flow diagram shape), 103
user testing, 107
User Voice (website), 194

V

Vaynerchuk, Gary (marketing great), 236
venture capital, 15
version number format, 273–274

video editing software, 70
video producer, 70
VideoHive (website), 72
videos, as promotional tools, 201, 236
Vimeo, 72
viral flow chart, 47
viral goodness, mixing in of in app, 46–49
Vision Board app, 128
vital few, law of, 278–279
Voices app, 199
Voices 2 app, 7

W

wallpaper, 236, 238, 239
Warren, Frank (app creator), 63
WDDR Intermediate Certificate, 176, 177
Weather Channel app, 82
web design gallery (search term), 73
web hosting, 243
web view, 99
"Webcam 101 for Seniors" (video), 227–228
website creation, 17
website for your app
    importance of, 33, 242
    micro-test, 65
    preparing of for app launch, 198
    rolling out, 218
    teaser site, 73, 243–245
    tips for effective one, 245–247
Wee Rockets app, 8, 58, 59, 80, 110, 111
Wee Subs app, 8
Wee Taps (app company), 2, 8, 80, 110, 111
Weightbot app, 7, 196
welcome screen, 132
West, Mae (actress), 10
Wetherille, Patrick (VP Lose It!), 7, 40
WhatsApp Messenger app, 114
whitespace, guidelines for, 21
Wikipedia, testing of keywords in, 210
Wildcard App ID, 178, 180, 181
Williams, Robin (author)
    The Non-Designer's Design Book, 122
wireframe/wireframing, 108–113, 138
Wood Camera (website), 2, 225
word-of-mouth marketing, 224, 225
WordPress blog, 69–70
Words With Friends app, 49
WWDC, 155

X

Xcode
   asking prospective developer about, 156
   bundled with iOS SDK, 30
   cautions with beta versions of, 275
   creating special build with, 211
   described, 28
   guide to using, 171–175
   interface screen shot, 29
   for snapshot of app, 206
   turning off Apple's gloss effect with, 129
   Welcome screen, 171

Xcode 4.5, 176
.xib files, 156, 174

Y

YouTube, 70, 72, 224

Z

ZenDesk (website), 194